D1179308

The Wild Track

www.penguin.co.uk

Also by Margaret Reynolds

The Penguin Book of Lesbian Short Stories
The Sappho Companion
Victorian Women Poets: An Anthology

The Wild Track

Adopting, Mothering, Belonging

Margaret Reynolds

With Lucy Reynolds

doubleday

TRANSWORLD PUBLISHERS
Penguin Random House, One Embassy Gardens,
8 Viaduct Gardens, London SW11 7BW
www.penguin.co.uk

Transworld is part of the Penguin Random House group of companies
whose addresses can be found at global.penguinrandomhouse.com

First published in Great Britain in 2021 by Doubleday
an imprint of Transworld Publishers

A CIP catalogue record for this book
is available from the British Library.

ISBN 9780857527424

Typeset in 11.5/16pt Granjon LT Std by Jouve (UK), Milton Keynes
Printed and bound in Great Britain by Clays Ltd, Elcograf S.p.A.

The authorized representative in the EEA is Penguin Random House Ireland,
Morrison Chambers, 32 Nassau Street, Dublin D02 YH68.

Penguin Random House is committed to a sustainable
future for our business, our readers and our planet. This book
is made from Forest Stewardship Council® certified paper.

For Lucy
with Lucy

and in memory of
Mona Howard
Lisa Jardine
Adrienne Reynolds

CONTENTS

CONTENTS

I have seen the sun break through
to illuminate a small field
for a while, and gone my way
and forgotten it. But that was the
pearl of great price, the one field that had
treasure in it. I realise now
that I must give all that I have
to possess it . . .

R. S. Thomas, 'The Bright Field'

PROLOGUE

WE HAVE FINISHED the interview. My producer says, 'I'll just record a bit of wild track.' Anyone who works in broadcasting – in film or in sound – will know about wild track. You capture the substance: tape the interview; shoot the scene; lay down the number. But then you pause, everyone stays in place, and you switch on the microphone to collect . . . nothing, space, emptiness, silence.

When I started working for the radio, I was commissioned to present a documentary with producer Nicki Paxman. On that occasion we were talking to the composer John Tavener at his home, and this was when I first heard those words: 'I'll just record a bit of wild track.' Practically speaking, it is a recording of the atmosphere in the room, which a producer can use to bridge the gap between one section of interview and another. So it is a tool in the editing process. But the track has to capture the same ambient sound as when the interview was conducted. And sound is affected by bodies – breathing, beating and simply being present.

So we all sit there – producer, interviewer, interviewee – listening to the distant traffic, a dog barking, someone far off asking a question, water gurgling in the pipes, birdsong. I was enchanted. Such a beautiful term for simply paying attention to silence, to living.

But I have since come to regard wild track as a parallel to and a parable for so much that happens in life. You go forth with a task. You ask some questions, you receive some answers. Those questions and those answers are what you came for, what you intended to collect, what you planned to create. You get to the place and you think it is the place; you think you have arrived where you are meant to be. But then, in a space that is entirely separate and specific, you just listen, in a meditation that opens out beyond the moment, to wherever the moment takes you on the wild track of its own intimate revelations. You never know where it will lead.

FIRST LIGHT

World is suddener than we fancy it.

World is crazier and more of it than we think,
Incorrigibly plural . . .

Louis MacNeice, 'Snow'

THERE IS A little picture that I look at every day. About twelve inches by nine, oil on board – eighteenth century, maybe. Very fine brushwork. In the left foreground is a large tree, its wide-spreading canopy arching over a path, with rocks to the right, mountains in the far distance, all under a pellucid sky. And in the middle is a tiny figure, dwarfed by the landscape. Hard to tell if it is male or female, but wrapped in a red shawl and walking undauntedly towards the light of the sky, towards the dark of the mountain. It is just one person; a lone being. But then, one day, it seemed to me that the questing figure was not alone. In my imagination, voyaging alongside that person was a smaller being – a little child, held by the hand. And together they were moving out of the shadow, into the light of the bright field. Every day they marched stalwartly onwards, and yet every day they were still there, still speaking to me of purpose, challenge and hope.

It is hard now to recall when she – if she is a she – came into my life. It must have been winter. One of those early morning hours of pale light when the slide from dream to wake is fitful, reluctant, slow. There might have been snow – dulling sound, filtering sight. But it brought a clarity of thought, and a vision of the possible. On this snowy morning, quiet and half dreaming, I asked myself, 'What is it that I would like in my life, that I could have now, and could not have had before?' And the answer came clearly. A child.

When I wrote this account, some months later, I was staying with friends in Scotland. But the idea was still with me. It was hot – an August bank holiday. The sun burnished the terrace, shimmered in the lake below, illuminated the hill of purple heather and the dark trees that framed it all. Some of the party walked the path below us. Someone else was reading the newspaper. Two others chatted quietly a bit further off. I picked up my notebook and wrote, then paused to think about my wish for this child, about the children I knew and had known, about the parents I knew and had known.

The friends I am staying with – David and Helen – have three children, grown up now, or nearly so in the case of their youngest. When the elder of their two sons was born, we were all in our early twenties, and I conjure up the distant memory of meeting the fair-haired baby. He was the first baby in our contemporary circle so it was a new experience for all of us, and one which I encountered unprepared; conscious, all the same, that it was testing out my feelings. I was wearing a vintage cardigan covered in sequins and beads, not suitable at all for cuddling a newborn. But if his little face was scratched, no reproach was made and I have clearly been forgiven.

I wonder now, as the desire for a child takes hold in my mind so late in the day, how it was that I did not feel it then. I wonder too if perhaps I did. But then David and Helen still offer me a splendid model, for they unabashedly adore children – everyone else's along with their own – and read bedtime stories, kit them out for fishing, cook up special treats.

So why a child? And why now? What for, anyway? What makes me want to be a mother? What makes any woman want to be a mother?

The answer is: a lot of things. Many of them obvious, most of them not so, but to begin with, watchwords might be 'love', 'purpose', 'joy'. Finding something or someone to love sounds simple, general and vague, but it also suggests a structure, making a commitment that has be renewed daily – a commitment that tries and shapes the self.

Around the time of that vision of the possible, I made a programme with Sara Conkey about Christina Rossetti's 'A Christmas Carol' – better known as 'In the Bleak Midwinter' – for the Radio 4 series *Soul Music*. I spoke about the ways that Rossetti envisaged winter as the time for lying fallow, watching and waiting, letting yourself go into the dark, letting the water lie on the land – so that the light may come, so that the flowers may flourish. I might have been speaking less about the poem and more about myself. The well-known final verse – with its many repetitions – works because the form and the meaning of the poem are exactly matched:

> What can I give Him,
> Poor as I am?
> If I were a shepherd
> I would bring a lamb,
> If I were a wise man
> I would do my part, -
> Yet what I can I give Him,
> Give my heart.

That insistence on 'I' is everything. It is a poem about you and me, about here and now, about what we can do, about what we can give. But I had always thought – in a typically academic way – that the first 'I' of the penultimate line was purely decorative, a stage-managed repetition in the question, and that the last line was the answer to that question. It was only when I heard the final broadcast version of the programme that I realized my error. Only then did I see that those two final lines are not odd and contrived and arty at all – they make perfectly simple sense. That is, they are a resolution – 'What little I have is what I will give, and that is my heart.'

Giving your life, making sense of your life by being someone for someone else – that makes a sense of motherhood. But it also exerts an enormous pressure on every mother, perhaps on every parent. As I tried to think this through, one sentence kept coming into my mind: '[. . .] it drives someone mad if she is not able to love.' That seemed to me how I felt – that there is a need somewhere to be able to love, but not one that needs reciprocation, as one might expect of a romantic relationship.

The words resonated in my mind and focused on that little figure walking alongside the person wrapped in the red shawl: '[. . .] it drives someone mad if she is not able to love.' Eventually I looked them up. They come from a book by the Australian psychoanalyst Neville Symington – *A Healing Conversation: How Healing Happens* (2006) – and I was astonished to see that I had forgotten the context, because it is specifically about mothering, or a difficulty in mothering.

Symington was working with a distressed woman who knew not only that she had been conceived inadvertently as the result of a one-night stand, but also that she was born only because her mother's faith forbade an abortion. This mother told the child constantly that she loved her, but her many neglectful actions spelled out a different story. The mother could not admit that she did not want this child because, as Symington says, 'It may have been that this is not a feeling that a mother is supposed to have.' She may not have been able to admit to it, but the hurtful things this mother did made the lack of love clear, and so the child was unable to trust her. As Symington says, '[. . .] love of another is only possible when the words spoken fit with the emotional behaviour.' As a result, this child – now a woman – was 'not able to love' either her mother or herself.

There is 'an old proverb' (variously attributed): 'God could not be everywhere and therefore he made mothers.' But how is any woman, anyone, supposed to cope with this imperative? As Symington quietly remarks, feelings of regret or rejection or lack of interest or hatred or ambivalence are not things 'that a mother is supposed to have'. But surely any mother might feel any or all of those things depending upon her specific situation, and at any given moment in time, however fleeting they may be?

Psychoanalysis has shown us that this is often the case, and in the past, writers from Simone de Beauvoir to Melanie Klein and D. W. Winnicott have raised the question of the difficult relationship between mother and child. Since the 1970s, many others, especially as women themselves began to speak about motherhood, were forced to acknowledge the challenges and tackled these questions with bravery and honesty. Here is the acclaimed American poet Adrienne Rich, writing privately in her diary in 1960, words she then went on to publish in her groundbreaking work of 1976, *Of Woman Born*: *Motherhood as Experience and Institution*.

> My children cause me the most exquisite suffering of which I
> have any experience. It is the suffering of ambivalence: the
> murderous alternation between bitter resentment and
> raw-edged nerves, and blissful gratification and tenderness.
> Sometimes I seem to myself, in my feelings towards these
> tiny guiltless beings, a monster of selfishness and intolerance.

Following on from Rich, many more women began to write on mothering, specifically and calculatedly letting motherhood be in their work. They even welcomed motherhood into their writings because it could give them, as the late Irish poet Eavan

Boland put it, 'the grand permission'. Despite women of my mother's generation, such as Rich and Sylvia Plath, already doing this, it was still a relatively new thing when Eavan Boland began to publish her work in the late 1960s. Boland then felt that the poetic tradition within which she worked did not allow her to express her own experience. This is what she says in 'The Journey':

> And then the dark fell and "there has never"
> I said "been a poem to an antibiotic: . . .'
> . . .
> so every day the language gets less
>
> "for the task and we are less with the language."
>
> I finished speaking and the anger faded
> and dark fell . . .

But in 1982 Boland published a collection called *Night Feed*, and by 1992, when I first interviewed her in 'Four Woman Poets', a documentary for BBC Radio 4 with producer Beaty Rubens, she remained clear about her justification to choose subjects that come out of the ordinary lives of women who may also be mothers:

> When I lived in this house, and I had two children under the age of three, a washing machine was a *big* item to me. I did not see why a washing machine could not transit from being outside a poem to inside a poem. The Irish poem had really very very little place for a washing machine in it.

While writers such as Boland, Plath and Rich were putting mothering into their poems, other women were questioning the traditional ways in which mothers and motherhood had been presented. You need to read Buchi Emecheta's 1979 novel, *The Joys of Motherhood*, to understand the irony of her title. In a colonized Nigeria, Nnu Ego longs to achieve the status that motherhood will bring, but as she eventually succeeds, she finds that her children are rather more of a burden than a blessing.

The Bulgarian-French philosopher Julia Kristeva noted in an essay called 'Stabat Mater' that 'we live in a civilization in which the *consecrated* (religious or secular) representation of femininity is subsumed under maternity . . . ' Originally published in 1977 under the French title of '*Hérethique de l'amour*' ('heretical-ethic of love'), Kristeva balances – quite literally, as part of the text is set in two columns – the idealization of the 'maternal body' effected through religious iconography and the real experience of women who are mothers.

In 2005 Kristeva extended her earlier observation about the conventional consecration of the idea of the mother by saying, 'Today motherhood is imbued with what has survived of religious feeling.' But that does not mean that it is a true feeling.

It was with the 2001 publication of Rachel Cusk's challenging memoir, *A Life's Work: On Becoming a Mother*, that the trials of motherhood, as opposed to the sanctities, became a key topic. Cusk's account of physical pain and mental misery made her a target for a barrage of negative criticism. Years later, in reviewing Rebecca Asher's *Shattered: Modern Motherhood and the Illusion of Equality* (2011), Cusk was still thinking about mothers and what the experience of mothering may mean for a woman, and she was still trying to discriminate between the general and the particular:

> . . . a woman is never more of an individual than in her response to the conformity of motherhood: it is her individuality, after all, that is being questioned. This is one of the things that makes the culture of motherhood so difficult to grapple with. Motherhood may look like a genre, but in reality it is an infinitesimal network of secret pacts and compromises, of private bargainings with the self.

Since then, motherhood and mothering have remained in the public eye, in both fiction and academic discussion, and what is intriguing about contemporary reactions to these works is the way that people cling to the 'religion' of motherhood. Is it possible then to reclaim motherhood – a real motherhood in all its complexity and variety? I would like to think so, and in *Mothers: An Essay on Love and Cruelty* (2018), Jacqueline Rose concludes that it should be. She says that motherhood could 'be left to get on quietly with its work'.

In a book published just a short while later, Sarah Knott set out to find all those various and varied mothers. *Mother: An Unconventional History* (2019) positions the title as a verb. She tells the story of how she came to mother her two sons while she investigated the ways in which other women in other times, places and cultural settings worked to mother their own children. The record – being largely women's history – is fragmentary, made up of scraps from diaries, asides in letters, palimpsests in doctor's records, between-the-lines in newspaper reports, overheard whispers from anthropologists and 'shards' from the archives.

What emerges is a complicated story across time and space and experience about wishing, conceiving, quickening, swelling, birthing, weeping, waking, nursing, advising, succeeding, failing, reading, listening, remembering, othermothering, working, raising, collecting, training, trailing, and then conceiving, birthing, working, succeeding, failing, working as it starts all over again.

What we need to remember is the simple point that Julia Kristeva made in a talk she delivered in 2005, titled 'Motherhood Today': 'motherhood is not an "instinct".' Nor is it a universal or a general – there is no sameness here. To mother – to be a mother – is layered, multiple, various, variegated, diverse, disparate, intricate, intimate, or as Rachel Cusk put it, that 'infinitesimal network of secret pacts and compromises'.

There is nothing safe or sanctified about this, for motherhood can and does take women to the bitter extremes of experience. Which is what Clover Stroud says in *My Wild and Sleepless Nights* (2020): 'Motherhood hurts.' Becoming a mother impacts your body and the changes can go on for years. But there is more. For any mother, whether a biological parent or not, motherhood can negatively affect your physical health, your mental health, your sleep, your sense of self, your identity, your work, your achievements, your family relationships, your creation of a home, your friendships, your ability to cope with responsibility and with disappointment, your capacity to handle fear and failure, anger, shame, guilt, and anxiety, your level of tolerance when faced with criticism, condemnation and disgust.

In the UK, the Infanticide Act 1922 was designed to recognize the extremes of physical and mental pain or psychosis that might be suffered by women who had recently become mothers, and the death penalty was revoked for a mother who may have, sadly, killed her newborn. But nearly a hundred years later, in October 2017, *Time* magazine published an article by Claire Howorth entitled 'Motherhood Is Hard to Get Wrong. So Why Do So Many Moms Feel So Bad About Themselves?', where the cover carried the strapline: 'The Goddess Myth: How a Vision of Perfect Motherhood Hurts Moms'.

If, on the one hand, to wish to be a mother is not 'an instinct', and if it includes many powerful contraindications in different situations, what then is it? Kristeva says that 'it is a reconquest that lasts a lifetime and beyond.' It is a lived process, renegotiated every day, and fraught with danger but also with prospect.

Today, the ways in which people have children, the ways in which women become mothers, have also become multiple. Only two of these ways are long established: biological parenthood, with all its possible difficult situations; and (mostly) informal or private or opportunistic adoption, with all its possible difficult situations. But now we also have sperm and egg donors; infertility treatments, including surgery, IVF and surrogacy; complex legal and official adoption, both inter-country and domestic.

To read the stories of parents who have travelled these paths is to enter a strange, Gothic world of pain and horror countered by sublime vision: of dreams and nightmares, of apparitions of what might be, and of even more terrifying apparitions of what might not be. Of loss of blood, loss of self, loss of sanity; of dark nocturnal scenes and overlit corridors; of small spaces and labyrinthine passages, whether of the body, the hospital or the offices of authority.

In 1998, when Jill Bialosky and Helen Schulman were compiling an anthology of writings called *Wanting a Child*, they commissioned essays from many writers, but not all of those pieces materialized. 'As uplifting, funny, courageous and hopeful as many of these personal histories may be, they are also full of pain and yearning,' they wrote in the introduction. For some, those memories were too hard to revisit. These are difficult stories to tell.

If Eavan Boland felt she was taking a new path in writing about mothering, today, a great number of fine poets make this a key subject of their work – Sharon Olds, June Jordan, Rachel Richardson, Gillian Clarke, Margaret Burroughs, Asha Bandele, Jackie Kay, Alicia Ostriker, Carolyn Kizer, Carol Ann Duffy, Alice Walker, Jorie Graham, Audre Lorde and Margaret Atwood, to name but a few. And their motherhood is not one thing, but many, distinct and different, as their children are many, distinct and different. These writers, these mothers, may share some experiences – we may even be able to acknowledge some commonality in their works – but it is impossible to categorize them under one heading.

All the same, I might try. And, as I think about my own wish to be a mother, it seems to me that two of my own watchwords might bring them together, and these are the second and third terms that I started out with: 'purpose' and 'joy'. For some women, a child may just happen – setting her or him going 'like a fat gold watch' in Plath's phrase from her poem 'Morning Song' – with the beginning of a heartbeat, whether the man and woman consents or no, whether they actively wish for it or no. But for many others it is a choice, a decision. The child is first conceived in their mind, in their imagination. Once this imaginative conception is acknowledged, then motherhood – or maternal purpose, or mothering – can encompass all categories: biological mothers, adoptive mothers and social mothers. But let's face it, this is only about the adult that already exists – it is most certainly not about the child (at least, not until they have that 'ticking' life).

Only the adult that already exists can be the one who seeks the purpose, seeks the joy. And we do. Carol Ann Duffy's poem 'Lessons in the Orchard' was written for the Charleston Festival, which takes place each year in Sussex at the one-time family home of the artist Vanessa Bell, sister to the writer Virginia Woolf (who also lived near by). Duffy's poem ends with an evocation of everything that Bell's home came to be – to herself, to her children, and to her friends and the intellectual community – and an invocation to the many artistic endeavours that took place there:

> And the dragonfly's talent for turquoise.
> And the goldfish art of the pond.
> And the open windows calling the garden in.
> This bowl, life, that we fill and fill.

Is this not the point? We have just so much life. Pretty soon after we come into life, we learn that it is finite. So how to use it? How to fill it?

But the 'bowl of life' that Duffy uses here is borrowed, or referenced or reverenced, from Virginia Woolf's autobiographical essay 'A Sketch of the Past'.

If life has a base that it stands upon, if it is a bowl that one
fills and fills and fills – then my bowl without a doubt stands
upon this memory . . . It is of hearing the waves breaking, one,
two, one, two, and sending a splash of water over the
beach; . . . and feeling, it is almost impossible that I should be
here; of feeling the purest ecstasy I can conceive . . .

'Conceive'. An interesting word. To have an idea. To imagine
something. To make a child.

Once, I decided to keep hens. There was the room. Surely it
could not take up much time? And feathered things are a blessing. Why not? I read a book. Why not?? Because hens contract
unpleasant diseases and attract infestations of red spider mites;
they get taken by foxes, snatched by eagles, plagued by rats. That
was the end of that idea.

Years later I felt differently, and built a hen run with wire dug
down in trenches (for the fox) and more wire above (for the
eagles) and a guard of cats (for the rats). I gave them vitamin sup-
plements, put apple cider vinegar in their water, scrubbed their
hen house every Saturday and let them forage in the garden. Of
course, the fox still took them, they still got sick, or died for no
apparent reason (though never did see an eagle). But I took the
risk. We pretend that we have control in our lives when there is
no such thing. There is only planning, crossed fingers, and risk.

But as I thought about my hens, I realized something. On a
simple, elemental level – both then and now – it makes me very
happy as I go to sleep at night to think about my birds roosting
in their clean straw, my cats well fed in front of the fire, my dog

snoozing safely on her bed, my pony in his own field, with a proper stable and a warm rug protecting him from the weather. I like looking after them. I like looking after living beings.

At the end of 'Snow' – another of Carol Ann Duffy's poems that is important to me as a guide – Duffy asks, '. . . what will you do now / with the gift of your left life?' This is the question I was asking myself when I decided that I wanted to take the risk of wanting a child. And this includes belonging and being needed and making patterns and becoming a different self, perhaps a better self.

In an interview with Bill Moyers (11 March 1990), the writer Toni Morrison explained what it meant to her to be a mother. She described it as 'liberating', because of the particular demands her children made on her: 'to be a good manager, to have a sense of humor; deliver something that somebody can use . . . The person that was in me that I liked best, was the one my children seemed to want.'

And what else do I want? I want the shared long history, the making of memories. The *do you remembers* that can make a pattern of our lives, giving them shape and form. I want the marks and traces that testify, however briefly, to the fact of our existence. All over the world families do this, quite literally, marking a wall or a door jamb with notches and dates, tracking their children's growth.

This is something I want. I want to watch a life unfurl, unfold, fulfil. The fragments of the ancient Greek poet Sappho speak about her daughter, who may have been called Cleis like her own mother: 'I have a golden child for whom I would not take all

Lydia . . .' But Sappho seems to link her daughter Cleis to other mothers watching over their children. Mothers such as Demeter who mourned her daughter Persephone, 'a tender girl picking flowers'; mothers such as her own who said that 'in her youth a purple headband was a great adornment'; mothers who provide a place for their children every day, as night follows day: 'Hesperus, the evening star, calling everything back scattered by shining Dawn . . . you bring the child back to its mother.'

Long ago, when a close friend of mine gave birth to her first child, she said to me that when you have seen birth you understand death.

Back in the 1980s, led by H. V. Morton's lyrical description from *A Traveller in Italy*, I went to see Piero della Francesca's *Madonna del Parto* in the tiny mortuary chapel for a cemetery outside the Tuscan town of Monterchi. The Madonna is young and unlined, but she has a sad, dignified face, her eyes downcast. Her hair is bound with ribbon in the style of the 1450s and finished with a netted circle, which might be a halo or some fashionable headdress. She wears no ornament other than this. She stands inside a pavilion with two smaller angels – mirror images apart from the colours of their clothes – lifting the fabric like framing curtains. She is dressed in a simple gown of blue, laced at the sides and in the front. Her left hand seems to support her aching back, her right hand slightly opens her dress over her swollen belly. She is utterly recognizable, frank, intimate, dear.

And yet the iconography is complicated and profound. The tent or pavilion represents the tabernacle that contained the Ark of the Covenant, carried through the wilderness by the Israelites fleeing Egypt. So the Madonna herself bears the child, emblem of the promised new covenant of the Messiah, and her dress and her very flesh become two other veils holding and containing the sacred child.

The material of the canopy is decorated with stylized pomegranates, a symbol of fertility since ancient times because of its many seeds, but also associated with the flow of blood and with death, because the ancient Greeks believed it to have sprung from the wounds of Adonis. In the book of Exodus, in the Old Testament, pomegranates adorn the hem of the robes of the priest, symbolizing blessing and royal prerogative through the little 'crown' on the top of the fruit. This simple, realistic-looking woman, so familiar and ordinary-seeming, is also an allegory of power, sanctity, fruitfulness and the giving of life.

But the veil that the angels draw, the slits in the gown that expands to accommodate the baby, and the body that will be torn to expel the child suggest the correspondence between life and death, just as the two mirror-image angels imply the duality that shapes all our lives, poised as we are for a brief moment between birth and death.

The summer day of this visit was hot, and in the early eighties, cars were not air conditioned – or not the kind of car my then husband and I could afford anyway. We drove on to a shabby little café by the roadside, the metal signs for Fanta and Peroni rusting under the sun. In the bar an older man passed through the beaded fly screen and called for his wife to supply our *limonata*. She too came through the fly screen – slowly, wearily. She was dark-haired and young and heavily pregnant. I wondered if she frequented the mortuary chapel, if she had lit candles, placed flowers. She stayed in my mind, she is still in my mind. But her child will be grown up now – middle-aged, even – with children of his own.

When Morton visited the Madonna he did see two pregnant women light candles in the shrine, and wondered about this 'procession of life to a cemetery' where birth and death must often 'meet at the door of this chapel'. Today you will no longer find the Madonna in that sacred collateral space. Since 1992 she has had her own dedicated museum in the town. But I am glad I saw her there in that isolation and remember her suspended in the landscape that Piero once looked upon, at the end of a double row of cypresses.

I am still left with the question: why do I want to be a mother? What do I know about mothers, about mothering, about mothers and their children?

My own mother was an impatient person, but this is a Fisher family trait that we – my siblings, my aunts and uncles, my cousins – all recognize. Her mother was the same, but in her case it was compounded.

My grandmother, Louisa, got married at the age of thirty (late in life for the time) to a much older man (though she did not know that at the time). She had many roles and little leisure: she was the doctor's wife with a social position to uphold in a remote country town in Australia; she was also the chief nurse and assistant; she superintended the small private hospital they built; she was the life and soul of the party, always laughing in public; and, last of all, least of all, she was a mother.

My uncle Eric, some years older than my mother, says Louisa

was nurturing 'in her own sort of way'. But everyone knew that everything had to be done according to her way, and my own memories of her are of someone stern and rarely approachable.

My mother, Adrienne, had mostly not very happy memories. She recalls a terrible afternoon from a time when she was very little – about two and a half. It might have been in Sydney, or back at home in West Wyalong. She was hot, thirsty, tired, and yet her mother led her over a long diagonal path across a barren, empty lot where the sun was beating down. Her mother urged her on, insistently, commandingly, but without compassion, and refused to pick her up.

Only much later did Adrienne realize that Louisa was experiencing a miscarriage at the time. Only then did she understand that the real terror felt by her child self was the psychic communication of heightened suffering and emotion that her mother could not, and never would, express.

Another memory is more endearing, though still sad. Until my uncle Coll was born, when my mother was nearly eight, she and her older brother Eric were mostly looked after by the maids who came in. There was Frannie, whose family had migrated to Australia from the Channel Islands, and who walked with a pronounced sideways roll because of a congenitally dislocated hip, then Edie, who started work in the household on her fifteenth birthday. Not much older than the two children, these women were the ones to whom my mother and uncle turned for sympathy, for comfort, for reassurance and for safety. But one day, Adrienne came home from school to find her mother ensconced by the fire in the sitting room, darning socks: 'It was lovely.'

My mother must have been in her seventies the last time I heard this story, but the wistful longing in her voice was still there. These memories are not mine. But the vanishing traces of that difficult relationship between parent and child remain, even though the events themselves took place nearly one hundred years ago.

'You parent the way you are parented,' the psychologists tell us. In my mother's case this was not a great beginning. Her parents always said 'no': when she pleaded for a birthday party to keep up with her friends; when she wanted to go to school in Sydney like her brothers; when she won the New South Wales junior swimming championship and was invited to train for the Olympic team; when she asked about singing lessons; when she would have liked to go to university. And that's before we start on any of the teenage barbecues or dances.

It was not much better when she became an adult. Christmas 1965 and we went home to Grandma's for the summer holidays. I would have been eight. As we drew up at her house on Court Street, she was in the garden. We children piled out gleefully – we had not been here for a whole year and had been travelling for seven hours. My mother opened the car door and stepped out, smiling. 'That skirt's too short,' was Grandma's greeting. My mother said not one word. She turned back to the car to pick up the baby.

So my mother had a lot to resist in the parenting stakes, but she did, and she made a point of trying to be unlike her own mother. When we were little she was at home when we came back from school, she organized sumptuous birthday parties with coconut ice and soda cream drinks, she put together little picnics, she bought the impractical tapestry coat I desired, she helped when we planted a herb garden. When we were older she never asked questions, tried hard not to criticize, worked at being positive, and carefully did not tell us what to do.

My mother became a mother because that was what you did in the 1950s. As it turned out, by the 1970s she was forced to learn to regard her parenting as a duty, a requirement, a profession.

But the fact that she had children gave her a lot of pleasure in her later years. She liked the company of her family, and she was immensely proud and fulfilled by the fact that her own four children knew their Australian cousins – her two brothers' seven children – and knew them well. As cousins, we were friendly, caring – close, even, despite living 12,000 miles apart after our migration to England in the 1960s. That meant a lot. To her; to us.

In the past, children were often a social and biological given, as they were for my mother – the result of love (one hopes). But children could also have been the result of desire, force (physical, economic, communal, political), strategic allegiance, inheritance, self-realization, commercial exploitation, cultural expectation.

All of the above still apply. But today, even though there are also other choices to be made, a person's desire for a child is accepted as the normal state of things, the status quo of human life. Politically, scientifically, socially, we sanction that 'desire for a child' – with the legal and acceptable growth of fertility treatments, for instance. Children are now what they always have been, though perhaps in a different way – a desirable commodity.

Much more usually, those who are without children are regarded as the oddity. There is a difference between the 'childless' and the 'childfree' – one indicating loss, the other insisting on choice – but how can we know, without being privy to the specific situation, which is which? Whatever the case, a glance at the internet shows how both the childless and the childfree are treated with suspicion. To be childfree is to selfishly expect other people's children to pay the taxes that will provide for social care in old age; to be childless as a woman makes you unfit for public office and all the rest. But what concealed decisions, what secret pain may go into this?

There is the woman who longed for a baby but whose partner was adamantly against it and so, in the name of love, she acquiesced. Or the woman who actively did not want a child but felt it unfair that she was forcing her husband to be childless, so she too, in the name of love, acquiesced (but only the once). And there are the other women – and men – who might wish for a child but are denied that possibility, perhaps because of physical reasons such as infertility or illness, or perhaps because of social or personal situations that make it a difficult undertaking, ruling out alternatives such as surrogacy or adoption.

So often, the wish to have children relies upon external considerations, though sometimes that can mean no consideration at all. In the wealthy West, social expectation sets it up as a regular human desire, entirely normal and natural. So people often do not think about it. They assume that it is what they want, what their parents want, what everybody expects and wants. So instead of asking 'Why do I want a child?' they ask other, sidelong, questions such as, 'Do I want a child with this person?', 'Is this the right moment to have a child?', 'Do I have the room/money/time/ support for a child?' Their true intention is displaced.

But whatever the reasons, whatever the decision-making process, few hopeful parents consider the child in this endeavour. Of course, some people do think about the child, or about themselves as children, and come to the realization that they do not want to be a parent. But there are others who want to reclaim and recuperate their own lost or painful childhood, and look to remake a fairy-tale version for their own offspring.

Of course, my wish for a child was by no means unusual. But in my case it was more complicated, without any of the usual social considerations at play.

At the time of that snowy morning – when I had that first light, that vision of the possible – I was in my mid-forties. Late enough in any case, but for me a child was a biological impossibility. I had experienced a sudden early menopause in my thirties – hidden to all, of course, but dramatic and disconcerting. I had been due to co-chair a huge international summer school in Oxford when, having just set off, I started to bleed. Heavily, copiously. Fortunately I had been assigned a room in the centre of the college and managed to cope by leaping up every ten minutes and rushing back to base to sort myself out. This went on for the whole five days I was there, and beyond. There was no time to think about it, and no one to talk to, so I kept the fright to myself and put the worry off for later. Then it stopped.

I went home, felt fine, thought no more about it. Some while later I realized I had missed my period. Twice. A blood test showed that I was perimenopausal. The doctor offered me HRT. Interestingly, there were no questions asked about how I might take this news, how I might feel. True, I had never raised the question of my fertility – or now, rather, lack thereof – but nonetheless, at that moment I felt as if I would have liked some acknowledgement. Some commiseration, even.

Because my reaction was bizarre. Before that point, I had been resigned to not having a baby. But somehow that was still just a temporary acceptance. The possibility was there on the horizon – if it were to come over me, if circumstances were different. And now that possibility was gone. I was oddly upset, and looked at the friends around me who had young children with a new perspective. And with a new kind of something that I can only call envy.

But then, at that time in my mid-forties, I also knew that the wish for a child wasn't about me. I mean, it was not about my body, my DNA or my desire to make a curly, redheaded, miniature me. I do not care about DNA or physical inheritance, and I know that I didn't care about it then either. It was not that drive that was causing me pain.

All the same. Once, at the opera, I ran into a man who had been my first boyfriend, and whom I had not seen for many years. 'Any children?' he asked, quite casually. 'No,' I replied. 'A shame,' he said. I think he meant it as a compliment. Or was it a judgement on my failure? People ask this question so easily, so thoughtlessly. I acknowledge having done it myself, but I think now that I am more careful, because I can see that look in the shadowed eye. And I have heard the tart response that I gave on this occasion: 'It's a bit of a sore point.'

*

I don't feel that my wish to be a mother was to do with bodily experience. Unlike some women, I had not ever thought much about carrying a child or the prospect of giving birth.

Nonetheless, as one of four siblings with a tribe of cousins, I had indeed taken family life for granted and vaguely assumed that there would be children. That no steps were needed. But things did not turn out that way. When I was young and contentedly, happily, lengthily married, there were other priorities. He worked hard and put in long hours. I needed to finish my PhD and get a teaching job, then a permanent job. Like so many, I thought that there was plenty of time for tomorrow.

Later on, for a long time, I lived with someone who did not want children, and I accepted this situation. Which is why, when I went through that sudden menopause, it should have made no difference; it should not have mattered.

But then this relationship abruptly came to an end. And many months later, as I emerged out of the dark of that time, the pale light of that snowy morning gave me this new idea.

In spite of my certainty that this desire of mine was not being driven by biological craving, for a fleeting moment I did consider IVF. For rather more than a fleeting moment, in fact, because I made an appointment with a private fertility clinic to discuss the question. There was a talk with a very scary lady ('All I need is a healthy womb') and a scan. And that was it. I was accepted on to a scheme. Obviously it required both a donor egg and donor sperm. The waiting list was long.

A year later, when I had quite forgotten all about it, the clinic rang me. They had a donor mother. I asked for one day to consider it. But by this time I had made a choice, and for me, it was the right choice and a first choice. I had a new plan. And so, the following day, I called back to say thank you, but no thank you. They were pleased. I had made a good decision for me. And I had passed on a hope to the next woman on the waiting list.

Lisa Jardine, a dear friend, much loved and much missed, took up the post of chair of the Human Fertilisation and Embryology Authority (HFEA) in 2008. A brilliant choice, because Lisa was both a scientist and a humanist: she could understand the technical questions, but she recognized the feeling, the emotional dimension. When Lisa announced her retirement from that job in 2013, she said in an interview with Jenni Murray on BBC Radio 4's *Woman's Hour* that her biggest regret in departing her office at the HFEA was that she had not made it clearer to women considering IVF just how difficult and how much of a gamble this kind of treatment is. Of course, I know many children born in this way, and they are a delight to their parents and to the world. But it was not for me.

At one point during the year I was on the books of the fertility clinic, I went to stay with Lisa in France. We worked in the morning, swam in the afternoon and talked over our lives. Always direct, even then Lisa advised me against IVF: 'There is a child already in the world who needs you.' She was backing my other plan, my new plan.

I set aside all external considerations. I had no partner to take into account, no biological urges to contend with, and no expectations from my family or anyone else. But I still wanted a child. I thought about words, fertility words, birthing words. 'Hormone', from the Greek: meaning 'to set in motion, to urge on'. 'Conceive', from the Latin: meaning 'to take in, to take up, to contain, or to hold'.

Soon after the time when I had dreamed that first light, one kind friend, quite coincidentally, was thinking over my new and hitherto unlooked-for options. 'How about this?' she said. 'Have a baby.' Well, that was out the question. 'Adopt, then,' she replied.

So that is what I decided to do. I 'took in and took up' this desired child. I 'set in motion' and 'urged on'. Adoption was the answer. And, in spite of the long deliberations set out here, that answer came to me quickly and clearly. Once the germ of the idea of an adopted child was there, it took hold and grew rapidly.

It was my answer, but it was also my choice. And it was by no means a provisional choice, a conditional choice or a 'settling for what I could have' choice. As you will see, it was to become more and more certain in spite of the many obstacles I had yet to overcome. Because the path towards adoption is not straight – there are many bends in the road, many hurdles, many frustrations, many times when you seem to be at a dead end. Even the earliest stages of the process are arduous, gruelling, difficult.

The choice to 'urge on' and to 'set in motion' had been made, and that decision was crystalline in its conviction. But the results of that choice were to challenge me in ways I could not have imagined.

I F

ADOPTION WAS THE new plan – the one that Lisa did like. As she then said to me, 'There is a child already in the world who needs you. Why go through the agony and risk of failure? And besides, with adoption, you still have your body, your health and your strength.' I went on with the 'Adopt, then' advice. How easy it is to say. The reality is quite another matter.

Before I go further, I must make it clear that I was not looking for a child to remedy my life. It was a positive decision to seek out something that I had always vaguely expected but that had never been mine. In acknowledging this clear desire, in making this choice, I was re-connecting with a core: a self that was really me and not the me made by relationships with others or by chance and circumstance.

Anyone who has experience of the adoption system will know that it requires dedication and determination, and, per-haps most of all, a willingness to examine honestly one's own life and values. It is also a system that requires an excess of commitment and scrutiny far beyond anything that birth par-ents may undergo.

There are many different kinds of parenting patterns, or ways to become a mother, but for now let us consider six that may pertain in the UK. First of all there are birth parents, which is a form pretty much unregulated – you get pregnant, you have a baby, no one questions your right to that child. Then there are birth parents who come to that position through medical intervention, which may involve a degree of regulation and some interrogation. Then social parents, where a child may be looked after by another family member – again (for the most part) unregulated, unexamined. Then step-parents, also generally unregulated (though in some cases Social Services, or even the family courts, may intervene), but a situation that is delicate and needs subtle negotiation – neither too little, nor too much. Then fostering, where a child in the care of the state is placed with 'parents' not related to them, which is highly regulated but also financially supported by the state. And, finally, adoption, which is highly regulated, and where the parent is rigorously examined, where officials make all the decisions, where the law is invoked to revise the child's story. It is neither generally supported financially, nor much supported practically.

As the idea of adopting a child grew in me, I knew that there were particular things in my past – specifically in my own childhood – that needed addressing, and part of this chronicle is an account of that endeavour. Then there is the preparation: the volunteering, the courses, the knowledge that needs to be acquired in order to demonstrate commitment to this new life.

There were also more practical things. As an Australian living in England from the age of eleven, I had to consider, in the largest terms, my home situation, my allegiances, my sense of identity and belonging. More simply, I also had to think concretely about what kind of home I would be offering to this notional child. That is all here too.

In the very beginning I made a big mistake. Because of this, and for many other reasons, this is the story of nearly seven years. But seven is a magic number. It is not ended yet. There never will be an end. But this is the tale of how it began.

In a very short time, I leaped from the germ of the idea of a child to an idealized picture of what my life would be like with that child. I began to imagine her – if it was to be a her – always beside me, and I began to plan. We would travel, as I had done in my own childhood. We would go to the opera and to the Schubertiade festival, for surely that would be small enough and intimate enough for us to sit at the back and leave if the child were to grow restless.

Gradually, this notional child was always there, even on a trip to the dentist. Now, I love my dentist. She rescued me from a botched job many years ago, and little catch-ups with Estella and her colleague Cara are a pleasure. After one appointment I stepped out into the street feeling merry. Across the road was a dress shop and I turned in idly to browse the rails. And there was a little coat – a child's coat with a hood in a heavy cotton that looked like a brocade, spring green trimmed with cloudy blue. It was absurd, but I bought it anyway and carried it home triumphantly, my secret held close. Later that night, the figure wrapped in the red shawl in my picture walked alongside a small child in a green coat with a hood.

*

These were happy thoughts, but once I had settled on adoption, I also knew that this was about the child too. That this (as yet only imagined) child was also a person, highly likely a sad person, suffering from loss. The hope of my personal fulfilment was predicated, necessarily, on that child's pain. This is a difficult element for adoptive parents to contend with, but one that they must recognize and acknowledge.

In one way I already knew this, and it was something that drew me. Years before, the late Julia Briggs was then the general editor of the Penguin series of George Eliot's novels. We had never met, but she asked me to come and see her, and she suggested that I take on the job of editing *Adam Bede*. It is a novel with painful subject matter. Hetty Sorrel, pretty and vain, is seduced by the grandson of the local landowner. When she finds herself pregnant she flees the village to seek out her lover. Giving birth to her child during this journey, distraught and alone, not knowing what to do, she leaves the baby in the wood, but then returns, haunted by the child's cry, only to find it gone. The baby dies. Hetty is tried for child murder. Eliot herself said that she wrote these parts of the story 'rapidly' and 'without the slightest alteration of the first draught [sic]'. But in the novel we never learn anything else about this child. Not its sex, not its looks, not its marks, not its name – if it ever had a name. This child is a lostling.

I asked Julia, 'Why me? Why me for this novel?' And she replied, 'I want to see what you will make of that child.' At the time, it seemed an odd response. Now, as I begin to move forward with this decision in my life, it feels like a premonition.

*

In telling her stories about mothering, about the verb 'to mother', Sarah Knott sticks to one enterprise. She was, at the time of writing the following passage in *Mother*, newly delivered of a four-week-old child, and her research method was governed by that fact:

> I turn the spines of my pile of books on maternal loss or
> foundling hospitals against the wall. Their subjects make
> me retch, or panic. I hold, yet more urgently than before, to
> the guiding topic: the living mothering of a living infant.

By choosing to adopt, by choosing to try to become an adoptive parent, I am taking a different way, a different topic. I knew that then. What I did not know was how that sidelong, ancillary subject would become the central subject; how my vision of the possible would move from a focus on me and my wish for mothering to a focus on the child, and on the lostlings, foundlings and changelings who are all around.

But first of all I had to get there.

I began by trying out the idea of adoption on my friends. I talked to Marianna Kennedy, an artist and a beautiful person I had known for years. Marianna, always optimistic, slapped my knee, spilling her coffee, 'Let's go for it!' In particular, I spoke to my friend Jacqueline, herself the mother of a young daughter. 'Yes, absolutely,' she said. 'When you have that kind of love in you, you must put it somewhere.'

But where to begin? I knew nothing. I had no idea.

I wrote a letter to Social Services and waited. I resolved to do something every day to further my plans or improve my knowledge. This was a good discipline. Being an academic, I read books on adoption.

But I also took new directions. I had to decide where I was going to live, and this meant thinking about identity, allegiance and home, both my old childhood home and the new home that I would make for my child.

HOME

I lost two cities, lovely ones. And, vaster,
some realms I owned, two rivers, a continent.
I miss them, but it wasn't a disaster.

Elizabeth Bishop, 'One Art'

WHEN I FIRST saw the house where I live I had no idea that it would become my home. But I vividly remember that first sight of it. It is possible to be haunted by the future.

It was September. I was moving from London and had driven to the country to meet a surveyor at my new property. On the way back to the city, I happened upon a shortcut through a village where the houses were ranged around a wide green. There were two tiny, mirror-image, semi-detached cottages, set well back from the road. And the whole of the substantial front garden was laid down to dahlias. There were round red pom-poms and spiky white blooms, some with delicate pink petals and others brassily sturdy in yellow. I stopped and stared. It was so spectacular, so old-fashioned, so much of the stuff of fairy tale, that I would often tell the story, though the place then meant nothing to me.

Many years later I had no home because my house was to be

sold. My friend Jayne, who lived just outside the village, called one day in August to tell me the cottages were for sale by auction. I collected the keys from the estate agent and the house drew me in.

The first cottage was near derelict. Kitchen and bathroom were in the same space – sink in one corner and a bath in the other. The toilet was outside. But there were original stone flags on the ground floor, wide elm boards upstairs, and a huge inglenook fireplace that had ideas above its station, fitted with a cute 1930s Rayburn. The second cottage did have a bathroom – in avocado. But it too had the wide floorboards, and a fireplace with a good-looking Victorian range. I stole a tiny, old, glass lemonade bottle from a niche in the stone wall as a spell, promising that I would bring it back when the house was mine.

The cottages were to be sold at auction in a pub, which was new territory for me. The only other person I could think of to have bought a house at auction in a pub was Virginia Woolf. In the summer of 1919, she and her husband Leonard happened across an auctioneer's placard: 'Lot 1. Monks House, Rodmell. An old-fashioned house standing in three-quarters of an acre of land to be sold with possession.' The following Tuesday, on 1 July, Leonard and Virginia presented themselves at the White Hart in Lewes.

'I don't suppose,' wrote Woolf later in her diary, 'many spaces of five minutes in the course of my life have been so close packed with sensation . . . The room . . . was crowded. I looked at every face, & in particular at every coat & skirt, for signs of opulence, & was cheered to discover none. But then, I thought, getting L. into line, does *he* look as if he had £800 in his pocket?'

But the house did go to them. At £700 the auctioneer's

hammer came down, 'to our thanksgiving – I purple in the cheeks, & L. trembling like a reed.'

Before long it was also my turn to do this. It was September again and the auction was taking place at the end of the day as the late-summer light was beginning to fail. I drove up by myself, and arrived absurdly early at the Old New Inn. I chose a seat at the back where I could see the competition. Then I changed my mind, and moved to the front where the auctioneer could see me.

People began to fill the room. Most came in little groups and sat down with their pints, chatting as the auctioneer set up a little podium and the estate agent handed out brochures for the cottages. A few of my friends arrived, but I was not in the mood for conversation. How could they all be so calm, so unconcerned? Was this person my rival? Or that? The man studying the particulars – does he display an indication of affluence? Or that woman sitting alone – is she gearing up for battle? In fact, as I later discovered, most people there were from the village, come to see the fun.

Cannily, the done-up, avocado-bathroomed cottage was auctioned first. But it was the neglected one I wanted. So I knew that I had to get the other too. Whoever succeeded in purchasing Avocado Hall would have the incentive to bid on for the second cottage. That competition had to be seen off.

The auction began. The sums were fairly low and hands went up all over the room. I sat tight. A friend, perched behind me, began to get desperate: 'Why aren't you bidding?' she hissed impatiently. Well, I may only have bought a few shawls and cheap Victorian paintings at Christie's, but I knew the form. If you come in as a new bidder when the price is already quite high, then the punters think you really must have the zlotys. In the end, it was me and one other man. Just when the amount of the bidding was reaching a little bit over my maximum, he gave in. A sigh all round.

The bidding for the second cottage began. My erstwhile foe bid half-heartedly. I waited. My friend started the agitated whispering again. I could strangle her. When the price was nearing what I thought it was worth, I began to bid. Most others fell away, but one persisted. My overexcited friend fussed, 'Keep going, keep going.' Spotting this, the auctioneer encouraged, 'Listen to your adviser, madam. Listen to your adviser.' *I will* strangle her.

Suddenly, a woman I'd not even noticed began to bid against me, but by then the rises at each new bid were tiny. I took a quick glance at her, insofar as I dared to take my eyes off the auctioneer. The lady was white-haired, plainly dressed, with no sign of obvious monetary power. I did keep going. One last little flurry and the cottage was mine. Both cottages were mine. My defeated rival stormed noisily out of the room.

As we left the pub amid kisses and glee, my friend Ron, who had come along for moral support with his wife Barbara, said, 'Don't do that again, Peg. My heart can't stand it.'

I won't. Neither can mine.

My heart longs for a home. When I was a child, we never lived anywhere for more than two years. My father was a schoolteacher, and under the system then obtaining in New South Wales you could only get a promotion by moving. When I was born he had a one-teacher school with nineteen pupils, aged from four to sixteen, in a settlement on the appropriately named One Tree Plain. Booligal – notoriously celebrated in A. B. Patterson's 1896 poem 'Hay and Hell and Booligal' – consisted of a church, a pub, a courthouse, the schoolhouse, and seven outlying farm stations.

Some time after my sister was born, we moved to a dusty little town where I drove my third-time-pregnant mother to distraction by dragging my two-year-old sister up from her afternoon nap, climbing out of the laundry window and hauling her along the dirt roads. We once saw a peacock on the street in this way, its tail spread in full glory, escaped from who knows where.

Then there was a larger town in sheep-farming country, along with a new little brother. After that came a town in a coal-mining area, which has since become world famous as the wine-growing district of the Hunter Valley. And another small brother. Each time, we moved further away from the country and nearer to the city and the sea.

In one way it did not matter. I made friends and I lost them. Strange places became familiar, then familiar places became strange. Through it all there was the continuity of my grandmother's house, four hundred miles into distant country that had once been the site of a gold rush. Every Christmas we decamped there for the whole of the summer holiday. And there were my two doctor uncles, the collection of 1930s *Batman* comics under the bed on the back veranda, the backyard toilet, the plates set on a display rail high up in the formal sitting room, and all my gang of seven dear cousins who, each year, would be coaxed and corralled into performing our Famous Christmas Day Show. It was close to home.

But then my parents – objecting to Australia's conscription

policy introduced as a result of participation in the Vietnam War – decided to leave. The choice was between Canada, favoured because of the scenery in the film of *The Incredible Journey*, and England – where my parents had been married and where lived Litzi, a beloved friend to my mother who, as my uncle Coll once observed, was 'more of a mother to her than her own mother'.

It was to be England. We embarked from the long-distance passenger dock at Circular Quay in Sydney on an Italian cruise ship called the *Castel Felice*. Uncles and aunts and cousins all came to wave us off. We children tore up and down, enchanted by the cabins and the bunk beds, the deck, and the sailors in their black-and-white uniforms. Then my cousins all got off, and the truth became plain.

As I tell this story I wonder about child migrants. How bewildering it is, how overwhelmingly painful, even when your family is still with you, let alone if they are not. I have returned to Sydney many times since this departure. Circular Quay now houses fancy restaurants and hotels, where people sit out in the sun, drinking, chatting, laughing. But in 2005 I sat there alone, watching, my heart full of long-forgotten misery and dread.

The voyage was miserable too. There was a school on board, but it was in a room right over the engines. The smell, the noise and the vibrations made me sick so I did not go. My siblings and I liked the menus that came each day with a different pirate story: Blackbeard (Edward Teach), Israel 'Basilica' Hands, Richard Hawkins, and our favourites, Charlotte de Berry and Anne Bonny. But my only real pleasure was sitting in to watch the rehearsals of the am-drams who put up with the lonely kid in the front row.

My baby brother got very sick and nearly died on the journey.

My mother spent the night making up her mind to beg the captain to put his little body in the freezer if the worst happened. I made a promise to God that I would give up the dress rehearsal that I had been so much looking forward to so that he would be safe. He was. And in the morning all the sailors and waiters and workers smiled and gestured to us children, crying, '*Il bambino, il bambino.*'

After six weeks at sea we docked at Southampton. It was February and we children had no coats, which horrified my mother's friend Litzi, who marched us straight off the boat-train and on to Oxford Street to supply the deficiency.

Because the boat was two weeks late landing in England, my father lost the post he had arranged before leaving Australia. We had no money and, to begin with, lived in a modest hotel off Russell Square on a diet of cream crackers. While my parents searched for a job for my father, we older children were sent to a school near by. A school where the corridors smelled of toilets and overcooked cabbage, where the children mocked our accents, where my sister – a frail child with a small appetite – was made to sit all lunch time over the food she could not eat, and where the only place to play was on a roof surrounded by twelve-foot-high mesh fences.

It was cold. It was dark. I missed my cousin Jenny. I made up an imaginary friend who lived in the hotel plumbing, and I whispered my troubles to her through the waste overflow in the bath.

My brothers and sister and I admire our parents for their bravery, for their commitment. But now I wonder. A psychotherapist once remarked to me, more or less in passing, that this move was 'not a very child-friendly decision'. In an exhibition titled 'The Children's War', which was displayed at the Imperial War Museum from 2007–10, there was a quotation from a man called Jim Bartley:

> At the time I was evacuated I used to tell myself that one day the war would be over and I could go back home. After the war . . . I made my way back to where I used to live. The whole area had been obliterated during . . . the Blitz and I was quite unable to find the spot where our house once stood. That happened more than fifty years ago . . . but somehow I am still waiting to go home.

Recalling the psychotherapist's remark, I stood before this placard for a long time, wondering about my own childhood experience of displacement and how it has shaped me in invisible ways.

The smell is familiar as soon as I step off the plane: eucalyptus, giving way to sea salt. At Avalon, on Sydney's Northern Beaches, shoppers with green bags chat their way around the supermarket in bare feet, towels wrapped around their swimmers. Almost everybody wears a hat. Absolutely everybody has some sunscreen sticking out of their bag. No one is really bronzed. Those days are gone. My paternal grandfather suffered from skin cancer and ended up with a false nose and a false ear. Nothing fancy. Just plain, vivid, pink plastic. His party trick for us children was to take them off. At the 'Stop, Kiss and Leave' sign by the school gates, the blond children peel away and flutter off. The straight-down light makes everyone look beautiful.

One calm day we take the ferry over to the Basin. We are greeted by the cheery lady ranger collecting our $6, and then by a swamp wallaby with a joey in its pouch. On the ferry is a couple golden with sun. They carry two towels and an esky. She wears a skimpy green bikini and a white silk sarong. He, long baggy shorts and a T-shirt. Under a Scots pine they arrange themselves at right angles, her hand on the flat of his stomach.

The lagoon is exquisite. A curve of blue sky, green and grey in the steep wooded slope fretted by the pink-and-white bark of the gum trees. The water is still, pale yellow, clear through to the sand, then dark green where the shore drops away and the water deepens, and then, further out, blue under the curve of the sky.

Two young girls sit on their towels under a tree. Their picnic bag is tied high in the branches, safe from the marauding goanna. The dark-haired one sings along to her iPod. She laughs, and offers an earphone to her blonde friend.

Am I at home here? I love the slopes and the water, the birds and the smell of the sea. I like being surrounded by Australians and their easy ways. I relish being able to call up my cousins and run over for dinner. The old goanna lumbers past the golden couple. Green Bikini tracks him with her camera. Two myna birds screech and a whole flock attacks, swooping low at the lizard. And the constant cicadas.

Am I at home here? As I fall asleep in the house looking out over Pittwater, I can see water and sky. There are no buildings, no light except the stars. Just the same as it would have been thousands of centuries ago when what is now the Ku-ring-gai Chase National Park would have been a home to the Guringai people.

In Shaun Tan and John Marsden's *The Rabbits* – a parable about the darker side of Australia's past and present – Tan has illustrated the endpapers with shallow blue water, bordered with black, and dotted with delicate birds and water lilies. The story is a sad one. 'The rabbits came many grandparents ago,' appears on a page rich with ochre red and deep lapis blue.

The 'rabbits' in Tan's vision are angular and pointy of head, ear and limb in their stylized eighteenth-century costume: 'They ate our grass . . . and stole our children.' On this page the small, red, curly creatures are individually packed into hundreds of square white kites trailed on strings by black aeroplanes. A black-suited regiment of rabbits oversees the proclamation. Small on the horizon, the yearning, red, curly parents lift their hands to the sky.

As you turn the pages of the book, the images fade from vivid colour to barren tones of sepia, grey, and then to black. 'Where is the rich, dark earth, brown and moist?' the book concludes, ' . . . Where is the smell of rain dripping from gum trees? Where are the great billabongs, alive with long-legged birds?' It ends, 'Who will save us from the rabbits?'

This is a story about home. But it is also a story about a lost home, or a home snatched away from those to whom it belonged. When I decided that I wanted a child, when I decided that I would try to adopt a child, I thought a lot about children and loss and home and belonging. Part of my task at this time, during these months in Australia, was to think over my own childhood there.

But I found myself thinking also about displaced children, and specifically about the ways in which so many children suffered because of the policies of past Australian governments. Tan's illustrations in this book are beautiful, as is all his work, but the text reminds us of the shocking facts of the Stolen Generations, when Aboriginal children were calculatedly taken away from their families, from their homes, from their own lives, in an effort to integrate and eradicate a whole cultural history.

As a child I had a double vision. We hardly ever saw any indigenous Australians in the lately-come gold-mining-then-sheep-farming white-settled towns of western New South Wales. There might be a few, glimpsed fleetingly, as we drove past the occasional shanty town on the outskirts of suburban sprawl. In fact, it seems to me now that we rarely saw anyone who was not of White British origin. There was the Chinese family that ran a little farm shop just outside the town where my grandmother lived. We liked to go there to see the turtles in the tank. There was the cast-iron figure of a black boy eternally waiting for someone to hitch his horse on the High Street at Maitland. That was it.

My experience is not unusual. In her book *The Tall Man* (2008), about the death of Cameron Doomadgee – the Aboriginal man who died in police custody on Palm Island in November 2004 – Chloe Hooper says much the same:

Like most middle-class suburbanites, I grew up without ever seeing an Aborigine, except on the news. The Reconciliation Movement – our country's fitful attempt to bridge relations between the first Australians and all who followed – is a cause pursued by thousands who do not actually know any of the 2 per cent of the population who are Aboriginal.

But this was Australia in the early 1960s. A place where the White Australia policy restricted immigration by those of non-European ethnic origin, and where Aboriginal and Torres Strait Islander peoples were not counted in the census. A place where men went into bars, while women and children waited in the car outside. A place where a favourite saying was, 'If it moves, shoot it. If it doesn't, chop it down.' A place where my father was known for his wit: 'I don't get headaches. I give 'em.'

But then I had other stories. My great grandmother was born in 1857 and her family lived on Dumaresq Island in the Manning River, near the Queensland border. An Aboriginal group shared the island and my great grandmother, Margaret Alicia, had a special friend in Topsy. (Yes, really.) As an old lady she would tell my mother – and then my mother would tell me – stories about Topsy. And every time they began with the same story. That of how Margaret Alicia was the stranger, the odd one out: 'Margarlissabar, Margarlissabar, why you got blue string in your veins?'

My great aunt knew all this, told to her by her mother, my great grandmother. Auntie Lil was the youngest of Margaret Alicia's ten children, and she was born on 1 January 1900.

By the time I knew her, Lil lived in a weatherboard house on an orange farm owned by her brother in the area of the Central Coast. As a child, she seemed to me much of a child too, with bright blue eyes and a frank delight in the everyday. Her house was a fairyland: the fragrant beauty of the orange trees in blossom, the big banana tree by the back door, the mosquito nets over the beds, the dunny stationed well away from the house, and the set of ebony elephants ranging from a foot high down to one barely half an inch tall. It was Lil who first introduced me to *Anne of Green Gables*. And *she* could possibly have begun by reading it as a young girl when it was first published in 1908.

When I went to look for Lil's house recently, I found the country still beautiful, just as I remembered it. But many lovely old houses had been left to decay, while smart new bungalows preened alongside. At the local hotel, pop music blared out, the pure landscape of willows and water, dragonflies and bright avenues tamed by the inanity of canned sound and banal suburban platitudes.

Yet when I arrived at Lemon Tree, I knew the track and turned the car instinctively. I knew the house, and the shapes of the landscape felt familiar. The orchards were gone, but the spirit of place was the same. The shifting grey-green leaves, the layered palimpsests of coloured bark. What surprised me was the green Europeanness of it all. I had expected to find one home there, but I discovered two. Maybe it explains my love of the flickering English willow, of water and green and soft hazy skies.

Here. The robin, a woodpecker's yaffle, the *pink-pink* of the chaffinch. Most deliciously, the long, drawn-out display of the blackbird in the summer evening. At other seasons, the pigeon, the pheasant, the cuckoo, the rich tapestry of sound in the early light. A dog barks. Sometimes a horse neighs. In the spring, the lambs cry.

There. The kookaburras at dawn, the raucous cry as the sulphur-crested cockatoo sweeps by, the sweeter sounds of small coloured birds, the pink-and-grey galahs, the bright rainbow lorikeets and, over all, the incessant cicadas. At Yarramalong they are deafening, and you can see them, two inches long, scattered up the white bark of every gum tree.

I decided to apply for a British passport. If I was to adopt a child, it suddenly seemed to me sensible to claim an absolute right of residence.

In my Australian passport there is a stamp that reads 'Given leave to enter the United Kingdom indefinitely'. The wording on the stamp was changed a few years ago. It used to say 'Given indefinite leave to enter the United Kingdom'. I puzzled over the different word order. Had I more rights, or fewer?

I went to the post office for a form. First of all, my lovely (South African) postmistress, explained that I had to apply for naturalization. Naturalization. A word apparently transparent, but it has a history. Today, the Home Office website explains it with these words: 'The criteria and process have changed over the years but for successful applicants the end result has been the same: that person is granted the same legal rights and status of a natural-born British citizen.' But that 'natural-born' is suspi-ciously indicative of assumed privilege and power, and the granting of such rights to others has usually occurred in the light of some perceived benefit to British commercial interests.

Most notoriously in recent years, the British Nationality Act of 1948 allowed for all 'British Subjects' in the colonies to become a 'Citizen of the United Kingdom and Colonies', wherever they lived. Many workers migrated to the UK under this system, but by 1962 the Conservative government – in a move that was clear racial discrimination – declared that only those with official employment vouchers could settle, and the Commonwealth Immigrants Act of that same year made all those from the ex-colonies subject to immigration control.

As I think about all this, I remember something. On one occasion, as I passed through Heathrow travelling on my Australian passport, an immigration officer detained me to enquire how I had acquired my 'indefinite leave to remain'. I explained that I had come here as a child, that I had been to college here, that I worked here, that I had lived here ever since. He was not much impressed by any of this. Then he asked, 'Did your father have a work permit when you first arrived in Britain?' 'I don't know,' I replied indignantly, 'I was a child!' He was clearly not satisfied. Reluctantly, as it seemed to me, he let me go. But then, I reflected to myself ruefully as I walked away, my skin is white.

At the time that I applied for naturalization, the Home Office website offered a choice from some thirty different forms depending on your specific situation. There was then no online application: you had to pick the appropriate form, print it and post it off. I cannot remember why, but I found it very difficult to find the one that applied most closely to my position. There was a telephone number offering assistance. I rang first thing in the morning. I rang at elevenses, at tea time, at half-hourly intervals throughout the day: it was always engaged. So I gave up and tackled the many different forms again. Hours later I had narrowed it down to key elements, such as my Commonwealth status and my 'indefinite leave to remain'. But I still could not choose between two forms. In the end I filled in both of them and posted them off together.

After six months I received a letter acknowledging my application and my Australian passport was returned. The letter's heading read 'Who to contact with an enquiry'. Underneath this it instructed, 'Do not contact us'.

After another few months I was sent my Naturalisation Certificate and, later on, my new British passport.

The Home Office rules have changed since I applied, and the system is meant to be more streamlined, but there are many hurdles. A glance at their website will show that it is complicated and longwinded. But I did get the passport quite quickly and, being a Gemini, I am rather pleased with my dual nationality.

I am an immigrant. My mother is an immigrant, as our ancestors were once immigrants in the other direction. In London, my place is in Spitalfields, home to Huguenots in the eighteenth century, Jews fleeing Hitler in the 1930s, Indians displaced by Partition, Bangladeshis, Bosnians and Serbs, Poles and Czechs. My friends there come from Canada, the US, the West Indies, Afghanistan, Portugal and Ireland. Britain's mongrel heritage gives you a pedigree there.

This is also a story about home.

MAYBE

SIX MONTHS AFTER I had first written to Social Services enquiring about adoption, I received a letter from the local authority. An initial visit was arranged with a social worker. Claudia arrived promptly. I made her a cup of tea. She was directly on the case and asked me my reasons for wishing to adopt. This is rather a big question at a first meeting, and it is difficult to know where to start when the reasons are many.

All my thoughts about why I want a child, why I want to be a mother, what I feel I could offer a child, what I feel a child could offer me, are the things I begin with. Those seem to me the key reasons, needing no further explanation. But this is at once too general and, apparently, too unnecessary. In a funny kind of way, adoption social workers often take it for granted that people just do want children, and so they don't require long philosophical musings on the subject. They are frequently used to dealing with couples – married and not – who have had fertility problems, of whatever kind. So they want to know two things, really: how stable the relationship is, and how effectively these prospective adopters have come to terms with their infertility.

I am a slightly different case. And – I can see – a bit of a puzzling one. First, because I am older and have apparently tolerated my childlessness for all this time, and second, because I am single; I want to do this on my own, without any significant other with whom I wish to make a family. I don't fit. But Claudia listens to my explanation about my commitment to parenthood, and she seems to accept that as enough. She explains that in order to proceed, we will need to embark on a 'home study'. This will take at least six months, and involve numerous visits to discuss my family, my finances, my employment position, my relationships, my capacity to parent, my life.

But before any of that can start, Claudia wants to know what sort of a child I am looking for. I had not considered that this would need to be decided upon so soon. I had vaguely thought that you got approved and then identified what kind of child afterwards. Pretty quickly, though, I see what she means: the home study needs a specific focus, needs to have the desired end result in mind. In fact, I had indeed already thought about this question of 'what kind of child'. It was obvious, really, I thought foolishly – children start off as babies, so I wanted a baby. But I knew very well from all that I had read that, in my case, at my age, there was only one route available to me that might lead to a baby.

So I told Claudia that I had decided on inter-country adoption. In Britain, babies are relatively rarely taken into care and hence available to adopt. This has not always been the case: in the past, social opprobrium led many young unmarried women to relinquish their babies. For the most part, children come into care today through the intervention of Social Services. That usually only takes place when a child may be subjected to neglect and abuse, and by the time that is recognized, such a child is no longer likely to be a baby. In any case, as an older prospective adoptive parent, I was not likely to be offered a baby through agencies in the UK.

I had also already asked myself which country: that too has to be settled before you begin the home study. Many different countries at different times have permitted overseas adoption, generally for reasons to do with political or social circumstances, such as war or extremes of poverty. So this can make for an uncomfortable narrative, balancing perceived Western security and wealth against the exigencies of less developed or disrupted nations.

Agencies dealing with overseas or inter-country adoption ask that prospective adopters have some recognizable connection to the child's country of origin, and require that they respect and maintain their cultural heritage. When I realized that one had to make a choice of country, I considered India simply because I knew it and had loved my time there. But a brief conversation with a member of the Overseas Adoption Support and Information Service (OASIS) made me realize that I did not have a strong case.

Once, it had been relatively easy for foreigners to adopt from India, but by the early 2000s the authorities there – as in so many other countries – were becoming reluctant to release their children for adoption overseas, and looked to place them at home. My contact on the phone explained that some people had succeeded by becoming involved in the life of a particular orphanage, but these were people who had lived and worked in India for years, so their links to the country were much more active and substantial than mine. Of course, discovering all this had taken a while, so there was some imaginative investment here, but I could certainly see this point of view and quickly came to accept and understand the reasoning behind everything that the adviser from OASIS had outlined for me.

Claudia and I discussed all this at the preliminary meeting. She was worried about being able to make a case for India because, other than my fondness for the place, there were no clear connections or practical associations. Claudia suggested we step back and consider all the possibilities. At this time, in the early twenty-first century, a number of countries were still prepared to permit adoption overseas, each of them for very different reasons. In a way that seems to me almost callous now, we reviewed the regulations and requirements for prospective adopters. At the time, I fleetingly noticed how this reviewing process was only about me, only about the point of view of the hopeful adoptive parent, and their desires and the potential out-come. The children – all those many children so in need of a safe and committed family and home – were hardly part of the equation.

Russia was no good because they had an upper age limit for adoptive parents and I was already well past that threshold. Peru would not do either, as they only allowed single adopters to apply for children over the age of six. Many other countries were out of the question because they accepted only married couples. And so on. I should have taken notice of this. I should have paid atten-tion to just how conservative these values in and around the bureaucratic processes of inter-country adoption were. But I didn't.

'How about China?' Claudia said.

There were advantages. At the time, the China Center of

Adoption Affairs (CCAA) – the body with overall responsibility for the international adoption of Chinese children – accepted single women as prospective adopters. The CCAA was also, at this time, flexible about the age of adoptive parents, and would agree to consider applications from older prospective adopters. They were, in addition, a designated country, which meant that the Chinese adoption process was recognized by the British authorities. There was a clear and well-organized system for inter-country adoption from China, though it usually took two years from beginning a home study to being matched with a child.

The fact that there were so many children available for inter-country adoption at this time was due to official planning policy. This is not an easy subject, nor does it have any easy explanation.

The Asian studies scholar Kay Ann Johnson died in 2019. In 1991, while working on an oral history of a village in north China, she adopted a three-month-old baby. As it was to turn out, Johnson's daughter was one of the first of some 120,000 Chinese children to be adopted internationally in the 1990s and early 2000s. As her child grew, in trying to analyse and under-stand the truth of her own experience and that of her daughter, Johnson embarked on a major study in which she listened to the stories of fear and grief told by the desperate parents who gave birth to children 'out of plan'. She published *China's Hidden Children: Abandonment, Adoption, and the Human Costs of the One-Child Policy* in 2016. In the same year, Mei Fong published *One Child: The Story of China's Most Radical Experiment*, and she too recites a tale of heartache and coercion.

Of course I had no access to either of these books at the time, nor did I understand then – in the way I do now – the enormity of this ill fortune and suffering, which is often misrepresented in the Western press. At the time, however, this seemed like a sensible plan. A straightforward plan.

But for me, there was one major disadvantage.

I had looked at the website for the Department of Education, the relevant agency at the time. I had read all the rules for the CCAA. Although there were no specific laws at this time on homosexuality in the People's Republic of China, official attitudes were derogatory. However, the *Chinese Classification and Diagnostic Criteria of Mental Disorders* removed homosexuality from its list of mental illnesses in April 2001. It is generally said to be the case now that Chinese policy is 'no approval, no disapproval, and no promotion'.

But as I had read all the information available on the internet, I knew that the CCAA did not accept applications for inter-country adoption from homosexuals.

I had once been married to a man for ten years. But I had also lived with a woman.

I thought about the colleagues and acquaintances who had, I knew, successfully adopted from China. At least two of them were women in long-term relationships with other women, though this was before the days of civil partnerships, let alone marriage. I wondered how they had managed that. I felt I did not know them well enough to ask – but perhaps that would have been a wise move. I guessed that they had each just applied as a single adopter and said nothing about their relationships.

I thought about the implications for me. I would have to

ignore a large section of my past for the purposes of the home study. That would not be so hard. Those years were packed with teaching and writing, broadcasting and journalism. I had plenty to talk about. And in any case, I reasoned, this was about my life now. And now I was solvent and single and knew I could make space in my life for the child I wanted. So it did not seem so duplicitous.

Yet of course it was. But how do you measure moral culpability when the everyday assumptions and laws in one nation are contradicted and overturned in another? On the other hand, if I wished to adopt a Chinese child, should I not respect the laws of their sovereign state? After thinking about the problem for a while, I decided that I had better ask for some advice. I called the helpline for one of the independent support groups for inter-country adoption. 'Well,' said the adviser on the other end of the line with a sigh, 'that's a tough one. But you can offer this notional child a whole life. I should just get on with it and forget about that bit.' So I did. Sort of.

I called Claudia and agreed that we should apply for China.

After I had paid the first half of the fee, we started on the home study, examining all the circumstances, present and future, that would impact on my capacity to parent a child. In domestic adoption there are no fees payable, whether you are assessed by a local authority or by an independent agency. With inter-country adoption, however, a fee is payable by the applicant – usually half up front, and half at the stage when the applicant is approved. The rates varied, but were generally in the region of £4,000–7,000.

I should also say – as I now know so much more than I did – that in a domestic adoption an applicant will hardly ever go straight to the home study. The first stage will be a long interview – which is intense and searching – followed by rigorous adoption preparation groups. These preparation courses usually take place over the course of four or five consecutive days, or six or seven evenings a week. They are designed to make you think carefully about the implications, requirements and consequences of adoption. The best of such courses address general issues to do with the upbringing of any child, but they also help you to contemplate the special need for therapeutic parenting. Children who have been exposed to trauma – which might have been while they were in the womb, or during their early years, and is not necessarily the result of an abusive past – have high cortisol levels, which makes it difficult for them to regulate their own behaviour. In order to support such a child, it is helpful to use caring techniques that are nurturing and comforting, avoiding punishment or shame, with the aim of making the child feel safer.

Again, the best of such courses have a dual purpose. They offer training to prospective adopters, but they are also formulated to allow the qualifying agency to assess you before they commit to your case. It might be worth noting here that biological parents are never asked to do any of this – to analyse their own capacities or abilities as parents, or to be evaluated by any authority as likely effective parents.

In this, my first experience of a home study, from January to July, Claudia came to visit me at home. Each meeting took two to three hours, and we met some ten, eleven or twelve times.

This is a big time commitment for the social worker. Add to that the travelling, the report-writing, the filling-in of official forms, and it soon piles up. You can see where the money goes. We talked about my childhood and upbringing, my family, education, work, finances, motives, attitudes to children, lifestyle, support networks, interests, capacities, expectations.

The point is to build up a picture of your life – as it has been hitherto, and as it is now – and to consider how the introduction of a child will impact upon and change that situation, and how you have prepared yourself for that eventuality. So I banged on obligingly about my mother and father, about my sister and brothers. I told about my youth and my marriage. I brought out my work contract, my accounts, my tax returns, my utility bills. At the same time, Claudia saw three referees and checked my council tax registration.

Some of this was easy and straightforward – as in the case of work, for instance. I had a job, and had been working at the same college for some time. The department was supportive and appreciative of all its staff, and the atmosphere there was positive and welcoming. More than that, the senior academic managers in my department were conscious of the family responsibilities that many younger lecturers had to balance with their scholarly life, and did as much as possible to make that work.

On one occasion famous in the School, when the person nominated to take on the arduous role of head of department announced that he and his wife were expecting twins, other colleagues rallied round, relieved him of that post and shared out its responsibilities between them.

With regard to my other work, the journalism was something

I could do from home. And the broadcasting for my radio programme came in clear sections of two months each, here and
there across the year. Of course, now I needed to think how this
working life might function with a child at home. There would
be official leave to begin with, but what about afterwards and as
the child grew? But even that seemed relatively straightforward.
I had plenty of friends on hand who would help in the less dire
emergency situations, as well as many people in the village. But
clearly that was not going to be enough.

When I was at work I had to travel to London, or to the BBC
in Bristol if I was recording. I needed someone always on hand.
And then I realized that there was just such a person – a compe-
tent woman, mother to three children all grown up now, who
needed work. So we set up a plan, long in advance of any of this
happening. We agreed that on the days in the future when I was
working away from home, I would pay her a retainer and petrol
money so that she could pick up my child from school and stay
with them in my home until I returned. Not only that, but she
would also make herself available on those days and ensure she
was near by in the event of an emergency, accident or illness.
That looked as though it was going to work. One thing crossed
off the list.

Other parts of this investigation into my life were much more
difficult. I discovered, rather belatedly, just how much the childhood move from Australia had cut across my sense of self. And
it was curious and unsettling to have to think about my parents
and how they parented. A great deal of this was painful to
remember as I described and analysed my relations with my
mother and, most especially, with my father.

The home study is a good tool, and I would not argue with the philosophy behind its principles or institution. To welcome a child into your life naturally involves it changing beyond almost all recognition, and the imperatives of self-reflection and analysis that the home study demands challenge conventional and sentimental expectations, which is helpful and as it should be. But – having now been exposed to a different version of the system – I have my thoughts about my experience of it on this occasion.

But this is only the outer work. The inner work had already begun and would continue throughout all this time. When I decided that I wanted a child I began to think about myself as a child. This, in itself, is a challenging task. Because we have all been children, it is too easy to assume that we know something about them; that we know what 'a child' is. But, as adults, we necessarily have different perspectives, and it can be hard to remember, to revisit, to reconnect to and reconstruct the emotions and viewpoints we once had. More than that, children's voices are rarely heard: they are often ignored, disbelieved, or belittled by the grown-ups around them, or else they are revised, superseded or misremembered by the adults those children become. But perhaps the one place when adults often do think about children and a child's vision is when they have children. This might happen to a reflective birth parent. It most definitely happens to an adoptive parent, because this process starts not in the body, but in the mind.

So, as I say, when I decided that I wanted a child, I began to think about myself as a child. And much of my childhood was dominated by my father. By his presence to begin with, and then, still more, by his absence.

So what is a father? What are fathers for? How much are they worth? What do they owe to their child? How much does a child owe to their father? I begin to realize that I must understand about fathers if I am to become a mother.

DADDY

Father, father, where are you going
O do not walk so fast.
Speak father, speak to your little boy
Or else I shall be lost . . .

William Blake, 'The Little Boy Lost'

I AM STANDING at the churchyard gate, waiting to go to my father's funeral. I am alone. This has to be a secret. It is hot, but cool under the yews. From this dark shade the sun strikes bright on the briar rose over the wall and the pebbly path winding up to the church door.

My route to the church had circled right around it. I had arrived early to find the way and spy out what is best to do. I had driven straight past the main gate, on to the village road, turned right, and then right again. In a little wood I stopped, got out and, holding my black skirt up over my knees, negotiated a path through the nettles to pee. The warm sun on bare skin, and even the bramble scratches on my legs, comforted me. Picking my way back again, I looked at my watch. Still fifteen minutes to go.

I waited a while, then set out again. Another right turn and I arrived at the back entrance to the churchyard. The car park was full. People were still climbing out of cars and taxis, greeting one another. I turned my car around and drove back the way I had come. Taking a little fork in the road, some way from the churchyard, I parked in the shade, collected myself, and put on my sunglasses.

I could hear the bell tolling as I walked towards the church. I looked at my watch again. Still seven minutes. I paused at a gate and leaned over to talk to a black-and-white pony and an old grey. A car pulled up in the gateway. The couple got out maps and a Thermos. Damn them. Still slightly too early; I would have to move on. I dawdle.

In the car park all is quiet. One man dressed in black – an undertaker? – lingers. I march purposefully up to the churchyard gate. And then I stop. I wait. I have a good view of the entrance from here.

A last few stragglers go in. Then I watch the coffin being carried in. I wait a little longer. Is it now? Should I go? It must be time. Everyone seems to be in. Time to brave it.

To my irritation there is still a woman in the porch. She greets me with a list and asks my name. I shake my head and say nothing. At the closed church door, I listen for a moment.

Music. It has started. Now it is safe. I turn the stiff door handle. I go in.

We hold a lot of contradictory ideas about fathers. What they are for, what they are meant to do, how responsible they are for what. On the one hand, we are now so used to the concept of the importance of the mother's role in a young child's life that fathers seem expendable. The family courts, for instance, will routinely grant custody of infants whose parents are divorcing to the mother, and pressure groups representing fathers have tried to question these decisions, which seem to deny the interests of fathers. On the other hand, fathers who, for whatever reason, do not live with their children are still expected to take financial responsibility for those children.

In the early 1990s the UK government was spending more than £6 billion – three times the amount it had been in 1979 – on supporting the children of single parents. A series of tortuous policy and legislative changes took place over the next fifteen years as successive governments sought to reduce the state's financial obligation for raising children in separated families and return that responsibility to absent parents. The Child Support Act became law in 1991 and led to the establishment of the Child Support Agency (CSA) in 1993. It was abolished and replaced with the Child Maintenance and Enforcement Commission (CMEC) in 2008; the Child Maintenance Group (CMG) in 2012; and the Child Maintenance Service (CMS) in 2013.

The website for the CSA stated:

We can help

- ensure partners who live apart from their children contribute financially to their upkeep
- make sure more children receive the maintenance they are entitled to
- take quick and firm action to make sure payments get made.

This part is all about money. But there is a clear, underlying gender bias. Not surprising given that in 92 per cent of separated families the parent with care is a woman.

What they are really talking about is fathers. Absent fathers; reneging fathers; fathers who have started second families and resent coughing up for the first; fathers who don't want to know; fathers who don't want to pay out for ever for a moment's fun. And what they really mean is that fathers are irresponsible, uncaring and selfish.

How has this happened? One answer, which often goes unnoticed, lies in the shift in the relative importance of the roles of 'father' and 'mother' that took place over the course of the twentieth century. Before that time fathers had legal rights in regard to their children – in effect, owning their children in a way that women did not. In the early part of the nineteenth century, women were, in the eyes of the law, minors, and that had consequences when it came to the custody of children.

The notorious cases of Caroline Norton and Rosina Bulwer Lytton brought this to public attention. Norton left her husband in 1836 when he accused her of 'criminal conversation' – adultery – with Lord Melbourne. Rosina Bulwer Lytton and her husband legally separated in the same year after she had endured years of horrendous abuse. In both cases, these mothers had their young children taken from them because, in law, the children were the property of the father.

Gradually, legislators began to prioritize the interests of the child, as opposed to the 'rights' of parents, but this was linked to new work in psychoanalysis. During the first half of the twentieth century, the dominance of 'the father' in the family was diminishing, and theorists such as Wilfrid Bion, D. W. Winnicott and especially John Bowlby emphasized the role of the 'primary care-giver' – usually, at that time, the mother – in the development of the child's 'mental apparatus'.

Today, these two key ideas – the primacy of the mother, and the possibility of analysing the psychological life of the child – have become so commonplace that many people would take them as 'natural' givens, not realizing that this was not always the case. But these essential ideas about the significance of the child's relationship with the primary care-giver, and the profound and debilitating effects of a disruption to that relationship, have become familiar to all.

What began, then, with research and thinking at the highest theoretical level in relation to the significance of the mother, has percolated down in a simplified and diluted form to colour everything from the decisions made in the family courts, to the establishment of the CSA and the screamers in the tabloids.

In *Mothers: An Essay on Love and Cruelty*, Jacqueline Rose argues that mothers have now become society's scapegoat: '. . . motherhood is, in Western discourse, the place in our culture where we lodge, or rather bury, the reality of our own conflicts, of what it means to be fully human.' This is true. But part of the reason for this is that fathers have often been written out of the picture.

From one point of view, society worries about children not having fathers. In June 2008, the UK government issued a white paper titled 'Regarding Responsibility' (published jointly by the Department for Children, Schools and Families, and the Department for Work and Pensions). It proposed that mothers registering the birth of a child should also name the father or face sanctions. The proposal was intended – they said – to deal with the 7 per cent of children (some 45,000) who are registered at birth in England and Wales with no named father.

At its most idealistic, the policy (which has not made it into law) was supposed to promote shared responsibility between father and mother. Its genesis, however, came directly from Sir David Henshaw's report to the government called 'Recovering Child Support: Routes to Responsibility', which recommended further investigation into making compulsory the naming of both parents at the registration of births – in order to make any future tracing of absent and non-paying parents easier for the state – and was driven by a governmental desire to enforce child support compliance and reduce the drain on the public purse.

As a society, we live with paradox. Built into the English language is an assumption about the dispensability of fathers. 'To father' a child is specific to a moment and simply refers to the provision of the wherewithal for conception. 'To mother' a child (or, indeed, an adult) implies feeding, cherishing, fussing, loving, listening and suggests the caring commitment of a lifetime.

We demonize fathers and we idealize them. We condemn them and we require them. Fathers themselves today seem not to be sure of their role. But there is evidence that they too are asking the question and (some) are wishing to be proper, 'better' fathers.

*

I do not know what fathers are for. But I know that they fascinate and trouble me, good fathers and bad. In Ethel Turner's *Seven Little Australians*, the stern Captain Woolcot is not a good father, even when he is present. He takes little notice of his children. At the climax of the novel, thirteen-year-old Judy dies – her back broken when she flung her body over that of her baby brother as a ring-barked gum tree (negligently never felled) crashed to the ground. At the end, her father is haunted by her memory, but he does not reform:

> The Captain never smoked at the end of the side
> verandah now . . . Judy's death made his six living
> children dearer to his heart, though he showed his
> affection very little more.

In E. Nesbit's *The Railway Children*, Father gets taken away abruptly at the beginning of the story, so he remains only an idealized absence throughout. The novel ends as he is finally released and Bobbie brings him home to be reunited with his wife and children. The narrator takes us quietly away from that scene:

> He goes in and the door is shut. I think we will not open the
> door to follow him. I think that just now we are not wanted
> there.

But the part that everyone remembers, reinforced by the 1970 film starring Jenny Agutter, is the moment Father steps off the train and out of the mist of steam after his long estrangement, and Bobbie flies towards him, crying, 'Oh! my Daddy! my Daddy!'

I do not know what fathers are for. But I know that they are a puzzle. I think of Roger McGough's poem 'The Way Things Are'. He speaks there about the distance between a child's inventive perception and the more down-to-earth realities of adult life. He ends, in the voice of the all-knowing father, by warning that no 'trusting hand' waits for the falling star.

And what did my father show me about the way things are? That someone can fire you up with ambition, driven alternately by an unexpected present of a recording of a Mozart clarinet concerto and the threat of the belt. That someone can frighten you a bit with their aspirations for you, can dance delightedly around the dining-room table, reading out your exam results. And that someone can leave, quite suddenly one weekend, without saying a word and taking all the money. That someone can leave when your mother is seriously ill with a life-threatening disease, when she has just had a major operation and has been in hospital for six weeks. That someone can leave when your one brother is only twelve, when your younger brother is only eight. And that someone can never see you, write to you, or even ask about any of you ever again.

In my father's universe, 'the way things are' included the lesson that you just cut off. If someone lets you down, if they hurt you – or you hurt them – you cauterize that part of your life. I learned then that not only was there no trusting hand to catch the falling star, I learned that there was no trust, and that there are no stars.

*

Rationally, I do know what happened. We came to England in the late 1960s from an Australia that was still in the 1950s. By the early 1970s, sex and drugs and rock 'n' roll had hit my father pretty hard. Two of them, anyway. He arrived home one day in a new purple shirt. Being fifteen, I told him he looked ridiculous. He went to 'library meetings' on New Year's Eve. Then he took a new job in a different part of the country and disappeared.

One autumn after I had come to the decision that I wanted a child, I also came to the conclusion that I had had too much loss in my life. I needed to acknowledge grief before I could choose happiness. I needed to shed my problems if I was to take on a child with their own complicated needs.

I made up my mind to go to a therapist.

A friend had given me a number ages ago. I didn't want to do it back then. Why would I want to talk about any of this? She obviously thought I should. But I had kept the number. Maybe now I was ready. So eventually I picked up the phone.

When I first met Luke I told him all my griefs, beginning with my father, and ended my spiel by saying, 'And you're not going to make me see him, are you?'

He laughed. 'No, I don't think that will be necessary.'

On a spring day eight months later, after we had been working together consistently all that while, I reminded him of that moment in our first consultation. On this occasion we both laughed. Because just recently, something quite unexpected had happened.

Eight months into my work with Luke, my sister Antonia called me about a letter she had received from our aunt – my father's younger sister. The letter explained that our father had been taken into hospital with fits and was likely to die. He was living in England. We knew he had been in Spain and in Australia, but he had come back to England. At the time, I thought that it was only for about four years. It turned out to be more than eleven.

My aunt's letter had been sent to my sister from Australia by express, overnight delivery. But something had gone wrong. Its postmark was a whole month before it arrived in England. Whatever the failure of the mail, my sister and I both recognized the implication. A month had gone by. He might be already dead.

Suddenly I realized how important this was to me. I knew in that moment, when any chance of understanding or determination might have been taken away, that I had to resolve things. I knew I wanted very much to see him. I grew desperate when I thought that it might be too late.

I didn't have an address. I knew that he lived – had lived? – near a certain market town. I looked it up in the phone book and called the community hospital there. 'Where would someone living in your area be taken in an emergency?' 'Banbury or Oxford.'

I tried Banbury first.

'Do you have so and so there? I am his daughter.'

'Hold on. I'll put you through to the ward.'

It is a beautiful day in April. I make a little posy from the garden. Tulips striped pink and white, Solomon's seal, grape hyacinths, deep-blue vinca major. In the hospital car park I am horrified to find that you have to pay. What is this preying on the anxious, the hopeful, the sad, the despairing?

At the locked door to the secure unit I have to press a buzzer and announce myself to the intercom. Even that is hard – to own him, to declare into the robot void, 'I am his daughter.' The doors open. My pulse is racing. I know that this is the bravest thing I have ever done. Because it is the hardest. I breathe in. It is more than thirty years since I last set eyes on the man who is my father.

Sackler Ward, Mellon Ward. I press another bell at another locked door.

A uniformed nurse greets me and I explain. She says that he is just finishing lunch. Will I wait?

The television is on in the lounge. It is Camilla and Charles's wedding day and the nurses want to watch. The patients don't know who Camilla and Charles are. But then, the patients here know very little. The patients don't know who they are themselves.

Then I see. A tall man comes tottering down the corridor on the arm of a nurse. I know him at once. He always was a fine-looking man. And I think. And I feel. 'It's my Daddy.'

VENTURING

. . . and home
is a long-distance love affair
with loss . . .

Vahni Capildeo, 'Windrush Lineage'
from 'Windrush Reflections'

MY FATHER'S EYES wobbled. I know now that this is nystag-
mus, a neurological condition that is, most commonly, present
from birth. It was strange to watch, as his pupils rapidly shifted
from side to side. And it made all face-to-face confrontations
peculiar. If he was pleased with you, if he was angry, if he was
questioning something, this visual tic was disconcerting. It nearly
stopped him from being allowed to become a teacher. In the
1950s, the NSW education board refused to accept anyone disabled on the grounds, apparently, that such a person could too
easily be teased and would not be able to command the appropriate authority in a classroom.

Looking up the condition now, I realize a number of things.
That my mother thought it was something to do with the circumstances of his birth, but it was more likely to be genetic. That

while the affected individual is unaware of this involuntary movement, the condition may limit or distort the vision. (But my father was far too vain to wear glasses.) That the condition is sometimes called 'dancing eyes'.

There was some strange back story in my father's family. He was one of six children, only four of whom survived into adulthood. There was an older brother, who died as a baby. And another brother, the youngest of them all, who died at four years old when he fell out of an upstairs window. Soon after that, my grief-stricken grandmother – still a young woman – also died. My mother held the theory that my grandmother and grandfather had had to get married because she was pregnant with that lost first child, and the death of the last was too much to bear.

Adrienne and Ken, my mother and father, first met on the steps of the library at a school in Young, NSW. She was saying goodbye to a friend when Ken hailed her: 'Wait for me, beautiful!' This was our story of origin. But Adrienne was not keen. She had just escaped from her home town and wanted to hold on to that free-dom. Unlike her two brothers, she had not been sent to school in Sydney and therefore had spent all her childhood and youth in West Wyalong. There was no prospect of all but the most rudi-mentary of tertiary education, so she trained as a PE teacher. Young was only seventy-five miles from home, but it was a start.

And besides, Adrienne already had a plan. She was going to England, as far away from home as possible, equipped with let-ters of introduction to Henry Carney, the brother of a country neighbour, who lived in London with his Austrian wife, Litzi.

And, in 1951, the only way to make the journey that was not prohibitively expensive was by boat; in this case, the *Berengaria*. The photographs of Adrienne's young self on that first voyage to Europe show no signs of the sea sickness that always plagued her.

True, later on, she told my brother Jeremy that she did suffer: 'All I wanted to do was lie by the pool.' And yes, she is there in a swimming costume by the pool. But she is also playing quoits on deck; she is glamorously dressed for the evening; she is taking one excursion after another – in Freemantle, in Perth, in Suez.

'Ted and Ade', 'Adie, Ted and Mona', 'Ade, Ted, Tom, Edna, Joan', 'Adie and Ted' are the labels in my mother's neat hand on the small black-and-white photographs in her albums. They touch, their arms around each other's shoulders. Now, looking over these pictures, my sister and I have no idea about Ted. Not who he was, nor what he meant to her. We wonder, we surmise.

For Ken had decided to follow her. In 1952 he also took ship – the *Otranto* – for England. On board with him was his friend Tom Savage. He told Tom about Adrienne and confided that he had decided to ask her to marry him. They agreed that Tom would be best man. Ken wrote home to his father and his younger sister. Everything was dazzling.

27 June. Dear Dad and Shirl,

The last four weeks have simply sped by. Yesterday morning we got up at 4 to see the Isle of Capri. It was very hilly and very different from what I had imagined. I saw the sun rise over the Bay of Naples at 4.30 and it was really wonderful. The Bay of Naples must be one of the loveliest views in the world.

6 July. Dear Dad,

I have the most wonderful news in the world. Adrienne and I
have become engaged. We plan to be married about the middle of
August, when we come back from the Games. We are very very
happy and I know neither of us shall ever regret it. She is a really
wonderful girl and I am sure she'll make an even better wife. All
of Adrienne's friends here are in flat spins with excitement. We
bought the ring on Friday afternoon – 5 diamonds with a
platinum setting – yellow gold band. Yesterday we went down to
Stratford on Avon . . . Tomorrow I'm going to see about a job.

12 July. Dear Dad & Shirl,

Have now been in London over a week and really, it seems as
though I've been here for ever. This is such an *easy* place to live
in. There is no hustle and bustle, no noise, etc. like Sydney, and
it doesn't matter if you miss a train or bus. There's always
another along in 2 or 3 minutes.

Spent yesterday afternoon looking over the Tower of London.

18 July. Dear Dad,

Have been to see a lady about a position and more or less got it
teed up to begin when school begins on Sept 1 . . . What with
engagement rings, etc., it soon drags the banking account
down. Could you lend me £25 on account?

Adrienne was convinced: 'I thought he must love me. He had
followed me all the way from Australia.' After all her resistance,

she had agreed to marry Ken pretty much as soon as he had arrived in London. In her photograph albums, there are no more pictures of Ted.

That summer Adrienne and Ken travelled on the ferry from Harwich to the Hook of Holland and then by train through the Netherlands on to Copenhagen, Stockholm and then Helsinki for the Olympic Games. Back in England they moved in to a shared flat at 63c Highbury Hill.

16 August. Dear Dad and Shirl,

Today has been showery and rather heavy at times. Well, it's only the second or third time I've seen rain in London . . . Dad, could you start sending me the *Sunday Herald* or something each week? . . . Shirl, you asked me about food parcels. I notice Adrienne gets one every month from home – worth about £1/15/0. It costs 10/6 to send. Adrienne says there's not much we really need – but dried milk is something – like sunshine . . .

. . . Arranged this week for the flowers, photographer, etc. There will be about 25 at the wedding – Henry and Litzi Carney (whose house Ade is going from and who are giving us the reception); Leslie (a friend of Carney's – who is giving us the wedding cake); Litzi's mother and father; Henry's brother and his wife; Joan Parker the bridesmaid and her Ma & Pa who came from W. Wyalong; Tom, the best man; Eric, Adie's brother; Phil Hordern; Andy Martin, from the *Otranto*; 4 friends of Ade's from Saint Margaret's Hotel and a few other folk here and there. So far, we are all organized . . .

On 23 August 1952 they were married at St John's in Hampstead. Ken had a Catholic background but Adrienne did not want her children to be brought up in the Church. Later on, my mother would wonder if some part of him thought he was not properly married.

Tom Savage was best man. Eric Fisher, my mother's older brother – then in Germany as part of his training as a doctor – gave the bride away. Litzi and Henry Carney held the wedding reception at their flat in Belsize Park.

26 August. Dear Dad & Shirl,

Well, here we are down in Canterbury. The wedding went off extra well . . . It was a lovely day and the sun shone – after 4 wet Saturdays . . . We left about 10 to 7, and just before, they sang 'Auld Lang Syne', 'Wish Me Luck' and then 'Waltzing Matilda'. It was really very good. I wish you all could have been here, but I guess you realize how impossible it was . . . Today we are going to Whitstable, about 20 minutes away on the coast. This is one of the oldest places in England. It was in this part of England that St Augustine came to preach hundreds of years ago. In the cathedral, which is magnificent, was murdered Thomas à Becket: many of the places are 1,000 years old. This hotel has parts dating back to the fifteenth century . . .

Ken and Adrienne both loved the history they found in Europe, but this was a time dominated by more recent history. At the end of the summer Ken got a job at a residential centre run by

International Help for Children, dedicated to assisting poor children, refugees and orphans.

5 Sept. Little Pond House, Tilford, Surrey
Dear Dad & Shirl,

At the moment, we are all singing, waiting for the rain to stop so the photographer can take a picture . . . This house is in a lovely place. All around the fields are green . . . This house belongs to the International Care [sic] for Children and various people like the L.C.C. send their children here for recuperation. Children also come here from the various countries of Europe – Italy, Greece, France, etc. We spend our time going for walks, paddles in the pond, rowing on the lake and so on. They do not have any school lessons. We have 25 boys. They are very very dull and backward. Many of them cannot even speak properly. They come from very poor homes. Those without good clothes & shoes are given such things when they come here . . .

By September Ken had a permanent job in a school for the 'sub-normal' – so called at the time – while Adrienne taught in various schools around Islington and Pentonville.

26 Sept. Dear Dad & Shirl,

The new school is not so bad. I have the 14-year-old boys. They are big lads with not a brain between them . . . The days are getting colder now. The trees are beginning to lose their leaves and take on a bare appearance. Seats are available

for the Coronation from 15 to 50 guineas – that is, in shop
windows, etc. along the procession route. The Yanks will pay
£50, they say. Of course, no ordinary person could get near
the Abbey.

In the end, Ken and Adrienne did not buy one of those 15 guinea
seats, but camped out in Trafalgar Square to witness the coronation procession. There is a photograph in which you can clearly
see Adrienne's face among the hordes. Looking at these pictures
now, it is striking to notice how youthful the crowd is, cheering
on the young queen, rationing still with them, the war only eight
years behind them and a new era ahead.

But not for my parents. Three years later and it was time to go
home. Ken volunteered for 'country service' and was appointed to
the one-teacher school in Booligal, nearly five hundred miles
from Sydney. Even now, it is eight hours' drive from the coast,
and the old One Tree Hotel, a lone sight on the plain and halfway
between Hay and Booligal, is derelict. 'Heat, dust, flies, rabbits,
mosquitoes, snakes, drought, lack of facilities and unpopularity
with shearers and drovers appear to be the major complaints,'
notes an article from the *Sydney Morning Herald* (8 Febraury 2004)
about the area. My uncle Eric remarked that this seemed like
some terrible cosmic joke.

But my parents made the best of it. Daddy became expert in
discovering and mapping Aboriginal carvings and cave paintings. I recall tiring hot treks through the bush while Mummy
pointed out the wild waratahs. When we moved to Cessnock,
Mummy would take us to the nearest cultural equivalent to her

London life – the Newcastle Gilbert and Sullivan society. On the long Christmas drives back to West Wyalong, we children would look out for the landmarks – the radio telescope at Parkes, the collection of farm letterboxes at the end of red-dirt tracks around Forbes. These were the maps of my childhood.

ALMOST

WHILE THE HOME study with Claudia was still going on, I kept up my campaign of trying to do something every day to learn more, to promote this new life growing inside me – in my head, if not in my womb.

My hopes and wishes were so bound up in it that every conversation turned on it. I found myself talking to strangers. One taxi driver listened. Then he told me that he and his wife were foster carers. How many children have they looked after? 'Oh, I don't know. Not sure. Eighty-five? Ninety?'

Everything I read turned on it too. There were mothers in every text. Some not very helpful, such as the one in Audre Lorde's poem 'The House of Yemanjá':

> My mother had two faces
> and a broken pot
> where she hid out a perfect daughter
> who was not me
> I am the sun and moon and forever hungry
> for her eyes.

Others were a great deal more affirmative, such as in Jackie Kay's poem 'The Telling Part', from chapter six of *The Adoption Papers*, which is especially important to me. The poem robustly answers all the anxieties and all the fears that thoughtless people raise with adoptive parents, and which you rebut with vehemence, hiding (for the moment) the terrifying fact that those fears still hover in the corner of your mind.

> I was always the first to hear her in the night
> all this umbilical knot business is nonsense . . .
> I listened to hear her talk,
> and when she did I heard my voice under hers
> and now some of her mannerisms crack me up . . .

Then it was July. Time to plan for going to the approval panel. At this point, Claudia decided that we needed a reference from my ex-husband. I had not seen him since we were divorced, fifteen years previously. I had had only one communication with him during that period, some five years later, when – quite bizarrely and accidentally – I had discovered that he was getting married.

It happened in this way. My partner and I were selling our house in London. The estate agent sent round a 'Mr Burford' to view. He turned out to be Bill Buford, at that time the editor of the literary magazine *Granta*. As both my partner and I had had dealings with him in a professional capacity – I had interviewed him for the BBC, she had written for him – we all found this very funny. Having shown him round the house, we invited Bill to stay for a drink. As we chatted, we asked if he had seen any other houses he had liked. 'Yes,' was the reply. 'One in particular.

In a square. Rather over-the-top Victoriana. Very nice man selling. He was getting married again.' My girlfriend and I looked at each other. 'What exactly is the address?' she asked. It was my own old house.

So I wrote my ex-husband a card. I posted it in Broad Street in Oxford. It said that I hoped he would be happy. I knew why this reference from him was required for the home study. In the 'Brighton & Hove case', four-year-old John Smith died in December 1999 as a result of injuries inflicted by his adoptive parents. He was covered with bruises and adult bite marks. The child, with one of his sisters, had been placed with these adoptive parents six months previously. The couple each received a prison sentence of eight years. In the course of the subsequent inquiry, it was discovered that the man's former partner had not been approached for a reference and she was aware of his potential for violence. As a result, adoption procedures were changed, and so these days, it is generally a requirement in the UK that all ex-partners – whether they were married or co-habiting – are asked for a reference.

As a courtesy, I wrote to my ex-husband at his work address to explain that he would be receiving this request. By return, I received a kind letter wishing me luck and sending best wishes to my family. I wrote again, gushing with thanks.

And then: nothing. Weeks went by. I called. Claudia called. My brother called. No response. I called again. 'May I speak to X, please?' 'Yes, of course, who is it calling?' 'Y.' Silence. 'I'm sorry, I am afraid he is in a meeting.'

The panel date, scheduled for August, was cancelled – postponed indefinitely. Hiatus, ellipsis, aporia, gap, empty space, stop.

At the end of September Claudia rang me. She had, at last, received the reference from my ex-husband. But no, she could not discuss its contents with me, just as she could not share all the other references she had already collected. So I did not know what any one of these referees may have said, but, of course, what I did know was that – for the purposes of the home study, because of the restrictions around inter-country adoption – I had deliberately done some forgetting about one part of my life.

The home study method used in the approval of prospective adopters is a peculiar thing. It is, yes, a record of what is past, but it is also a performative. Every day, every moment, the person being scrutinized plays the character of the person they need to become to meet the requirements of the system. What you wear, eat, drink, say and do are all being observed and assessed and judged – quite often in meetings and transactions with one social worker or another, all the time by the self that acquiesces in the process. The life that I was living at this time was authentic and whole. It performed both the reality of my existence and fulfilled the necessary requirements for the process. All the same, there was still that one little bit of forgetting.

Still, I went on with the work, inner and outer. I booked piano lessons. When I was reading *Children Who Wait*, published by AdoptionUK, I came across an advertisement calling for 'independent visitors'. Until this point I had not known anything about this volunteering role. Children who are in the care of the local authority – 'looked after children' – are entitled to an independent visitor. Someone to befriend them and support them. It sounded like a good thing to do, an interesting thing to do, and it would help me to think about the question of children who are displaced from their biological parents.

So I applied to become one. Then I went to my next-door neighbour and asked which nursery her two young children had attended. She put me in touch with the organizer there, and I began to volunteer one afternoon a week.

I read more books. I went to seminars. One seminar that I recall in particular was with the adoption expert Daniel Hughes. He told us that the key thing with adopted children was to remember the mnemonic PACE: 'Playfulness, Acceptance, Curiosity, Empathy'. The hardest one of those, he explained, but the single most important, is 'playfulness'. Little did I know that coming towards me was a testing time. I was going to need all of these attributes, and for myself, rather sooner than I had thought.

All these new projects were enriching. Apart from anything else, I met new friends at the seminars and through the nursery. I have those friends still. But I also learned new things. As a teacher, classrooms are my stock in trade. But these were different and unexpected lessons, and I had to reassess the classrooms I have known and the classrooms I would now encounter.

CLASSROOMS

Paper that lets the light
shine through, this
is what could alter things . . .

Imtiaz Dharker, 'Tissue'

MY FIRST SCHOOL is a blank, but when I was seven I attended a one-room school, which I walked to across two or three wide dirt streets. It was a mining town in New South Wales, criss-crossed with storm drains that never carried any water. There were not many pupils and my memories are few. But two things stand out clearly in my mind.

There was the daily milk – plain, but chocolate- or strawberry-flavoured if you were lucky. It came in little glass bottles and I recently found some of them in an antique shop on the Northern Beaches in Sydney. They were expensive, but I had to have them.

The other thing was my own propensity to build a wall around the edges of my desk, piling as many books as I could and as high as I dared, so that I could isolate myself and read behind them.

Later, in England, there were a few really magical things about my senior school. It was an old-fashioned girls' grammar, housed in a beautiful eighteenth-century mansion with one grand, stone staircase and one winding, secret, servants' staircase – deliciously mysterious to most, because only the staff and the sixth form were allowed to use it. The grounds had been laid out by Sir Humphrey Repton and included a Greek theatre. There was a fireplace in the fifth-form classroom, decorated with Victorian Minton tiles of scenes from Shakespeare, and there was a library in the old nursery, still with bars on the windows, as well as stupendous collections of L. M. Montgomery and Dornford Yates.

But the most magical thing – as it should be – was the teaching staff. My two English teachers in particular stay in my mind. Miss W, who was tiny, white-haired and pretty, and who wore neat tweed suits be it summer or winter. We all made up a story about how she was 'Miss' because her young man had been killed in the trenches of the First World War. Of course, she was not old enough for that. And I am older now than she was then.

The other – Miss B – was intellectual, funny, and moved by literature in a way that was feeling, inspiring, demanding and kind. When I failed to get into Cambridge at the first attempt, she told me tartly to stop walking round school like a tragedy queen. When a genuine hardship came into my life after my father left home, she was my support and my guide. She got me through Latin by coaching me on Sundays. She also got me through my second entrance exam – that time successfully.

Being a selfish teenager, I never quite realized that she was seriously ill. And she died before I had time to tell her what she meant to me. When I gave the prizes at my old school recently, I was able to say something of this. It didn't necessarily come out quite as it should have done. As I started on that part of my speech, I made the mistake of looking at my sister sitting in the audience, and saw my own tears mirrored by hers.

My PhD supervisor, himself a Dickensian scholar, was appalled when he discovered that I had never read any Dickens. 'Right,' he said. 'You must start at once. Read *Our Mutual Friend*. And for now, come on – come with me.'

So Andrew marched me down from Malet Street, past the British Museum, across Oxford Street and into Monmouth Street in Covent Garden. 'Look at that!' he said with a sweeping gesture.

I saw a row of boarded-up shops, derelict and depressing. I saw litter being blown along the gutters. I saw broken windows, graffiti, torn posters and billboards. 'At what?' I asked.

He sighed. 'That' – he pointed to a stone column at the crossroads – 'is the Seven Dials monument. This is Dickensian London, just as it was in his day. Look up. Look at the windows, the shapes of the buildings. Look at the old glass. Look at that door knocker.'

I was hooked. I read *Our Mutual Friend*, *Bleak House* and *David Copperfield*. I forgot all about my PhD for six months and neglected Elizabeth Barrett Browning shamefully. When I realized that I had worked my way through his every novel and every essay and had nearly done, I was bereft. I saved up *Martin Chuzzlewit*. I could not bear to contemplate a world where there was no more new Dickens to be read.

I think a lot about Dickens. About how his own miserable childhood marked him. 'I do not write resentfully or angrily; for I know how all these things have worked together to make me what I am; but I never afterwards forgot,' he wrote in his auto-biographical fragment. But he was resentful. He was angry. And he did forget. Because in middle age, Dickens turned into a monster and made his own children miserable. 'My father was like a madman . . . He did not care a damn what happened to any of us. Nothing could surpass the misery and unhappiness of our home,' said his daughter Kate Perugini.

During this strange waiting time, my Contemporary Writing class was reading a recently published book about a difficult childhood – difficult in both subject matter and form. Thinking about my students, I could anticipate potential problems and confrontational perspectives tugging at each other. My university was and is, proudly, very mixed. I did not want to duck the tensions, but I also wanted to make these students see one another's point of view – somehow.

Eventually, I decided on a method. I began with a straightforward talk on key theoretical perspectives. But then I planned to invoke the feeling.

'OK, everyone. Polly and Sarah and Elizabeth are going to come round with pieces of coloured paper. On the green one I want you to write one positive thing about your childhood that has contributed to your sense of identity. And then, on the blue piece of paper, I want you to write the very worst thing that has happened to you that constitutes part of your identity.' A frisson runs around the room. 'Don't worry. It will all be anonymous. But if you can bear to, I want you to tell the absolute truth. And Polly and Sarah, Elizabeth and I – we're all going to do it too.'

When the students started writing, the emotional temperature was high. I remember looking at Polly and the other teachers and wondering if I should have done this. Once they had finished filling in their slips, we collected them up and read them out at random.

I had known the range of experiences would be immense. But I had not imagined the extremes. Alongside exile and death, grief, immigration, terrible accidents and random violence there was also rape, and abuse and persecution by the state. As we four teachers took turns to read out the slips, the mood was sombre but deeply attentive. I was close to tears a lot of the time. I could see the others were feeling the same way.

And then a strange thing happened. I heard my own piece being read out in a voice that was not mine. I had written about the pain of being condemned to remain childless. But for a split second I did not recognize it. And for a blissful, releasing moment it did not hurt in quite the same way.

As we came to an end there was a collective release of breath. There was something in this experience that was cathartic for us all. Certainly, everyone looked at each other slightly differently.

As I dismissed the students to their seminars, I asked Polly and the team to lunch. I needed to wind down. We had all had brilliant sessions but we were drained. We agreed that the plan had worked. But I'm not sure that I would try it again.

In spite of the stalling of the adoption process, I persisted in focusing on all the new learning I could do and began to think also about the classrooms that we do not notice – the ones that teach us life lessons when we do not even realize we are the pupil. For these classrooms are all around.

My mother, for instance, was a keen gardener. She understood the wild naturescapes of Australia, and at each of our homes made gardens that drew on native plants and worked with the climate. Later on in England, we children all grew very bored as she exclaimed, 'Look at that beautiful eleagnes' or 'Well, I've never seen such a pretty astrantia.' Then, one day, riding out with my friend, I realized we were peering over walls and fences and saying, 'Isn't that Jackmanii lovely!' Or 'I must get some alchemilla to plant under my Bourbon roses.' And so on.

It comes to everyone, so they say. I am turning into my mother. For I find I know the names for every flower when I never even noticed I was learning.

One of the peculiar effects of both the official scrutiny and the self-examination that goes on during a home study is the way in which it makes past and future collide. You are doing this work in the present, agreeing for the time being to go through this strange and intrusive process in order to make a new life, a different life as a parent. And yet this experience forces you to think about a past which, by definition, is gone and will probably not bear any relation to the future you are working towards. But maybe there are connections even where you don't expect them; perhaps finding those connections is also part of the learning.

When my husband and I were young and first married, we had very little money, but we made a game of it. We kept an 'expenditure book', wrote down every penny we spent and tried to pare away wherever we could. I made packed lunches – 'Karachi pasties' were our favourite – for him to take to college, me to the library. We cycled everywhere, even in the rain. On Friday afternoons, just as the traders were clearing up at Chapel Market, we would collect any vegetables being given away and planned our meals out of them.

But we had two luxuries. We haunted the cheaper antique shops, first of all along the Blackstock Road; later, in Camden Passage. We made friends with all the dealers, listened and asked questions, and learned what we were looking at. We bought sparingly and worked on the furniture. I learned how to repair veneers and inlay. He became a dab hand at French polishing. What pleases me about this now is that I know what I am looking at, whether it is on show in a stately home or at a car boot sale, and that knowledge enhances appreciation. It also means that when I spotted some original William Morris peacock and dragon fabric I knew how much to pay.

The other luxury was the opera. I have no idea why we decided that we ought to learn about opera. For some reason it drew me, but it took quite a while before it began to mean something; before we began to understand. When I heard a positive review of a production of Massenet's *Manon Lescaut* we went to see it, but we were not as drawn in as I had expected to be. Some friends asked us to Covent Garden to see *Così fan tutte*. Today, though I can hardly believe it now, I do recall being so bored that I made myself examine the costumes minutely, starting with the shoes and working up in inches, just to keep myself sitting still. The problem, of course, was a lack of knowledge. How can you recognize the value of anything without understanding?

So we began again. We joined the local library, carried home great boxed sets of LPs, and sat down dutifully with the libretto in hand. Sometimes one or other of us would read it aloud as we went along. But we still didn't really get it.

Until one day we decided to just listen while we decorated the spare room. We painted on steadily, unmoved, until 'O soave fanciulla' floated up the stairs. My husband put down his brush. 'Did you hear *that*?' He rushed to move the needle back again.

And that was it. We bought cheap seats, went to everything, and studied each opera beforehand. After a while we looked forward to hearing an opera completely new and did away with the preparation. We hung about at the stage door and got our programmes signed by Joan Sutherland, José Carreras, Placido Domingo. And we cycled home through the silent streets on a high.

This was a past education but now it marks my present life. For everything I learned there as an amateur (in the true sense of the word) also made me an expert. I have since given talks and written programme notes for many major opera houses, I have reviewed and broadcast on opera.

And now I do understand. It works because of the totality of that effort: the skills of the composer and the librettist being brought to life by so many supreme artists all at once, not to mention the commitment of everyone backstage and front of house. And the singing – that sound, made by a human body – goes straight into your body, as into the bodies of all those around you in the audience. Which is why it is so transformative; why it can so powerfully take you completely out of yourself or beyond yourself. And all of this I will now be able to give to my child.

*

There are also occasions when things from the past stay with you. In this case it was a living thing that is still very much with me.

I was forty before I learned to ride a horse. One day I came home to find my girlfriend finishing off a phone call. 'Ah well, Don,' she said, 'the truth is that you *should* teach an old dog new tricks.' She had booked us in at the local riding stables and we dutifully trailed off to buy hats and jodhpurs. 'What is the point of living in the country if you don't do country things?' she said.

So there we were, with cohorts of teenage girls shouting us around the manège: 'Sit up! Kick him on. Turn your toes in. Hands down. Kick *on*.' One of the girls had a cartoon pinned to the wall of the office hut. It showed a Thelwell pony with a girl sitting on him, hands tied to the saddle, heels roped securely down, a broom handle parallel to her spine with the brush sticking out the top, and the voice of the invisible instructor in the caption shouting, 'And now RELAX!' That was about my experience.

But I soon learned to love it. I looked forward to the lesson and longed to be allowed to hack out. But that also had its trials. In the school I could climb on to my pony from a mounting block. When we started being taught how to get on from the ground, I groaned and complained mightily. I was never, ever, ever going to manage this. 'But it's easy!' exclaimed the humiliating teenagers, demonstrating lightly. I began to fantasize about the possibility of carrying a little aluminium ladder round with me, so that I could get back on if I had to dismount. Now, in fact, I can get on easily and swiftly from either side, and never cease to be pleased with my ability.

My girlfriend gave up after a bit and started going to the gym instead. But when the riding stables had to close, we bought one of the ponies – a black-and-white cob called Billy. And I kept him through everything that happened afterwards. Once our house was sold, it was, in some ways, a madness, because I had nowhere to keep him. But I could not part with him. My commitment was for life. Eventually Jayne (the friend who had found my cottage for me – her speciality is always coming to the rescue) introduced me to a farmer who kindly agreed to let us have a paddock where Billy lived out, winter and summer, for many years, until I managed to acquire my own field nearer home.

So this is another place where the facts of the past might gesture towards the future for which I am now striving. It was difficult to keep Billy, but I did it. My loyalty to this living creature might help me to cope with the – as yet only imagined – person who will need a similar dedication. So Billy and I hack out round the lanes, catching a glimpse of the kingfisher or a herd of deer, and then we stand on the hill we call Boadicea's Bottom and admire the view while we think about the child who is already in the world and who is coming towards us.

'Good afternoon, everyone.'

'Good aaafternoon, Mrs Turner. Good aaafternoon, Mrs Bexley. Good aaafternoon, Miss Reynolds.'

'Good afternoon, everyone.'

I am still volunteering at a local nursery, partly to gain experience with children and partly for the purposes of the home study – to demonstrate to my social worker my commitment to adoption.

All the same, I love my quiet times there. The children do bits of simple maths or they pick out words as we read aloud. We go into the art room, and while they run up and down with dried leaves, snowflake doilies, cut-out tulips and stripy buckets, I chat to Mrs Bexley. The seasons pass. I learn to pay attention in the moment. I learn to try to decode the children's behaviour when they do not yet have the capacity to explain. I learn a lot about small joys and a lot about laughter. I confide my hopes to Mrs Bexley. I even go to the nursery directly from my father's funeral. They know about this story too and, guessing from my black dress where it is that I have been, they greet me with ready sympathy.

One little girl with shiny brown eyes and shiny brown hair takes a shine to me. And I to her, I must admit. We like to read an old-fashioned book together about growing grain and making bread. She calls it 'the quiet book'. She takes to hiding when I arrive. The other children call to her, 'Miss Reynolds is here!'

At the end of the day Mrs Turner has them all sitting on the carpet while she reads a story. It is *Mole and the Baby Bird* by Marjorie Newman. Mole finds a baby bird and looks after it. As it grows bigger, he builds baby bird a cage. Grandfather Mole takes him to the top of the hill and shows him the free, swooping birds. At last Mole understands. ' "Birds are meant to fly," said Mole. He opened the cage door and he let his bird fly away, because he loved it. Then he cried.'

Mrs Turner looks up. 'Oh dear, we've made Miss Reynolds cry.' We all laugh. The Shiny Girl looks up at me a bit anxiously and nuzzles her head against my leg. 'It's OK,' I tell her. 'It's a happy kind of crying.' And it is.

BUT

AT THE END of February, Claudia decided that the home study was complete. She had done all she could, including interviewing yet another referee. We were given a date for the approval panel. I was as prepared as I could be. On a practical level, I had rehearsed: worked out how to get there, where to park, what the room looked like. I chose an outfit that was muted and understated. The performative again.

There are usually some fifteen to twenty people on such panels, including social workers, a medical officer, solicitor, and often adopted people and adoptive parents. The routine is that your social worker goes in first, comes out having been interviewed, then you are invited in. They ask questions, you are released, and your social worker stays for a final grilling.

I witnessed the process in operation on that day because Felicity and Stephen – a couple I had met at a preparation group, and who were planning to adopt from Russia – went in first with Mary, the social worker who had carried out their home study. Mary was in for five minutes, Felicity and Stephen were in for five minutes. Mary came out almost at once. They were through. Hugs and kisses all round. This moment in the lives of adoptive parents is a curious happiness because it is so remote. There is nothing concrete here, only an official permission that makes it possible to take a path that is still complicated and fraught. But on this occasion, Felicity and Stephen were happy and I was happy for them. And I was encouraged. Why should not my experience be the same?

Then it was my turn. The chair of the panel came out to meet me. Was it my imagination, or did it seem that she was reluctant to shake my hand? Claudia went in. She was a quarter of an hour. I was invited in. They asked me . . . Why did I wish to adopt from China? How would I cope with the child's uncertain medical history? How would I support her cultural heritage? How helpful were my support networks? Then, I was out.

Claudia stayed. And stayed, and stayed. Ten minutes went by. Twenty minutes. Twenty-five. People came and went in the lobby. Then Claudia was out, smiling. Yes, she nodded, it was OK. As she sat down to de-brief me she remarked that it was not unanimous, but she assured me that that was not unusual. Slightly crossly, she told me that someone on the panel thought I was 'too clever'. As I wiped my eyes, I replied, 'Well, even clever women want to be mothers.' But I wonder now what was meant by that remark. Perhaps it was not so much a comment on intelligence as on what they saw as a deliberate strategy.

Afterwards, I felt dazed. After all this time, after all this effort, could this be it? Could this really be the beginning of where I wanted to be? It was, by now, more than eighteen months since I had first started on the home study. But it was well over two years since I had had that vision of the possible, since I had begun to long to be a particular person alongside another small person who needed me. Since I had wished so much to be a mother.

I wanted a calm space, so I turned into the nearby cathedral. I lit a candle. In the shop I bought a book of prayers for children and then found a lovely replica of a small William Morris stained-glass Madonna, bent tenderly over her child. The vivid colours of her blue robe and golden halo glistened in the shadowy light. 'She's the last one,' said the assistant. 'She is so beautiful. I will miss her.'

In the early evening I received the customary phone call to say that the agency decision-maker had orally endorsed the panel's recommendation. I went to the ballet with my friend Jacqueline and her mother. We had dinner, we celebrated.

Three weeks after the adoption approval panel, I got in to work to find a message on my answerphone from Claudia, asking me to come in to the office in three days' time 'to discuss the next steps'. This was slightly odd. She knew I hardly ever answered that phone. Why had she not called my mobile? Or rung me at home? But I called her straight back to say, 'Yes, of course.'

Arriving at the council offices at the appointed hour, I was ushered into a little waiting room. Then Claudia appeared with Martha, the team manager. They thanked me for coming. And then Martha said it: that since the date of the panel 'it had come to their attention that I had been in an eleven-year relationship with person X, which I had not disclosed.'

Looking back on it, I realize how horrible it must have been for them. I had driven up all jolly and innocent with no knowledge of what was in store. They, on the other hand, had probably been gearing up to this for days, even weeks; I pictured their stressed phone calls, fraught consultations.

And for me? It was a gruesome hour. They showed me snippets from articles and references on the internet. Most of the facts therein were wrong. The dates were contradictory and mostly wrong. The focus they came back to, again and again, was the fact that I had had a relationship with a woman. It felt as though this was my 'crime' (maybe it was, in their eyes). Struggling to control my own feelings in relation to this, I tried to concentrate on what I really had done wrong – the non-disclosure. I said that I had left it out because it was irrelevant. That the home study presented an accurate picture of my life now, and it was now that mattered. That I wanted to be judged for myself, and not on gossip. That I knew about China's rules.

Thinking about it now, I realize that I should simply have refused to discuss it there and then. I should have asked for another meeting with some other independent witness also present. But it has taken me years to realize that. And I was being asked to respond in a moment.

Well, everything I said was truthful, but it was by no means what they needed to hear. I fear that the situation was compounded by a prejudice against the thing I had left out, but even setting that aside, I had done the worst thing that a person applying to become a prospective adopter could do. I had breached the contract of trust.

The thinking goes that if a vulnerable child is to be placed with you, then you have to be honest in your dealings with them and with every professional involved along the way. You have to be able to demonstrate openness, willingness to seek help when needed, willingness to confide the most intimate of details, and willingness to trust that what the professionals say is so, is so. It would be true to say that I had failed to do that. From their point of view – and perhaps mine too – I had arrogantly assumed that I could manage something in a system that absolutely requires you to hand over all control to the professionals and the authorities.

Years have gone by since that time. I have struggled and struggled to overcome my mistake, to recover my position. I have told the story of this error over and over again to others, both to acknowledge my responsibility and to seek forgiveness. I have had to work hard to be given a second chance.

In retrospect I see two things. First, that for all my longing, maybe at that time I was still at the fantasy stage. I wanted to be a mother, but I had calculatedly taken a route where I risked being denied. It was almost as if I had courted the denial that eventually came. The second thing is that at that point I did realize what it meant to me. The jolt of this sudden reversal put my wish to be a mother into a new light. I suspect that it was at that time that I really became determined, that I knew I could not give up.

But at the time, on that horrible day, I just had to get through. I went home, sat in the garden and wept. I phoned my sister, my friend, my brother and wept some more. I awoke morning after morning to the enormity of what I had done.

Only at one moment did I laugh about it. I decided that I'd better do what I had never done, and I googled myself. Well, yes, there was stuff about my work and my books and broadcasts, but nothing else. What could the problem be? Nothing there was controversial. I puzzled and puzzled, and then I looked again. At the top of the page it said, 'Results 1–10 of about 2,360,000.' I had only looked at the first page.

*

When I received the letter from the agency decision-maker, revoking the recommendation and explaining my next steps, I pursued the appeal process as directed. I wrote a letter to the panel asking them to reconsider at their next meeting. I was not permitted to attend, but Claudia was to represent me, and she said she would support me. But in the event, they moved the time of the panel and so Claudia was not there, which seemed to me very unfair. The decision to revoke the original recommendation for approval was upheld. Now that I have seen so much more, know so much more, I have my thoughts. When the bill came for the second half of the fee for the inter-country adoption home study, I paid it. But I had my thoughts.

I applied to the Independent Review Mechanism (IRM), then newly established. I went to a specialist solicitor who suggested that maybe they could do something for me by recommending that I be approved instead for domestic adoption.

But when I got into the IRM meeting, the chairman explained at once that they could only adjudicate on my original application, and for that – by definition, because of China's rules – I was disqualified. I thanked them sincerely all the same. The whole experience of the review process had been swift, efficient, firm and thoughtful. They all sat there in silence and looked at me sadly.

As I left the room, one of the independent social workers on the panel – the only man, as it happened – followed me out. He touched my arm. 'Just start again,' he said. 'You have a lot to offer. Be honest, be patient, and start again.' It seemed there was still much more learning to be done.

CLASSROOMS

Expect nothing. Live frugally
On surprise . . .

Alice Walker, 'Expect Nothing'

I DID NOT give up. My brother Philip kindly said that there would be no shame in doing so. My friend Bel Mooney heard out the story. It stuck with her, because she later mentioned it in one of her advice columns for the *Daily Mail*, which described how someone she knew had been refused the chance of adopting and yet still chose to help out at a nursery, finding enjoyment even there, among the children apparently out of reach.

If I could not adopt, then could I foster? I called three local agencies – each one privately run – and explained my situation to them with honesty. Each one came to visit me and all of them agreed that they would take me on for training. This seemed to me to suggest two things that were rather worrying: that the urgent need for foster carers meant that all of these agencies were prepared to overlook my old failure in the contract of trust; and that the commercial interests of such fostering agencies were the paramount consideration.

I chose the agency that seemed to be the best, and again, I started on new training. As ever, it was interesting, but two particular stories stay with me – both about lost children.

The first was related by a young couple who were experienced foster carers. Mostly, they took children in the short term, for respite or in emergencies. But one little girl came to them at three years old and stayed for over a year. Then this couple found out that they were expecting a baby. Their happiness turned to sorrow when Social Services decreed that their foster child had to be placed elsewhere. Why? Because this poor child had been sexually abused and the social workers felt that they could not take the risk that she might abuse the new baby. Everyone was devastated – the couple, their parents, the child. The husband still had tears in his eyes as he spoke.

The other story was told by a mother who had a little girl – adopted from an orphanage abroad. Along with a number of other couples, she and her husband had travelled to pick up their babies. The orphanage director met them with all the designated children. But Anna's baby was lethargic and sleepy. During the night, the baby became entirely unresponsive and, calling the orphanage, they were advised to take her to hospital. The next day the orphanage director appeared at their hotel with a new baby. They took that second baby home and she was happy and well adjusted. But Anna and her husband still grieved for the first baby, the one they felt they had failed.

Once again, I am reminded of how much pain there is in all

of these children's lives. And of how it will be in mine if I succeed.

Because something else has changed now. By this stage I have spent a long time constructing an (as yet) imaginary identity as a mother. The 'performing' of my self that began during the original home study stays with me. Everything I do, every remark I make, every interaction with every person I meet, everything I wear, everything I buy for my home, gestures towards the self-as-mother that I am inventing, creating, bringing into being. I have also read a lot of books about children displaced from their biological parents, about adoption in practice and in theory. I have attended seminars addressed to adoptive parents. I have made friends with many adoptive parents. I have read *Children Who Wait* and *Be My Parent* month in month out, heard terrible stories and encouraging ones. I took a path that was foolish and it came to a dead end. But there were still other paths that might be taken, that might yet be open to me.

For the moment, just for the sake of it, I also did one last thing that was useful to me in resolving my feelings and attitudes, and which helped me to come to terms with the fact that I had been barred (strictly, always was barred) from adopting a baby from China. I signed up for an introductory one-day course run by the Inter-Country Adoption Centre.

We met adoptive parents and adopted children. One young man had been adopted from Peru as a baby. All his life, he told us, he had fantasized about his birth mother. In his early twenties he had travelled to South America and, because the orphanage still held the records, he was able to arrange to meet his birth mother. In his mind she was an Inca princess. The woman he saw before him was little, old, toothless and wrinkled. He was able to laugh, but it was still terribly sad.

At the end of the day I waited until everyone else had gone. I wanted to ask the social worker running the course one question – the key question, the question I should have asked myself in the first place. 'I am single, in my forties, I have been married and I have had a relationship with a woman. Should I be considering inter-country adoption?'

The answer was delivered gently, but was instant, firm and certain: 'No.'

What else could be done? By this time I had learned a lot about unsettled children and strategies for helping them to feel safe; for creating routines and making calming spaces. So thinking about this and what might be useful to such a child – and to me – I signed up for a course in aromatherapy massage. Touch can be a difficult issue for any child, but often particularly so for those who have experienced trauma in their lives. All children who are adopted or have experienced being in local authority care have, by definition, experienced trauma of some kind. Many practitioners working with care-experienced children advocate some form of 'story massage', which often takes the form of a simple tale about a dog going out, running in the park, coming home and feeling tired, accompanied by gentle back-massage strokes in a regular order over the child's clothing.

With all this in mind, every Wednesday night I betook myself to a shed in a suburban garden for the classes. Another girl was studying reflexology. So, as Classic FM played Ketèlbey's 'In a

Monastery Garden' or the 'Méditation' from Massenet's *Thaïs,* Rebecca practised on me and I practised on her. Our teacher was accustomed to invite all her neighbours in to act as subjects. I used to smile as I drove away with a vision of this particular corner full of relaxed inhabitants, chilled out, and at peace with themselves and the world. But it was another lesson about caring – about a calming, meditative, noticing practice that was helping to educate me for the shape of the existence I still wanted. It was a lesson that I could usefully take into that life.

Other lessons that turned out to be useful at this time were those that preached patience and acceptance. That June I attended a conference on the English sonnet at Ghent University. It was my birthday. Unfortunately, a friend had sent me a text which read 'Haqgy birthday'. I knew she had trouble with small print, but really. However, there I was, all dressed up and among congenial people. My close friend and much-admired colleague Angela Leighton gave a paper on Christina Rossetti's Sonnet VI from *Later Life: A Double Sonnet of Sonnets.*

> We lack, yet cannot fix upon the lack:
> Not this, nor that; yet somewhat, certainly.
> We see the things we do not yearn to see
> Around us: and what see we glancing back?
> Lost hopes that leave our hearts upon the rack,
> Hopes that were never ours yet seemed to be,
> For which we steered on life's salt stormy sea
> Braving the sunstroke and the frozen pack.

If thus to look behind is all in vain,
And all in vain to look to left or right,
Why face we not our future once again,
Launching with hardier hearts across the main,
Straining dim eyes to catch the invisible sight,
And strong to bear ourselves in patient pain?

This is a poem about absence, about lost hopes, and yet – as ever with Rossetti – with poetry comes power. Out of the nothingness of the present, past and future, she has made a kind of brave promise in her repetitions: 'Why face we not our future once again'. But this time with 'hardier hearts' and 'strong to bear ourselves in patient pain'. Another useful lesson. Another useful reminder of how to cope, how to keep going.

Angela's reading comforted me. I was becoming an Ancient Mariner, reciting my story to anyone who would listen. Another esteemed colleague, Isobel Armstrong, was there. I told her. She was shocked and indignant on my behalf. That also comforted me.

Back at work after a period of leave, I was asked to review for the radio part of the Bridge Project at the Old Vic. Simon Russell Beale was playing Leontes in *The Winter's Tale* and Lopakhin in Chekhov's *The Cherry Orchard*. Sam Mendes and his co-sponsors suggested why these two plays worked well together. Of course I saw that it is about time and regret and lost chances, but no one mentions the one thing that now stands out to me clearly.

With all my experience at this time – all this loss behind and insistent hope before me – I have become always alert to the presence of children. Both *The Cherry Orchard* and *The Winter's Tale* have a dead child in the margins. In the Chekhov, Ranevskaya's seven-year-old son Grisha has drowned six years ago. Where? In the river beside the orchard. How? Because everyone thought it was someone else's job to look after him. Why? Because everyone had other things on their mind.

> Father died six years ago, and a month later my brother
> Grisha was drowned in the river – such a dear little boy of
> seven! Mother couldn't bear it; she went away, away . . .

And if you look at the end of the play, that same crime of carelessness is reprised, except on this occasion with an absurd, expendable person – the elderly servant Fiers – who is left alone in a locked and empty house with no food or fuel. The snow is coming on and no one is coming back there again until the spring.

In *The Winter's Tale* the lost child is Mamillius, the young son of Leontes and his queen Hermione. Mamillius goes into a decline when his mother is wrenched from him and declared an adulteress, while his baby sister is reviled and abandoned. As Leontes defies the Oracle of Apollo and refuses to believe that Hermione is chaste, news is brought of the death of young Mamillius whose 'honourable thoughts, / Thoughts high for one so tender' cannot support the slandering of his mother.

Both plays are about the misuse of power, about class and exploitation, about tyranny and the failure of responsibility. And the people who are failed most are children. In both plays, people die. But the first people to die are children.

In Shakespeare's plays, children often are doomed. They come on stage sweetly prattling. But keep watching, because then they die, let down by the adults who should look after them: Mamillius, the two princes in *Richard III*, Juliet, Lady Macbeth's lost baby, Arthur in *King John*, Macduff's children, 'All my pretty ones'. Perdita and Marina survive, but only just, their names pointing always to their first lost families.

Suddenly I see the point of this. Historians now estimate that in the sixteenth century about one-third of children born alive would die in infancy. Today, we still fail our children. In the latter part of the nineteenth century, many Acts of Parliament were passed to help children thrive – to make sure that they got born, that they stayed alive after birth, that they survived beyond the first few months instead of being abandoned at railway stations or thrust into middens.

Many people worked for children, but children were the last vulnerable group to acquire a society dedicated to looking after their interests. The National Society for the Prevention of Cruelty to Children (NSPCC) was founded in 1884, modelled on a similar society that had been established in Liverpool in the previous year.

Just over a century later, in 1989, the General Assembly of the United Nations adopted the UN Convention on the Rights of the Child. It came into force in September 1990. By 2014, 194 countries were signatories, including South Sudan, which ratified the treaty in November 2013. Somalia deposited its ratification documents with the UN in October 2015. Ban Ki-Moon, secretary general at that time, called for the last remaining country to ratify. That country is the United States of America.

'Right. Now, if everyone could get into groups, please? Let's mix you up a bit. If we can have one group over by the window, one by the door . . . Hurry up and settle down, please.'

There are about twenty of us. All different: young and old, married and single, gay and straight. A variety of colours. A mix of lawyers and teachers, a full-time mum, a youth worker, a cleaner, a bus driver, and me. I am impressed that all these people have willingly signed up to do this. We have all been selected in the course of two interviews and a taster evening. We have all been CRB-checked.* We have all supplied the names of one professional and three personal referees.

The senior social worker running the course is fiercely accomplished, making sure everyone sticks to their tasks, but there are four others leading the training here too, and they join in with the different groups, observing us, weighing up our reactions, our prejudices, our sympathies and our behaviour. This course is both an education and an evaluation.

'All right, everyone. I am now going to hand round a sheet listing some situations involving children. I want you to look at the list and rate them in terms of risk. Fifteen minutes before coffee time. Off you go.'

---

* The Criminal Records Bureau (CRB) and the Independent Safeguarding Authority (ISA) are now merged under the title of the Disclosure and Barring Service (DBS).

At first everyone in my group agrees. 'Well, that's OK.' 'Yes, and this one is fine too.' And then someone raises a doubt. 'Well, I'm not so sure about this.' After ten minutes, tempers are rising: 'No, that would be totally out of the question.' When the course leader calls for order, no consensus has been reached. We're soon laughing, but this is all too serious.

Here are some items from the list:

1. An uncle takes photographs of his six-year-old niece in the bath.
2. A child tells you that she sometimes gets into her carer's bed for a cuddle.
3. Your decorator offers to take your four-year-old swimming.
4. Adults and children walk about the house with no clothes on.
5. A neighbour reads a bedtime story alone with the child in the child's bedroom.
6. Adults play wrestling and tickling games with children.

Some of the answers are 'definitely risky'. But most of them are marginal, 'maybe yes, maybe no'. We never did manage to agree, except that 'it depends on the circumstances'. And what were we doing? Training to become independent visitors for looked after children.

Under the Children Act 1989 and the Children and Young Persons Act 2008, any looked after child in the care of a local authority has the right to an independent visitor (IV). The requirement is particularly relevant when that child has little or no contact with their birth family. The child has to agree to an independent visitor being appointed. The role of the IV is to visit and befriend the child or young person. They may also help the child or young person by supporting them in exercising their rights, and may even (if appropriate) attend their regular statutory review.

Yet in 1998 the Joseph Rowntree Foundation (an independent social change organization working to solve UK poverty) found that many local authorities failed to provide IVs for their children. In 2012 the Ofsted report on IVs did not see much improvement. In January 2016, the National Independent Visitor Data Report compiled by Alexandra Gordon and Kris Graham stated that 'There are around 2,200 children currently matched with an Independent Visitor – 3.2 per cent of the total looked after children (LAC) population in England.'

I don't know if everyone on that course was approved. I was, and went on to be matched with a fourteen-year-old girl living in a privately run residential home. I was given some information about her, and had a talk with her designated social worker. The idea was that once a fortnight or so I would take Tiana out somewhere in her local area, either for a day or for a few hours, and that I would phone her every week at the same time to have a chat and a catch-up.

All our face-to-face meetings had to be carefully documented, and each time we met I was required to discuss with Tiana's social worker where Tiana and I would go, how long for and what time I would bring her home. I also had to discuss how much I could spend – on food, on admissions, on little souvenirs.

My time would not be paid for, but I would be given a small budget for petrol and expenses, as well as a sum to buy her a birthday and Christmas present – both of which had to be vetted. Finally, I had to sign an agreement that I would never take any pictures of Tiana.

I worried a bit about this last condition on Tiana's behalf, because it would mean that she never had any record of these rare days spent outside of school and the home. Though of course I could see that it was to do with safeguarding, as well as Tiana's right to privacy. Later on, I came up with an idea. How about if I were to give Tiana a disposable camera? Then I could use it to take photographs of her on these days out, and she could take the whole camera away with her at the end of our meeting to have the film developed later. Tiana's social worker agreed to this. But to begin with, she arranged to meet me at the residential home and introduce us.

On the agreed day I set out to drive to the home. The place where Tiana lived, with five other girls in care, was a once beautiful old rectory in the country. Each girl had their own room decorated with their own stuff. But the bathrooms were institutional, the garden neglected, the sitting room bland and dominated by an enormous state-of-the-art television. On this occasion, when I first spent an hour there, I realized afterwards that the phrase I had heard over and again was 'Bye-bye, all. I'm just off now.'

The point is that nobody *lived* there except the six children. There were always staff on duty, of course, but overnight the one staff member on the rota slept on a put-me-up in the office. When their shift finished first thing in the morning, another member of staff arrived and the overnight supervisor went back to their own home and family, marking once again the 'difference' these children suffered.

Any home preceded by a descriptive word is not a home. Care home, dogs' home, children's home, residential home: they all mean, by definition, that the inhabitants of such establishments are not in their own home, or any kind of real home. How were the children in Tiana's residential home to learn about continuity and family and security – let alone love and attachment – if the adults who looked after them came and went, and these children knew that they were less than the other, unseen, unknown children in their carers' lives? The other children who belonged to those adults, the other children to whom they rushed at the end of their working day?

One day, when we were out on a visit to an aquarium, Tiana said to me, 'So you teach in a college, and you work for the BBC and a newspaper. Do you get paid for seeing me?'

And then I realized. She was surrounded by professionals: social workers, carers, welfare officers, doctors, teachers, therapists. But I was the one and only person in her life *not paid* to be with her or to do something for her. 'No, honey,' I assured her. 'I do this for fun.' And I meant it.

At one time the government was considering re-thinking its policy of housing looked after children in foster homes, and moving towards more residential care. This seems to me to be a very bad idea, unless the kind of homes that exist presently are entirely re-thought too.

In January 2014, Dr Maggie Atkinson, the then children's commissioner, made the same point in evidence to a Commons Education Select Committee. There, she said that many of the care workers running children's homes were often '. . . the least well trained, many of them very young, very inexperienced, sometimes very mobile and transient in their work, moving on from job to job.' She added that 'These are our children, these are the children of the state . . . The nation needs to be as outraged when children are less well served than they should be in residential care.'

Atkinson also suggested that part of the problem is that there is an unfair 'stigma' associated with being in care, which can be seen when communities oppose plans to convert houses into homes for young people. 'Being in care is not just about somehow being "in trouble"; in fact, it rarely is,' she said.

If residential care homes are really going to work, they need to be like modern boarding schools where the children live as part of a family, with a permanent carer (or carers) actually living on site with their own family. But that is a huge commitment. Those taking on such a job would have to be paid handsomely, and honoured and applauded with respect and social status. Is society prepared to invest in its lost children to that extent? I would like to think so.

In June 2018 it was reported that the number of children being taken into care had doubled in the last decade. In 2017, 14,490 children were taken into care in England – 40 a day – almost double that of 2008, when the figure was 7,440. As a result, in England in 2017, the number of children being looked after by people other than parents – by professionals such as foster carers and carers in residential homes – was over 70,000.

Unless they have had some direct experience of the care system, few people realize that it is a ghastly cycle. Children in care all too often grow up to have children who are taken into care themselves. Why? Because such children grow up in foster homes where they may or may not have consistency of care. Or else they grow up in a residential home such as the one where Tiana lived; privately run and geared to make a profit. They have carers, as Maggie Atkinson said, but these are professional carers – often young people themselves with little life experience, who frequently move on to different jobs. The children living in such kinds of care have no continuity and, above all, no chance of developing the secure attachment that is so crucial in early years.

This emphasis on security and consistency was John Bowlby's essential observation when he wrote his monumental volumes of the *Attachment and Loss* trilogy – required reading for social workers dealing with looked after children. But the practicalities of simply coping with the everyday crises of more and more children being taken into care means that too often this principle is forgotten.

It is the same with foster homes. There too, children are placed with professional carers. They may be experienced, they may be supervised, they may even be good at it – and many of them do it as a social duty and because they do care – but some of them, especially in the past, did it for money. And even if they are the best foster carers in the world, things change. People get ill and so cannot continue. They have problems with their own birth children who need them, and so they cannot continue.

Foster-care placements are almost never long term, and only exceptionally rarely does a child stay in one placement for their whole childhood. Some children move many times over. So again, how are they to develop a secure attachment to any primary care-giver? How are they to learn consistency, security, love? How are they to learn how to parent, or indeed anything about what it means to be a family?

When sibling groups are taken into care, they are frequently placed separately. Sometimes there may be good reason for this – to do with one child or another's safety, for example – but more often it is simply because there are no sibling foster placements available. Local authorities and foster caring agencies desperately need people prepared to take two, three or four brothers and sisters, but they are seldom to be found. So these children, already grieving their lost parents and wider family, suffer yet another loss. They are separated from the very people who most understand their experience because they too are going through it – their brothers and sisters.

In addition to all this, children suffering from adverse experiences in their early years need specialist care. Some foster carers are trained in therapeutic parenting. Others are not. That said, many agencies today put a lot of effort into such training.

Today, and for some time, there has been a shortage of professional foster carers, and there is little time or money available to provide training for the everyday attention to a child's psychological state that these children really need.

There is an even greater shortage of prospective adoptive parents. But initial preparation courses, and the processes of the home study (to some degree), should and do provide some consideration of the role of therapeutic parenting. Some flag the special efforts that will need to be made to listen, to attend, to watch and wonder in an effort to understand or simply to notice or hear how the child might express their particular needs. But there still isn't enough provision for this, and there most certainly are not enough prospective adoptive parents willing to take on these tough tasks.

Sadly, I think here of one highly respected independent social worker, who once remarked to me that the two terms used to describe children dependent on local authorities were both inaccurate – they were neither 'cared for' nor 'looked after'. I asked her which children count as 'hard to place' for adoption. She shrugged. 'Anyone over the age of three.'

UNLESS

BUT WHY DID I do it? At times I wonder why did I seek out the one thing – virtually in the whole world – that I could not have? At times, depending on my mood or my circumstances, I have found different answers to this question and placed myself in various positions ranging across the spectrum of guilt and innocence, blame and exoneration.

In a psychological mood I might ask if I was embarrassed or ashamed? I do know that I was not – most certainly not. I loved my girlfriend and she loved me, and we were happy and open.

On one occasion I went to a wine-tasting party with the father of my god-daughter. My hostess – not a close acquaintance – asked where I lived. 'Ah,' she breathed, when I told her. She leaned over confidentially. 'And tell me, have the dreadful neighbours gone?' 'What dreadful neighbours?' I asked. She lowered her voice, conspiratorially. 'You know . . . the ladies . . . the lesbians.' I looked at her and put up my hand. 'I am that dreadful neighbour.'

Only through such openness is it possible to combat prejudice. I know that lady would never risk similar assumptions of shared understanding – or the frank expression of such derogatory opinions – ever again. And I have now learned first hand how concealment gives permission for biased judgement.

By keeping silent during my home study I had indeed allowed others to deduce that I was ashamed – I had possibly even re-inforced their view that it was something of which one should be ashamed. As my friend Philip said to me, 'It plays into their hands. If you speak about it openly, they do not dare to air their views. If you keep silent, they can carry on with their belief that this really is the dark secret that they fear.'

No, it was not shame or anxiety that kept me silent, though I suspect that the IRM panel suspected me, and – psychologically minded as they might be – I can see why. At the time, having taken that first step in choosing to apply for inter-country adop-tion, I thought I was simply making a practical decision that only happened to require ignoring one particular relationship. From my point of view it was a decision that was not directly con-nected to the facts of the character of the relationship itself.

Recently, another social worker told me that she really had to be sure that I was 'comfortable with my sexuality'. Is it so very odd to have loved man and woman? It doesn't feel like it to me. I took to asking my friends, 'Do you think I'm comfortable with my sexuality?' They all laughed. 'Absolutely!'

But in another way there *was* a psychological problem. I had been hurt just before I decided to start on the adoption process, and that took me back to all the other hurts, specifically the losses of my childhood. I had recognized this when I first went to the therapist and said of my father, 'And you're not going to make me see him, are you?' But I was still not restored.

I believe now that this had consequences. If at that time I was still nursing my own affliction, then I think now that I was not then fit to adopt a child who would inevitably carry what Nancy Verrier has called 'the primal wound' – that is, the pain of having been separated from their biological mother.

Verrier wrote *The Primal Wound: Understanding the Adopted Child* out of her own experience with her daughter, who was adopted as a very young baby. As the child grew, she still suffered a great deal of emotional trauma, which Verrier eventually connected to her loss, even though she had been so young. This is what she says:

> What I discovered is what I call the *primal wound*, a wound
> which is physical, emotional, psychological, and spiritual, a
> wound which causes pain so profound as to have been
> described as cellular by those adoptees who allowed
> themselves to go that deeply into their pain. I began to
> understand this wound as having been caused by the
> separation of the child from his biological mother, the
> connection to whom seems mystical, mysterious, spiritual
> and everlasting.

Of all the things that I had done 'wrong', this, I now think, was the worst. That I was not really emotionally fit to take on this task back then. But no one said that to me, though I suspect that my therapist might have been trying, even at the time, to get me to see it. I have had to work it out for myself. But then maybe that, in itself, is a sign of how my grief has subsided, faded to a memory that is no longer painful. Whatever. The outcome was the same. I had been – in this instance, at this time – refused the possibility of inter-country adoption, albeit under rather cruel circumstances. And – dare I say – I am prepared to believe now, in the largest sense, that that was the right outcome. The right outcome, I mean, for any child who might then have come to me.

Most especially now, in retrospect, I wonder if it might also have been the right outcome for any child who might have come to me through the route of inter-country adoption. At one point, in the throes of self-reproach and self-accusation, I said to the adoption solicitor that maybe I really was in the wrong. After all, if the cultural mores of another country condemned homosexuality, then who was I to question that, challenge that?

I then went on to say, 'And besides, suppose I had had a child placed with me. And then suppose her birth mother – had she known about it – would have been horrified to know that her daughter was being brought up by a woman who had loved a woman.' The solicitor was robust. 'Don't be silly – this woman abandoned her child!' This discussion was entirely hypothetical. All the same, I don't know. This fantasy mother still deserves compassion. More than most. And she still deserves respect.

Of course I was no longer, nor would ever be, adopting through any inter-country path. But this exchange with the solicitor made me recall something that happened at one of the many preparation groups I had undertaken. A mother, who had adopted her daughter from an orphanage in another country where babies had been relinquished for various kinds of difficult reasons, warned us that people often do not understand how entangled your imaginative life becomes with the lost and – in her case – ultimately unknowable family history of your child.

Someone had remarked to her casually that it was really good that there would never be any birth family to re-appear in her child's life. 'But,' she said to us, 'I would give anything to be able to help my little girl with the knowledge; to find her birth family. It would mean so much to her. And to me. And besides, there is not a day that goes by when I do not think of her. That other mother is in my life for ever.'

For who can know what sorrow and despair is here? What are the extremes of distress and misery that can drive a woman – or indeed a man, or a family – to relinquish their baby? Make no mistake, there is no callous indifference here. These children, in countries all across the world, are often left in public places – by bridges, at railway stations, near marketplaces – in the fervent hope that people will come by, and that these infants will be found swiftly and safely.

And anyway, how can we know for sure who it is that leaves that baby there? It could easily be someone else, someone not part of the birth family, who has made that decision and intervened. As my own understanding of what mothering may be has grown, so too, in proportion, has grown my empathy, my feeling and solicitude for all these other mothers.

I am not sure now, at this moment of writing, how I feel about adoption generally. I know that adoption can be – very often is – a wonderful thing for the adoptive parent. Looking around me I can see the blessings, the delight, the whole-heart satisfaction that possesses those who can thus come to love and be loved. I can also see – I do see every day of my life – how the lives of adoptive children are enriched and enabled and progressed and promoted by their adoptive parents. How they, too, learn to love and be loved.

But now that I have witnessed, at first hand, what it means to lose home and family and school and place and name and identity all at once, in a moment, I know how difficult this is. And I wonder how much – or how little – does it matter if one adds culture, language, food, smell, conventions of dress, landscape, environment and racial sameness to that list of losses? Does losing all those things as well make it worse? Or is the enormity of loss just the same in spite of all the gains?

Having never experienced it directly myself, I cannot answer the question. But I can think of one person who has known it, and I recall her conclusions. In *My Fathers' Daughter*, the journalist Hannah Pool tells the story of the re-discovery of her lost birth family in Eritrea. At the time of the publication of her book, interviewers pressed her repeatedly on all she had gained through adoption, but she was insistent that for all that, if she could undo all that had been, she would have wanted to be a child who had remained with her birth family in Eritrea.

All the same, while I fully respect and accept Hannah Pool's conclusions for herself, they may need to be treated with caution and in a wider context. As someone who has grown up (by the circumstances of adoption) in a privileged environment, she knows the worth of all she has in her adoptive life, and – much more importantly – she knows what *it is not worth*.

The problem, as I see it, is this. Only if you *have* things can you know why you do not need them. If you *do not* have those things, then you cannot begin to comprehend their irrelevance. The child adopted contentedly (?) into a middle-class family might similarly say that her piano lessons, her reading, her travelling, her theatre, her possible career choices are as nothing compared to that which would have been hers had she been able to stay with her birth family. In one way she will be right. She has suffered the loss of the responsible, loving parenting given by a birth family that should be the birthright of every child. But it is only because she has lost what she has lost that she has ended up in a situation where she can understand what it is that she has lost.

Maja Lee Langvad is another adoptee who has thought extensively about the effects of adoption. Born in South Korea, she was adopted by a Danish family. Her book of poems *Hun er vred*, or *She Is Angry*, is a profound meditation on the impacts of her experience. But it is not easy reading. It is most especially not easy reading for an adoptive parent, whatever their situation:

> She's angry that she doesn't have an adopted brother
> or sister from South Korea who she can share her
> experience of being adopted with . . .

> She's angry that she is adopted.

Inter-country – or transnational, or overseas – adoption has become more difficult in recent years. In April 2016, one British agency, Parents and Children Together (PACT), decided to withdraw its inter-country adoption services. PACT chief executive, Jan Fishwick, said, 'It is with regret that we have made the difficult decision to withdraw from providing these services. Adopting from overseas has become increasingly complex . . .'

It is indeed more 'complex', and there are more rules. Just one instance. In the early twenty-first century, when I first began on this path, I met couples – I still know them – who adopted children from Russia. But since 2013, the Russian family code has stipulated that people from countries where gay marriage is legal cannot adopt Russian children. In 2015, only some fifty-eight children were adopted in the UK from abroad. But children's aid agencies reckon there are some 10 million children living in institutions across the world. And that there are another 60 million children living on the street.

It is difficult. There are no absolute answers. As the Australian writer and adoptive parent Carol Lefevre says, 'Now that I have had time to reflect, I believe, as I did not before, that adoption is a terrible thing. But the truth is that more often than not the alternative is more terrible.'

Adoption is 'a terrible thing'. For the child, always. For the relinquishing parent, almost certainly always. For the adopting parent, very often indeed. For even once you are through the studies and the panels, the scrutiny and the questions – all the things that are so exposing – there is still the child. And though you may do your best, the shadow of their lost past will for ever be there somewhere, and that can never be erased. Always assuming you make it to that stage at all.

I have seen many attempts at adoption that did not succeed, and all for variously complicated reasons that were not necessarily the fault of anyone concerned. Simply among people I know, I can think of one prospective adoptive parent who made it to the matching panel and no further. Another who got into introductions but could not go beyond that. Another who took the child home, but then the child wanted to go back to their previous situation. And another whose long-time partner suddenly decided that the prospect of an adopted child was all too much, and ended the relationship.

But then, 'more often than not the alternative is more terrible'. Because what are the alternatives? A childhood in an orphanage? A childhood on the street? A childhood with many different carers whose interest in you is primarily professional? And each one of those not-ideal childhoods is followed by an adulthood that is marked and scarred by the consequences of that childhood. Adoption, with all its pains for both the adopted child and the adoptive parent, is still the least worst answer for that child. Sometimes it may even be the best answer. But for me, at this time, as a hopeful adoptive parent, it was the best answer to the desire that started me on this path. I wanted a child. Now I know that I want an adopted child. And I know that I am prepared to accept, even embrace, both my own old losses and the losses that will be new for that child.

But I will also hope. I will hope that the joy I see in the faces of my friends who are adoptive parents will be mine. I will hope to see in my child's face the confidence and trust and contentment that I see in their children.

Eventually, I did take the advice of that kind unknown man who followed me out of the room at the IRM panel. As I write this, I wonder if that intervention was his spontaneous choice, or was it a planned action, out of earshot of the official minutes? I see that moment now as pivotal. And I am grateful that I heard those words. I made up my mind. I called the agency where I had been discussing the possibility of fostering and explained. They wished me luck, but said to come back to them at any time.

So I began again – with domestic adoption this time, for which I was fully qualified. There were more false starts – four in all – each one helpful, each one part of the process.

I wrote a letter to an independent agency based near me. Sheena made an appointment and came to see me. She had long dark hair and a thoughtful manner. I told her the whole story while she listened intently. Then she sighed. 'It's a shame,' she said. 'You should have applied for this in the first place.' Well, yes, I knew that by then.

So she came to see me again, and made careful notes of dates and times on all that had happened. She decided to take the unusual step of presenting my case to her panel and asking if they would take me on. They said no. But Sheena was nice to me. And sad for me. And that helped – she still believed in me.

I made an appointment with another local authority. Their offices, in a seedy part of town, were run down and gloomy. There were many people in the waiting room – patient, uncomplaining, suffering. I told the story again. The adoption social workers said they would have to consult. Two days later, the answer: no.

This rejection was difficult for me. From the little I had seen in that one visit, I guessed that they really needed prospective adoptive parents. But clearly I had made myself too much of a liability. On the other hand, maybe that was the point. They had so little in the way of resources, and so many demands on the little they had, that they could not afford to spend money on a home study that might not result in a placement for one of their waiting children.

The next attempt was with a local authority further away. There were two young women, both very attentive. For some reason, I wept through this one. Unsurprisingly, they said no immediately. I then went straight on to work to ask my head of department if I could defer the leave due to me. I told her the story too. I had to work. To be alone – researching in a library, trawling through the archives with no other human engagement, and nothing but my thoughts – seemed too much. I needed to see people, students, colleagues. I needed to teach.

Then another try, with another borough. I was subjected to a long interview, three hours of dense and detailed questions as to what exactly had happened and why I had done what I had done, along with other insistent questions on my past and on my present. I think again about the peculiarity of this process: no one asks all this of a woman who gets pregnant; no one grills them on their lives and their futures. I grit my teeth. But I clear this hurdle.

After this interview the agency agreed to accept me for a week-long adoption preparation course. And so I learned to make a 'life story' book – like the kind that is supplied to children living in care, designed to help them know about their past. I applied myself again to the need to heal, to the need for trust and honesty.

During this course I heard the stories of other prospective adopters. There was an Israeli couple who had already identified a little girl, just a bit younger than their biological daughter, who came from a similar background. There was a single mother with one birth daughter. There was a couple – Tim from Holland, and Robert, who was English. There was a young married couple who had one adopted toddler and who had already been matched with his younger sibling, still to be born.

As a measure of the difficulties that have to be overcome, only two of these other prospective adopters ended up with a placement. The married couple collected their new baby son a day after he was born. The two men adopted two brothers. But the Israeli couple had a terrible time: the little girl placed with them did not want a sister – she wanted *to be* that sister – and, in the end, they could not go on. The single mother decided to concentrate on her birth child.

At the end of the course, this local authority agreed take me on. But, they said, I had to live in London. I did not want to live in London. But I did want a child. What to do? I wrote myself a list of options headed 'Peggy's Difficult Choices'.

At this moment in the process of the story, I had been navigating the adoption system for nearly six years. But the point is that by that stage – as those many extra years had passed – I was so much more myself. I had my own home, and one that suited me in its eccentricity and its simplicity. I had come to terms with the losses of my childhood – both my motherland and my father. I had just a few secure friendships with people who supported me, exclaimed over each new rejection and cheered me on to each new attempt. I had congenial colleagues at work, at the opera houses and at the BBC, and this fostered my creativity as I developed my own courses and my own programmes. I had learned to become more and more certain that my wish to be a mother was proper and a real vocation. Most importantly of all I had learned about looked after children and had a great deal of experience both with them, and with children in general. I was certain of my own wholeness, which meant that I was in a position to commit to someone else's vulnerability.

In the end, the right adoption agency came to me by pure chance. A friend rang me one morning. 'Quick,' Gilly said. 'I've just heard the person for you on the radio.' I rushed to press the 'on' button. An independent social worker was talking about adoption on BBC Radio 4's *Woman's Hour*.

This woman did indeed sound brilliant. I looked her up on the internet and emailed her. She replied at once, we met in a pub, and she turned out to be the perfect guide – knowledgeable, wise and sensible. She put me in touch with a new independent adoption agency – now for my sixth attempt, including the first disaster. But the manager there – and everyone associated with them – was professional, efficient, scrupulous.

When I began this quest, when I first wished for a child, I found I could not help but begin to think about names. Both of my brothers have a penchant for fancy names when it comes to their children. Verity, Grace, Rose, Xavier, Gregory and Columba all figure – and my nephews and nieces all boast three names apiece.

To my own amusement, I found that I was just as bad. My friends with adopted children go for sensible options, such as Lily, Jade and Maya. I went more along the lines of Imogen, Kilmeny, Cordelia, Valancy, Perdita, Marilla, Blanche and – hippy-dippyest of all – Angel.

Soon omens appeared everywhere. The bus stop on my way to work is by Angel Alley. I realized that the walls of the college chapel were covered with winged angels. Early one morning I had an unsolicited phone call from some centre on the Asian sub-continent: 'Hello, this is Angel speaking. Are you happy with your insurance?'

Of course, I realize now that it is a bit of a fashionable name. I also realize now that I will never be using it. And that's fine, because she has, just the same, watched over me.

When I went for my first interview with the new adoption agency, I had taken down the address but I had not taken it in. Only as I arrived did I see it – and really see it – for the first time. It was on Angel Way.

VENTURING

I came to explore the wreck.

. . .

I came to see the damage that was done
and the treasures that prevail.

. . .

Adrienne Rich, 'Diving into the Wreck'

AFTER WE MOVED to England in the 1960s, my parents took up where they had left off ten years previously. We went to museums, the theatre, the ballet and the opera. I got Offenbach's *Orpheus in the Underworld* with Mummy. My sister got Britten's *Peter Grimes* with Daddy. At the time I thought she drew the short straw. She still thinks the same, but I feel very differently.

But the most important thing that my parents took up again was their friendship with Litzi and Henry Carney. Liberal, cultured, politically committed, Litzi especially was the key influence in my mother's life. She was to become a key influence in all of our young lives too.

Litzi was born in 1908. Her mother had been placed in a Catholic orphanage and was then adopted by a notable Jewish family. They had to promise to raise her as a Catholic, which they did, but she chose to convert when she was twenty-one. Litzi's father was a wealthy pharmacist. The family lived in the centre of Vienna and Litzi could remember witnessing the pomp of Emperor Franz Joseph's funeral in 1916. During the mid 1930s, Litzi met Henry Carney, a senior tax inspector, on a cross-Channel ferry. By the time they docked at Dover they had made a bargain. He needed respectability. She needed safety. I know all this is true because Henry himself told the story to my sister Antonia.

And so they married. They lived in an apartment on the ground floor of a house in Belsize Park. Henry's friend Leslie lived in a flat on the first floor. Henry set himself to work – filling in forms, attending interviews – to get Mutti and Pepe out of Vienna. (I was later to discover, entirely by accident, that he helped forty or fifty other families in the same way.)

Back in Vienna, the officer appointed to deal with the task of sequestering Pepe's property had taken a liking to Mutti. Playing for time, she would invite him to tea. 'After all,' he would say, '*you* are not Jewish. I will look after you and your daughter.' Mutti would smile and flutter her eyelashes. 'Let me think about it.' I know all this is true because Litzi herself told the story to all of us children, complete with 'come hither' gestures.

Eventually, Henry succeeded. He had to sign a paper promising that Mutti and Pepe would never become a charge on the British state. He had to find them jobs. Fortunately, Henry had a friend who owned a country house in Devon. Pepe became the gardener there. Mutti became the cook and housekeeper. Until then, she had never even boiled an egg.

By the time my mother first met Litzi in the early 1950s, Mutti and Pepe were living in one room of the ground floor of the house in Belsize Park. Henry and Litzi had the other, the third was the kitchen. Leslie still lived upstairs.

For us children, the Belsize Park apartment was a place of magic. Beautiful food was served on exquisite plates. A bottle of wine, ringed with a decorated drip catcher, was produced for my parents. Then there would be schnapps in a tiny painted bottle served in little painted glasses.

Henry seemed rather scary to me, my brothers and sister when we were young, though he became a good friend as we grew up. He collected old and precious glass, so we children tip-toed past that cabinet. He also collected Modernist furniture, so we children were not permitted to sit on the Gerrit Rietvelds or the Marcel Breuers (not that we knew then what they were).

Leslie would join us for lunch and talk to my mother about the theatre, or the Beatles, or the latest films. Then he taught us card games or did tricks for us.

And then there was Litzi. She had the most miraculous dressing-up box. Occasionally, she would get out the photograph albums of her youth. Sometimes she could tell us what happened to this or that of her cousins. Sometimes she could not, and all would fall silent. Always there were the coloured sugar crystals, the ritual of a 'mixture' of Chinese and Indian tea, her games, her presents, her secure presence.

This gracious way carried on into our own family rituals. *The Virginian* on television on a Friday night, with the treat of a Mars bar each. Daddy's speciality of fried scones if he was in a good mood on Sunday morning. Slideshow evenings when we would systematically review our Australian childhood, with an interval for chips, introduced by Daddy's special homemade slide – a view of the sea, on which he had written 'Anyone for a drink?'

And we travelled. No sooner had we arrived in England than we set off for the deep lanes of Devon that Easter, and then on to Stratford for a dose of Shakespeare. I recall camping in a field and being sent to the farmer to ask for milk for my little brother – which we were given, along with six fresh eggs and a pat of newly churned butter. As far as I was concerned, I had suddenly arrived in Famous Five country.

Then my parents bought a trailer tent. You pulled it up and over, and there was instant accommodation. Adding poles and canvas produced a living area, a kitchen awning. We always spent the whole of the summer abroad – or rather, that was the plan. Very often, we ran out of money. For the Easter holidays we travelled too, but in more southern European countries. That was harder and more chancy, because we needed to stay in the free, municipal campsites and they were not always open at that time of year. In this way we went all across France, Belgium and Luxembourg, Austria, Czechoslovakia and Hungary, Spain and Portugal, over the Alps to Italy, to Germany then north to Holland and Denmark.

One year we went to Austria to visit Litzi's friends, Erich and Jean Kuffner, at their apartment in Vienna, and at their summer house and allotment in the woods outside of the city. During the 1930s, while training to be a doctor, Erich had witnessed many Nazi attacks. Then, with the outbreak of war, he had been conscripted into the German army. Jean had refused to return home to England and left Vienna to hide in the countryside. Three times the village was occupied. No one betrayed her. When the war was over, Erich walked back to Vienna from Berlin to discover that their house was empty. But he found Jean in the end, and so we met them, with their daughter, Erika.

Inevitably, there were adventures for us too. Some more than one might wish.

That first summer we went to Austria, then on to Czechoslovakia (as it then was). In Brno, we returned to the car to find that it had been broken into. My father's camera had been stolen, all our money, all our passports. Daddy reported it to the police. They allowed him to drive us back to the campsite and then he was questioned at length overnight. (This seemed oddly heavy handed at the time.) Because Daddy was exhausted – as well he might be – we did not set off for Prague until the following day. There was no Australian embassy so we went to the British. Commonwealth citizens had rights in those days.

It was very busy. We hung around for hours as my father was passed from one official to another. There were little groups of people talking in lowered voices, gesticulating, frowning. Eventually Daddy was given a document guaranteeing our passage, and a loan of £50.

As we headed for the Austrian border, we saw a group of soldiers on the corner of a square and glimpsed a tank down a side street. 'That's odd,' said Mummy. At the border there were long queues of cars. Gradually my parents discovered what had happened. This was the end of August 1968. We waited. My father took his piece of paper from one officer to another. We were waved into a side queue. We waited some more. My little brother, cute and blond, and then only two, popped his head out of the car window and addressed a stern soldier with a machine gun: '*Danke schön, bitte schön*, please, Mr Policeman, open the barrier.' My mother hastily pushed him back into his seat and wound up the window.

Eventually one difficulty was overcome. The officials could not understand why we were going into Austria instead of straight back to England via Germany. I guess my parents thought the Kuffners might help. But everyone was suspicious in this moment.

Most of the £50 loan had to go on petrol. Racing across Europe, we caught a late-night ferry from Calais to Dover, and Daddy took his piece of paper down to the purser's office. He came back looking worn: 'He says he's never seen one of these.' As we approached Dover, Daddy went down to the purser again. This time he came back grinning. 'It's OK. The purser said, "Let's put it this way. I'm Scottish, you're Australian, they're English. Carry on."'

When Jan Palach killed himself a few months later in January 1969 I felt involved. And like many other people, I have never forgotten his name.

Was it reckless? Four small children and hardly any money? Yes. But it was wonderful too. For a long time my brother Philip drove his schoolmates mad. Any time a country came up in a geography or history lesson, he would fling up his hand. 'I've been there!'

Our shared young experience has coloured our lives and we are all similarly intrepid – or heedless. I would have only just turned sixteen when I first went to Paris with a school friend under my own steam. My siblings were the same. We were gifted the world.

But there was something wrong in our childhood sphere. Those mysterious 'library meetings'. The unexplained absences. The many 'conferences'. One day, searching through my father's jacket pockets for change for dinner money or some such, I came across a postcard. I did not know who it was from, or quite what was being said, but I knew it was not a good thing and that I had to hide it from Mummy. So I tore it into little pieces and put it at the bottom of the burning pile in the garden.

My sister and I now reckon there were at least three women at various stages. And then, one weekend, he left with no explanation to my mother or anyone else. After that, there was one day when Mummy put the four of us children on the train and we travelled by ourselves to see him. He showed us his new school. He took us to a restaurant for lunch. I hated every minute of it. Felt I should represent my mother, but had no idea how. Was cross with my little brother for being pleased to see him.

I need not have stressed. He did not attempt to repeat the experience. I am guessing now that the trip had been Mummy's suggestion anyway. I phoned him – at his office, it was the only number we had – when we were burgled. He came to sort out the insurance. Which meant that he turned up unannounced at Mummy's school during the day and took her out of the classroom into the playground, so that there was no time and no privacy for a conversation. He wrote to me when I had an emergency operation for a burst appendix. My sister saw him for ten minutes when she went on an organized trip near his new school. He chatted amicably to her teacher. And that was all. No letters, no visits, no contact.

In one way it was better like that. We children knew where our loyalties lay. In another way it was not so good.

DADDY

My father paces the upstairs hall
a large confined animal
neither wild nor yet domesticated.

                    Maxine Kumin, 'Spree'

AFTER THAT APRIL day when I first visited my father in the hospital at Banbury, I carried on visiting every Saturday. On one occasion my sister came too. And then, after that meeting, we telephoned our mother and told her what we had done. She was glad. I kept on with the visiting on my own account.

Which is how it came about that, some months later, I went to my father's funeral in that peculiar, secret way.

When he died, I again telephoned to tell my mother. She said, 'It is all right. I did my grieving long ago.' But afterwards, I discovered that she had fished out a picture of a young Ken in his graduation gown and had put it on the piano. 'That is my husband,' she would say to anyone who noticed it. 'He is dead.'

During those final months of my father's life, he did not know me. My sister and I joked over this: 'He did his best to forget us – and . . . he succeeded!' But he would pat my hand. He would sing sometimes. He would say – in a phrase I remembered distinctly from my childhood – 'We're all right.'

Correction. That is, mostly he did not know me. One day it happened that my visit coincided with that of his wife. He became very agitated. 'You stay,' he instructed her. 'You leave,' to me. It was emphatic – a strange will and awareness coming out of nowhere. I left. In the corridor one of the nurses touched my arm. 'I am sorry,' she said gently. I had told them all the story. 'I am sorry. Perhaps you remind him of your mother?' 'No,' I said, 'I look like him.' But she may have been right. There was too much unbearable memory there.

His wife and I got along fine. After this incident we agreed always to visit separately. But when Daddy died, quietly, without warning, she told me the funeral arrangements and said she was worried. No one in their circle knew that he had been married before. Nor did they know that he had any children. It was too *EastEnders* for me. And so I said I would not go. I told my sister I would not go.

But on the day, where else should I be?

I know the music the minute I hear it as I step past the solid church door. Kathleen Ferrier, Gluck's 'Che farò?' from *Orpheus and Eurydice*. My mother's favourite. The church is full. I take a seat at the back with the undertakers. One of them brings out a few more chairs and I move forward slightly. I can't reach an order of service without making a fuss, so I give up on that, though I would have liked to have had one.

Someone recites Dorothea Mackellar's poem 'My Country':

I love a sunburnt country,
A land of sweeping plains,
Of ragged mountain ranges,
Of droughts and flooding rains . . .

Someone sings 'Waltzing Matilda', rather quietly and eerily, unaccompanied. Someone tells a story about how my father grew up in a family so poor that he went to school barefoot. Not something I remember being told as a child.

Someone reflects on his laughter, his jokes, his lust for travel, his lack of a problem with a 'work–life balance'. Someone remarks that there was an element of the unknown about Ken. That he was a man of mystery. Now *that* I do recognize. If only they knew. No one here knows who I am. No one anywhere knows that I am here. No one here knows that my siblings and I exist. I smile bitterly to myself. I could explain that mystery.

It comes to an end. They move to carry the coffin to the back of the church so that the mourners can pass by. I can't be caught, so I get up and leave, as fast as I can, closing the heavy door behind me, racing back along the path and up the road beside the two elderly ponies.

As I drive back in my circle and past the church gate on to the village road, I see the funeral party lingering in the churchyard and the undertakers standing by the gate. One of them looks at me. I've got my sunglasses back on, but I'm pretty sure he recognizes me as the one who left early.

I expect he thinks I'm the other woman. But then, in a way, I am. If you count my mother and my sister, I am one of at least three.

*

There was one strange moment in all the many strange moments at my father's funeral.

Someone read a passage from a favourite novelist of my mother's. Later on, as a teenager, this writer was a favourite of mine too. The passage is so familiar to me that I find I can recite it word for word. The book was Han Suyin's *The Mountain Is Young* (1958). I have not thought of it for years, but I see at once a small piece of paper, typed out, that very paragraph, pinned to the home-made notice board above the desk in my teenage bedroom.

> 'But it is the same with me,' said Unni. 'Every day reveals new things. I had that feeling from the first day I met you, that we were setting out on a journey together. I didn't ask whether it would be long or short, and certainly I did not know how far together we would go . . . It was enough that I had found you, to walk with, a little moment or a long time . . .'

I cannot believe for one moment that my father ever read that book. Did he steal the passage from me? Did he see that paragraph and take it away into his new life? Were we so connected?

Later on, I thought again. The piece was typed. Had I typed it out? Or. Or had *he* typed it out for his own purposes, and was it all the other way around? Was it I who had purloined the found object? Who had borrowed this piece of his life from him?

In a way, it does not matter. We were connected. Somehow I knew what I did not know I knew.

But I still don't believe that he'd ever read that book.

*

It is indeed 'a wise child that knows its own father'. The proverb has its underside. If a child cannot know their father, then that father cannot know – or cannot be sure of – his child. And so – until now, until very recent times – it has always been. 'Sir, are you not my father?' asks Miranda in *The Tempest*. 'Thy mother was a piece of virtue, and / She said thou wast my daughter,' replies Prospero. Since the beginning of time, a woman said to a man, 'This is your child.' And he had to believe her. Or not.

Edith Hall once explained to me that in ancient Greece it was a father's prerogative to 'own' a child and to decide whether the newborn would be accepted, and reared in the family, or rejected, and exposed. If the decision was the former, a ceremony would be held on or about the tenth day after birth called the Amphidromia. The name means, literally, 'running around'. The mother presented her baby to its father and he would run with the child around the family hearth.

In Western culture the significance of the father's contribution to the birth of a child has always been afforded greater significance. For the Greeks, the father's seed contained the whole child – the homunculus, man in little – and the mother's body was simply the carrying case. This is made explicit in Aeschylus's *Eumenides* when Apollo's final judgement exonerates Orestes for the murder of his mother, Clytemnestra:

> The mother of what is called her child is not its parent, but only the nurse of the newly implanted germ. The begetter is the parent, whereas she, as a stranger for a stranger, doth but preserve the sprout . . .

In the Judaic tradition, while the line of racial integrity – very sensibly – is passed down through the mother, the emphasis is still on the male inheritance.

In spite of the knowledge that only one man's seed engenders the embryonic child, 'social fatherhood' has had a key place in Western culture. Sometimes that father knew that his child was not his biological child. Sometimes he did not. It is impossible to guess how many children have been brought up, loved, paid for, wept over, celebrated and adored by a man whose sperm did not do the deed. I suspect that it would be remarkably high.

You may think me cynical. You may cite the many women who draw attention to the fact that little newborn Bobby 'looks exactly like his father'. Again this is a commonplace. I am willing to admit that I have seen such resemblances myself. But no, apparently not. Recent research argues that mothers are the ones who insist on the child's likeness to the father in order to promote that bond so necessary for the support of the child. And fathers (and other interested parties) accept those links because that is also what they want to believe.

But this is not the only model. Among the cultures of Venezuela and Paraguay, some tribes practise 'partible paternity', a form of polyandry where responsibility for children is shared among fathers. Some of these cultures work with the understanding that a sexually active woman can be 'a little bit pregnant'. One man's sperm might begin the process, but for the fetus to grow, it requires regular 'anointing' with semen.

Recent work with the Bari in Venezuela and many other groups, for instance, suggests that the practice of partible paternity results in a higher number of live births as well as multi-fathered children being more likely to survive into adulthood. From a strictly biological point of view, it can be argued that mothers and babies in such cultures do better – most obviously and simply because more than one man will be providing them with food and protection. But women in such egalitarian farming societies gain still more in terms of promoting their reproductive investment: they (or their female relatives) get to choose their sexual partner(s); the network of women supports a woman's mothering; and women are not threatened by the effects of male sexual jealousy. On the other hand, from the man's point of view – and if we are focusing on only his reproductive success – that is best promoted with male control over women's sexual conduct, so that they can be certain of paternity, and dominant men thus may produce more offspring.

In terms of preserving 'the selfish gene', there is some point in this. There may even be some point where we are talking about the extension of royal dynasties or the retention of great estates, but in the ordinary run of things – even now – it still seems to matter to a man.

Today we have DNA testing. The practice of centuries – where a man had to take a woman's word – has been overturned. But perhaps the crisis dates back even earlier? I suspect that the secularization of sex in Western society has been a bad thing for men, and for fathers. I fear that it may also turn out to be a bad thing for women and children.

In the late twentieth century, women embraced a new ability to manage their own fertility. Women were persuaded that sexual licence promised individual freedoms, and some men were happy to go along with that idea. But the odd result is this. Sex is now (supposed to be) easy, informal, unconsecrated fun. It is separated from its age-old function as part of the ceremony of marriage, which itself was designed to accommodate the possible outcome (children). Thus sex is also separated from the ritual created to cement social responsibility in the presence of the whole community. And so men have lost their sense of identity. No longer can they claim the essential significance of their old social roles as husband and as father.

What effect will all these changes have on relations between men and women? On relations between fathers and the children? What will it do to fatherhood?

Some time ago my mother decided it was time to clear out our childhood home. She gave each of us children our accumulated childhood things: exam certificates, baby books, special Christmas sacks and, in my case (as the eldest), a collection of every card and telegram sent at my birth. The cards are deliciously period – sugar-pink cradles, storks streaming ribbons. But there is also a cartoon cut from a newspaper. It shows a man running out of a door labelled 'maternity ward' and shouting, 'It's a father! I'm a girl, I'm a girl.' Someone has written on it, 'Poor Ken!'

Reading Sylvia Plath's *Ariel* as a teenager, I don't think I understood her work then, and even when I began teaching her well-known poem 'Daddy', I fear I was groping in the dark. I don't doubt that I covered the imagery and metaphor, the form and the poetic structure. Anything to avoid the feeling.

Now, I still see the form. But I see it differently. This poem insists on one word – 'you' (which appears twenty-two times) – and it is that word and its rhymes – most especially 'do' and 'through' – that drive the poem.

It seems to me now that the anger in the poem comes out in these words – what 'Daddy' does and does not 'do', and how fraught is her relation to 'you'. So, 'I never could talk to you. / The tongue stuck in my jaw', leads on to the wild punning of the fourteenth stanza: 'And I said I do, I do' – as in the words of the marriage service – 'So daddy, I'm finally through' – as in 'through' to you on the telephone, or as in she is finally understood, or as in 'I am finished with you' – 'The black telephone's off at the root, / The voices just can't worm through.'

And so on to the end, where the corrupt relation is finally put to rest – or not:

> There's a stake in your fat black heart
> And the villagers never liked you . . .
> Daddy, daddy, you bastard, I'm through.

When I watched Ian McKellen in Trevor Nunn's 2007 production of *King Lear* for the Royal Shakespeare Company, I saw how the play hinges on two motifs.

The first is that of sight: Goneril declares that her father is 'dearer than eye-sight'; Kent advises the king, 'See better, Lear'; and in Gloucester's terrible punishment, both his own and Lear's blind wilfulness is represented – 'A man may see how this world goes with no eyes.'

The second image is that of nothing: 'Nothing,' says Cordelia when required to proclaim the quality of her love for her father; 'Nothing will come of nothing,' replies Lear; when she still cannot speak more than she means – 'I love your majesty / According to my bond; nor more, nor less' – then Lear offers to give her away, as she is, with 'nothing'. 'Nothing,' says Lear again. 'I have sworn; I am firm.'

I cannot watch the scene of Gloucester's torture. All such moments in the theatre are dark to me, eyes shut, fingers in my ears. But at the end I realized that the two images of seeing right, and of the 'nothingness' that must exist between father and child, come back again in Lear and Cordelia's reunion when Lear acknowledges his wrongdoing and Cordelia lets it go. He says that she 'has cause' to hate him. But she replies, 'No cause, no cause.'

There can be no accounting here. The child owes the father nothing except his having given her life. The father owes the child nothing, except his having given her life. In this equation, each debt cancels the other out. And yet, in that very 'nothingness' is everything. It is a reciprocal transaction that is so infinite as to be unspeakable. Which is what Cordelia knows when she says 'Nothing' at the beginning, and 'No cause, no cause' at the end.

I find my eyes are dark again. My ears can hardly catch the words. I thought I was better, I thought I had recovered. But I sit in the stalls, sobbing.

When I began the therapy sessions with Luke eight months before I found my father again, I agreed to write up my dreams. I would scribble them down in the night, then type them up the next day. I objected that this meant that they were already revised, but Luke said that was OK.

Here is a dream that came to me shortly after that day in April when I had first seen my father again, and Luke and I laughed over my old question to him: 'And you're not going to make me see him, are you?'

Some country setting – extending to Hope End and the Malverns . . . Someone is winning, betting on, trying to buy a prehistoric forest, a fossilized prehistoric forest . . .

As the forest comes into view I am told that it is mine.

See it very vividly. Am filled with emotion about it. Huge, huge tall walls of wide trunks that have grown together hundreds and hundreds of feet into the air, and in a ring like a barricade, or the stockade in *Treasure Island*. Someone asks me where are the leaves, but of course there are none – it is a fossil, not a living thing, though once living.

We fly high over it, high in the clouds. Feel great pleasure and contentment.

And another dream, a short while later.

Working on some archival project with two other people. A woman married to a clergyman . . . She is slightly inclined to the fanciful and the fictional, and does not do her research fast enough for me . . . But I don't mind that much. The man is quite scornful of her but I try to mediate between them.

I have a green jug, given to me by my father, which, on the
inside, is marked . . . with key words: truth, love, value . . .
You turn the jug to get the message. The jug is like my
Charleston jug and chipped like it too.

At the beginning of these sessions, Luke had warned me not to
let my professional urge to 'read' my dreams creep into my
account of them. That was his job. He was to do the interpreting.
But here I was pretty sure. Both dreams were about the past (the
fossilized forest, the archival project). But they were about a past
I owned, a past I happily possessed. It was Luke, though, who
pointed out that both the 'fanciful' woman and the critical man
in the second dream are probably versions of myself.

But the real point is this. The jug in the second dream is something I actually own. And though it is damaged, it is marked in
my dream with those key words: 'truth, love, value'. And, presumably, it still serves its purpose. It can still be filled with water,
or with wine.

This time I do know that I am better. That I have recovered.
There is for me now 'no cause, no cause'. I have been able to say
to my father, 'We're all right.' We're all right.

OR

THIS IS NOW my sixth attempt. But this time it is really happening. Here is the story of this final, successful attempt to become a prospective adopter.

After this new independent adoption agency – the one located in Angel Way – had agreed to consider me as a possible prospective adoptive parent, there was another preparation course, which took place over six days in the summer. In my experience, these courses vary considerably. The best timing for them to take place is before the home study. You are learning about the process and the commitment that it requires, but the agency is also looking at you, to assess your suitability before it goes on to the (serious) expense of a home study.

This particular course was by far the best, and the most demanding, of all those I had undertaken. The independent social worker running it was compassionate but uncompromising, and we all worked very hard. There was a lot of laughter and quite a few tears. I remember a searing video made by a young artist who had been raped by her father. Her work was beautiful, her subject matter appalling and horrific.

I also remember the woman who told us how she had been driving to the allotment when her five-year-old foster daughter began to tell her things about the child's past that she had never heard before. The woman gave up on planting the potatoes and kept on driving round in circles, just listening.

There was a training video about emotional triggers, the first scene of which was a teenager arriving home. Her adoptive mother's innocent question – 'Did you have a good day at school?' – was greeted with a barrage of shouting and swearing. Then we were shown the second scene – which was actually the first, because it took place in the past. The same teenager is still a child, maybe eight years old, and living with an abusive adult. This adult also asked, 'Did you have a good day at school?' but then said, 'Not that I care. Make me a cup of tea. You never do anything. You are so hopeless . . .' and much more in the same vein and worse, until the tirade ended with the adult seizing the kettle and throwing the hot contents over the child. We all flinched. My neighbour turned to me. 'So presumably the right response to the grumpy teenager is just, "I'll take that as a no, then".'

At the end of the course the independent adoption agency agreed to take me on and proceed to the home study. Which, thank goodness, could be in my own home. I didn't have to live in London. 'I know exactly the right person for you,' said the manager.

And she was right. Jessica, the social worker who was to undertake my home study, was wise and kind. But she was also fierce and challenging, and sternly honest about the difficulties ahead. We met at my home. We met often in my room at work. She interviewed all the same referees for me all over again. She asked my ex-husband for a reference. And she also – this time around – asked my ex-girlfriend for a reference. All of this was the same as in my last experience of a home study. But so many other things were different.

To begin with, I am changed and my expectations are entirely changed. As this is preparation for domestic adoption, there is no expectation whatsoever that I could be matched with a baby. I am far too old. So any child that may be matched with me will be not a baby, but an older child. A child, by definition, who has experienced neglect or hurt – probably both – who has suffered through omission or commission, a child who knows fear and loneliness, pain and change, anxiety and disappointment. A child with memories. Bad memories.

The general notion for adoption in Britain at this time was that an adoptive parent should not be more than forty-five years older than their child. Which meant that I could expect to be matched with a five- or six-year-old. But that is now fine by me. I know a lot more about children who are hurting. I know a lot more about the procedures and expectations for – as well as the likely experiences of – looked after children. I am intrigued by the prospect of therapeutic parenting.

Another thing is different too. In the process of the home study for domestic adoption you have to fill in a form. Well there are, of course, lots of forms, but this one is stark. It asks you what kind of child you will – and will not – be willing to take.

'A child who is the result of rape?' I tick that one. It is not the child's fault. But I do pause over how one might deal with that as a parent. 'Or incest?' I tick that too, but ditto. 'A child with learning difficulties?' Jessica intervenes here. 'No, you can't do that. You will be a single parent. You will have enough to do.' 'A child with emotional issues?' Jessica laughs. 'Well, that's all of them.' I tick yes. 'A child who is cruel to animals?' I know I cannot cope with that. I put a cross. A friend, going through the same process at the same time, has a different reaction to the question. She says she is OK with the animal thing. The one she could not tick was 'A child that is facially disfigured?' Her reason? 'I am too influenced by beauty. It would hurt me too much.' As ever, the willingness to examine our own weaknesses and capacities is tried and challenged.

The first time I saw a copy of *Children Who Wait* I turned the pages and wept. *Children Who Wait* is a magazine published by Adoption UK: prospective adopters can subscribe, and it includes photographs of children waiting to be placed and short profiles. All these smiling hopefuls with what terrible histories, what secret pain. But now I look at this blond boy or that little girl with spectacles and wonder, could I manage that?

Little by little, the prospect came closer. I went to approval panel in February. But this time everything was different. For a start, everything that happened in the past was on the table. Jessica was confident that she had addressed every question they could possibly ask, every reservation they could possibly have. Indeed, she told me that she felt more confident about my case than she often does about more apparently obvious cases, because she knew so much about me – not only in the long past, but in the recent past.

The panel asked me the dreaded questions about last time and about my culpability. But I knew how to answer: with the absolute truth. As the hour of the panel meeting wore on I realized that they were really listening. I realized that they were impressed with the resilience, the determination, perseverance and commitment I had put into this. As I left the room after my grilling session, Jessica nodded at me with a smile. It seemed as if she thought I had done well. She stayed behind for the final questioning and assessment. But – unlike last time – not for long. After just ten minutes she came out beaming. I am through. Once again I am an approved prospective adoptive parent.

Jessica was pleased. But she was wasting no time and she was straight on to the next step. She put the latest copy of *Children Who Wait* into my hands. 'Have a look through that. Let's get going.'

This time, I walked back to Spitalfields from Angel Way to tell Marianna and Charles and Jim, and all my friends there. As I did so I thought, inevitably, about that last time, but not with anger or recrimination, or even with regret. This feels right. This feels good. I wanted to be a mother and I wanted that for me. I would have been doing it for the child too. But now I really do know that I am most especially doing it – if I can do it well – for the child. As I pass by Wesley's Chapel just after Old Street, I turn in and sit in a pew and give thanks.

Now that I am an approved prospective adopter I am in a position to make enquiries about children who are available for adoption. I do phone about one child. She is called Alice. She is the funny little one with the spectacles. Her photograph and profile had first appeared a while ago in an issue of *Children Who Wait* and – rather prematurely – I had called about her then, only to be told that she had already been placed.

When she appears again in a new edition, I give it another go, especially as now I am in a position to investigate further. Her social worker is happy to discuss my interest because, she tells me, the placement had failed, which is why Alice's profile is back in the magazine. As we go on talking, the social worker reveals that this is Alice's third failed placement.

I consult with Jessica. She advises against continuing with the possibility of a placement with this particular child. She is right, and I do know why. Because those three failed placements suggest that this child is, presumably, challenging; difficult to care for. Why else have those other three sets of possible parents given up on her? Three times. The child must be in a terrible way. But then the shocking thing is that she will really be needing parenting, really be needing serious therapeutic parenting. Especially as each one of those failed placements will also have consequences, will also contribute to her – what? – anger, pain, hatred, resentment, self-loathing.

Full of regret for Alice, and with reluctance, I take Jessica's advice and decide not to pursue it. But the best – least worst – option for that child now will be permanent foster care. More likely, it will be a residential home. Or many moves and many fostering placements. Each one eating away at her self-esteem, each one taking her further from the likelihood of developing any kind of secure attachment, further away from any prospect of being loved and learning how to love.

There was one other enquiry that I made at this time. I had forgotten that I ever did this until I looked over my emails from that period. I called up about a little dark-haired girl called Angel. The name – the magic name – drew me and I could not resist. The profile in *Children Who Wait* suggested that she needed a two-parent family. I was going to be a single parent, but I contacted her social worker anyway.

I do not recall if I explained why I was interested in this child.

Almost certainly not. I think I would have been written off immediately as far too mystic. In the event, Pam, Angel's social worker, agreed to read my own statement and profile, and so I forwarded them to her. She called me back the next day and arranged a discussion with Jessica about the possibility of a match.

Just as I was coming out of that difficult time I was much encouraged by a poem by Louis MacNeice – 'Entirely'. It is about failure and approximation and settling for what is, while still striving for the ideals of what might be. Sometimes things go wrong, sometimes one does wrong, sometimes one makes mistakes. But none of that means that you don't go on trying.

> And if the world were black or white entirely
> And all the charts were plain
> Instead of a mad weir of tigerish waters,
> A prism of delight and pain,
> We might be surer where we wished to go
> Or again we might be merely
> Bored but in the brute reality there is no
> Road that is right entirely.

We might want certain things in life, but those things might not be what we can have. We might have to settle for something that is approximate or provisional (or, of course, nothing at all). I have wondered sometimes if, perhaps especially, this applies to the lottery of parenthood. Any parent, however they get to that position, invents their child to some degree, or imagines them. But then, one day, that child is there before them and has to be respected as their own self – an independent person quite separate from any expectations or hopes or wishes on the part of the parent. And so, that accommodation is necessary and has to be made.

But maybe, just maybe, what we get in the end, as we pass through this transitory 'prism of delight and pain', is actually the right thing all along. Is it too boring, too worthy, too full of platitude, to say that sometimes everything does work out for the best? In my case, that is exactly what happened.

Two days later Jessica is on my case. No, she has not yet had that discussion with Angel's social worker, because she wants to show me something. She emails me a profile for a little girl in foster care in a big city, complete with a black-and-white photocopied photograph. Now, this child, as it happens, has the same name as the Shiny Girl. Names again. She also has a sweet face and long hair down to her waist. When I show the picture to one of my friends, Rachel nods. 'It's right that a child of yours should have *hair*.' I pin the picture on my bedroom door. I look at her last thing at night and first thing in the morning.

Meanwhile, Jessica has been in touch with Catherine, the little girl's social worker, and is having discussions. Catherine has read my profile, heard my history. Jessica is certain from the start that this will be the right child for me, but she has to convince Catherine and the family finder from the local authority. After a week of talks and exchanges of information, Jessica calls me.

'They are looking at five families. But you are one of them.

Her social worker and the family finder will have to come and visit. Is Tuesday OK?'

I go upstairs and look at the picture pinned to my bedroom door. This is the first serious enquiry we have made. This is the first time of going through this. But then, chances are, it will not be the last. I remind myself that they are also considering four other families. But I look again at the little photocopy. The adoption advice books all tell you not to take the first child you are offered. Obviously, they say, you are desperate, but would you buy the first sofa you see?

I meet Jessica at the train station and she introduces Catherine, and Khadija, the family finder. They look over my house, the bedroom made ready for a child. We eat lunch. They try to get up the video they had made of this little girl singing 'Twinkle Twinkle Little Star' to supplement my black-and-white picture, but my broadband is not working fast enough. On the way back to the station they ask me the question I was hoping not to be asked. About last time. About my mistake. And I am driving. But I am used to this by now and answer simply, humbly. They will let me know on Friday.

So now it is just waiting. It is hard not to think about it, but I try not to. You are so powerless in all these situations when other people make the decisions, when everything is so out of your control. Even if we get through this moment there will still be other decisions to be made, again by others, always out of my own hands.

Friday comes. Jessica calls mid-morning on my mobile. I am in the garden. A garden bursting with May blossom. 'Yes,' she says.

'They have chosen you. She needs someone who can support her intelligence. And they feel that she would be best off with a single parent and no other children. Yes.' It looks like I am taking that sofa.

But that's still not the end, of course. Now that the social workers have agreed that I am the best family for this little girl, they have to swing into action and make their case. A vast file has to be prepared on me, a similarly vast file on her. She is not yet six years old, but there is still plenty to fill that file. The paperwork needs to be in place for the matching panel, which is the next obstacle. We are given a date for July.

In June I went to Cefalù in Sicily for a week with my friends, Angela and Harriet, who are often kind enough to invite me to share their holidays. We all get along very nicely, accommodating one another's interests and habits. One day we hired a car and drove to Enna, a city set on a steep rocky outcrop rising out of a plain and looking over Lake Pergusa. According to legend, this is where Pluto is said to have come upon Persephone, stealing her away into the underworld, and thrusting her mother, Demeter the earth goddess, into despair, and the whole world into a winter of mourning. I thought about mothers: mothers and lost daughters, snatched, stolen, taken away; lostlings and foundlings and changelings.

Mostly we stayed in Cefalù, sitting on the beach, reading, swimming, sleeping. We watched children negotiate new friendships. Then we watched their parents do the same: men standing in the surf, women seated under their umbrellas. We watched the traders selling beach towels and scarves, and girls carrying price lists for massages (though we never saw anyone take them up). We watch the hairy man in a singlet parade up and down, with a bowl of iced water containing coconut pieces held high, and shouting, 'Coco . . . Coconice . . . Coco!'

And we talk about her. How she might like this. How we would organize things. How we might manage to go on with our quiet holidays even after she arrives. We discuss how Harriet will teach her to sew. Angela says she is going to just listen. On the other hand, she could teach her Italian. That would be useful.

They happily join me in peering into shop windows displaying children's clothes. We wander out for the *passeggiata* and then come home for dinner, so feeding her early and putting her to bed would work fine. Their commitment to this imaginary life is total. Their belief in my future as a mother is complete. And that helps to make it real in my mind too. This was a calm time. As I recall, I was not anxious, nor trepidatious, nor excited nor apprehensive. This was simply the beginning of the fulfilment of my plans, and it was just a case of going on one step at a time.

A couple of years earlier, when my longing seemed so unassuaged, so unassuageable, Angela had written a poem. It was called 'The Sand Children' and she wrote it, I believe, watching children playing at the Lido del Faro in Capri. Now that the resolution of the wish is coming so close, I am reminded of what she said there – that children, these found 'sandlings', belong only to themselves:

    . . . Out of our hands, they are – so distantly composed,
    cradled from air and water, quartz and schist –
    children found
    in the making of what goes, and has to live.

Back at home again, with the matching panel date creeping closer, the meetings go on. I take a train to a large city to go to the hospital where the little girl was born. The option to meet with a child's doctor before placement is not always possible, but in this case the local authority were able to arrange it because she had been in their care for so long, and this man was still the official doctor for their looked after children. In any case, Jessica was anxious that I should have as much information as possible.

It is a surreal experience. Here I am at the hospital where the child who will become my daughter was born. A daughter I have never even set eyes on. For most mothers, of course, they are there in that hospital too. They will have memories. Likely ones of trepidation and anxiety, possibly of pain and distress, and perhaps even ghastly memories they don't want to revisit. Hopefully they will also have happy memories of seeing that little life, that particular little face for the very first time. I have never been there, in the sense of having that experience. But neither had I ever been here, in this hospital, in the very place where my daughter came into independent life. And I have no memories.

The meeting is with the doctor who has cared, in an official capacity, for my daughter for most of her short life. But she is only one baby; one toddler; one infant; one five-year-old among many. He looks over his notes. He tells me she is healthy. He tells me about one small concern but reassures me. He goes on to talk about the long-term consequences of pre-natal stress in the womb.

Then I have to go for a medical myself. The doctor prods and pokes and sends me through to the nurse to have my blood pressure taken. I have 'beautiful blood pressure'. Doctors often comment on it. But on this occasion the nurse asks me why I need a medical. As she straps me into the gear I start to explain about my little girl. 'Whoa!' she says. 'Stop there. Let's calm down and have another go.'

A week later I go to the Social Services offices to meet the little girl's current foster parents. Catherine, the little girl's social worker, will be there to introduce me, and Jessica is coming too because she also will need to work with them. I am not sure how to feel about this. Do I want them to like me? Do I need them to like me? Jessica is clear: 'No. *We* make these decisions on what is best for the child. And you are the one we have chosen.'

Moira and Bill have cared for her, on and off, for nearly two years. How many children have they fostered in all? Some huge number in the eighties. They can't remember. They also have three adopted children, grown up now. Towards the end of the meeting, one social worker present asks cheerily if they think I am the right adoptive parent for my little girl. 'No,' replies Moira. 'Only joking,' she adds, though I do not find it very funny. 'In the old days we would have gone on whether or not you looked like her. You don't. But it's all different now.'

I pondered this for a long time afterwards. At some times, physical resemblance was indeed considered an important matching factor by some adoption agencies. And there are studies that have suggested that adoptions were more likely to prove successful when parents and child felt that they were like each other, including a physical resemblance.

In a sense, you can see the point. Strangers will not look at you and your child and wonder. No one is going to blunder in and say, 'Is her father Italian?' or some such, just because you do not look like the child who is behaving in a way that clearly marks her as your child. But two things are problematic here. First of all, looks and appearance are not a whole person or a whole personality. And second, what then about trans-racial adoption? Does that mean that children can only ever be matched with someone who looks similar, even if, in all other – more important – ways that child and parent work together really well?

In my own experience, adopted children often seem to 'look like' their adoptive parents simply because they acquire similar mannerisms, gestures, emphasis, and other ways of speaking and behaving.

Everything is going well. But suddenly I am unaccountably low and cannot shake it off. Exams are over at college, so work is quiet, and my inbox is remarkably empty. Perhaps that's the problem. Too little to do except think. I have done all I can at home. Everything is ready. The house is tidy, the bedroom is furnished with a little box bed and a small cupboard for her clothes.

Now, with everything so close, I allow myself to go and check out the shop with children's clothes. I even buy a couple of dresses, a pretty striped blanket and some toys – a bear and a Peter Rabbit. On the administrative front, we have filled in all the forms. Jessica has drilled me in what to expect at the upcoming matching panel meeting. But my head is full only of what will be, and all of that is unknown.

When I am out riding Billy one day, a friend calls me. As it is not yet forbidden to use a mobile while in charge of a pony, I answer. 'You don't sound quite right,' she remarks. 'Look,' she says, when I try to explain, 'you have worked so hard for this, and now it's about to happen. Sometimes one does feel strange when the thing one wants is within one's grasp. Just keep going.'

I try the Angel Cards. My set is just tiny slips bearing an image and one inspirational word. I turn up 'willingness'. It is accompanied by a little picture of an angel tackling a huge pile of washing up. That's about right.

One day I turn into the local bookshop and glance idly over the section Anthea keeps for children. My eye falls on a picture book by Charlotte Moundlic called *The Scar*. It is about a boy whose mother has died. He picks at the scar on his knee to keep the memory of his lost mother alive. This helps me now to truly understand. I am happy about adopting a little girl. But she will not be happy. She needs this thing that will be a huge positive to me, only because she has had to suffer so much that is negative for her. My happiness is her sadness. So it is right that I should be sad. In fact, I begin to see now that it would be wrong to be entirely upbeat, entirely celebratory, because that would be entirely selfish. I remember those lines from Louis MacNeice: 'there is no / Road that is right entirely.' I buy the book.

At home I get out another picture book – *The Red Tree* by Shaun Tan. The illustrations are telling and powerful. It is a story about the terrible isolation of grief, or depression, or loss. But in the last image, the few scattered red leaves from the beginning multiply, the tree is bursting with red leaves and with a miracle of beauty, 'just as you imagined it would be'. In fact, when you look back through the whole book, if you search, you will see that on every page depicting sadness and loneliness, there is always at least one significant red leaf.

In July we arrive at the next important date. This is the matching panel, a big meeting held in the imposing offices of the town hall. The social workers on my little girl's side and on mine have agreed it all; I have met her foster parents, the doctor and the therapist; I have seen all the paperwork. A huge report has been drawn up on me. A second huge report has been put together for her. But now a select body of authorities is going to adjudicate on the propriety of the match between me and this little girl whom I have never seen.

I am terrified and anxious. This should be my last jump, last hurdle, last fence but, after all that has gone before, I cannot feel that I have arrived. On the other hand, Jessica greets me in a cheerful fashion. She is confident. John, tall, rangy and relaxed, shakes my hand in a friendly way. I have met him once before at the Social Services offices. He runs the department in the local authority that has responsibility for the child, so he represents the other side of the equation but, in the end, he is also the one who has to seek out and decide on the best outcome for her. He has taken the advice of his team and committed to me as the family most suited to her, so, in this, we are all on the same side. We three are here, in effect, as witnesses to be consulted, not as decision-makers in any way.

The officiating members of the matching panel are already assembled when we arrive, and the meeting has been in progress for some time as they go over the mounds of paperwork and hear from various representatives. We three sit outside for ages – as it seems. Then John and Jessica go in: professionals talking to professionals. I wait alone.

After a while, the meeting secretary comes out, and I am also invited inside. I am the last person to be seen, the last person to be consulted. But, as I take my seat, sitting alone on the vacant side of a range of four huge, long tables arranged in a square, I try not to think about the fact that while they make the decision, I am the only one here whose whole life is at hazard. But then there is also someone who is not here, someone who has never been consulted, and her whole life is at hazard too.

I look round the room. There are about twenty people present. I know a few of them – some of the social workers, the doctor, her foster carers – and I nod to them. I have seen this, or something like this, many times. Too many times for one lifetime.

I get asked the most difficult question right away. The one I always dread, the one about my past mistake. I answer with humility, acknowledge my wrongdoing. I see Jessica looking at me with a set expression on her face. So I pick up. I go on more positively, putting my case forward in a more upbeat fashion. I explain how I feel now that if I was wrong, I also feel that I was failed. I tell them how my hard experiences have taught me lessons: about how much this means to me and how much I am prepared to commit; about how much I know of what I have to offer. Jessica's look changes to one of approval. The questions continue. We seem to be getting there. Jessica, John and I leave the room.

But as we make our way back through the lobby to await the decision, I am worried. Thinking over it all, I had been somewhat thrown by one question and had pontificated about how I would look after myself as a single parent, referring to 'riding my pony' and 'listening to opera' and had ended by saying, 'And she'll have to get used to *The Archers* because I like that moment in my day.'

But Jessica is not fazed. 'Don't worry, you made them laugh with *The Archers*. It'll be all right,' she says. 'You'll see.' And John is calm. He agrees with Jessica. She laughs and points this out. They have had dealings before, with other children. 'Just remember,' she says to me, 'John has seen it all.'

Then the chairwoman comes out to tell us that the deed is done. Smiling, she shakes my hand. I am ready to burst into tears. I can hardly believe it. We say goodbye to John. He heads back to the office. Jessica takes me out of the grand town hall and into the nearest wine bar. She buys me a glass of champagne. And then another. 'I told you all along, didn't I?' she says triumphantly.

HOME

I shivered comfortless, but cast
No chill across the table cloth;
I all-forgotten shivered, sad
To stay and yet to part how loth . . .

Christina Rossetti, 'At Home'

AFTER THAT AUCTION in the pub, the two tiny eighteenth-century cottages became my home. I have no idea how many children must have grown up here, but I would guess quite a few. Now – and very soon – there will be added to that list a child who will grow to love this space. I can feel in the walls that there has been great happiness and contentment here.

There is a vegetable patch and herbs, there is a mulberry tree. The little old lemonade bottle is back in the niche by the kitchen door. The local vet has given me some tubers, so dahlias blow once again. There are new bathrooms, but I have kept the outside toilet too. It reminds me of my grandmother's house. There is Billy the black-and-white pony, now in his own field near by, and a fluctuating population of cats depending on how many kittens are coming or going. At present, there are only five cats.

Missy has taken herself off because while I was away in Australia my two god-daughters and their parents house-sat for me with their dog.

I wish she would come home.

With the matching panel all done and successfully negotiated, the social workers on both sides are hard at work to complete the process of moving this little girl out of her old life and into mine. I receive another email from Catherine. As part of the process of preparing the child for this huge move, Catherine has been making a life story book for her. It is one of the ways in which social workers try to mitigate the enormity of what is about to happen. The idea is that a child preparing for an adoptive placement can in this way learn something about her beginnings. But they can only work with what they have, and in this case it is very little. It is also, I realize some time later, rather odd. This child is five, very nearly six, but nobody asks *her* about the life that she has lived, the life that she remembers.

In theory, the idea of the life story book is an admirable one. In practice, such books have many shortcomings. Too often there is very little information that can be passed on. Too often there is no one who knows that information. Too often there are mistakes in the story – which is particularly difficult if the child is old enough to know the truth – but just as bad if they later learn the truth. Too often the story is told in a light-hearted manner, with the (inevitable) difficult areas glossed over. Again, as in many cases, the child will very likely know that none of it is true. Or they will one day discover that it is not true. And how does that help them to understand their life story? Story, indeed.

However, in compiling this book, Catherine has realized that I need to create one too, to help prepare the child for the upcoming move; a book about me and the places this child will be coming to. 'Make sure it is age appropriate,' she says. 'Things a child will be interested in. But remember,' she warns, 'nothing that gives any clue as to location.'

I begin by taking photographs. Of the new school, of the hens and the ponies, of the windows in a couple of shops, and of the little girl's new home. My niece Anastasia helps me put it together, drawing little flowers in the margins, popping in wisps of hay alongside pictures of Billy the pony. We are both very pleased with the result. I post it off.

Much later, I learned that when Catherine gave her the book, the little girl's foster brother joined her in looking over the pictures and scraps that Anastasia and I had put together, and sighed, 'You are so lucky.' But did she feel that way? I don't suppose so for a moment. How is one to feel when the home you know is being taken from you? How is one to feel when a new home is being forced upon you?

I realize then that the equation here, at this moment, is very lopsided. Throughout this process I was often troubled by my lack of agency; by the fact that others were making decisions that would radically affect my life while my input was minimal. But now that we have successfully negotiated the matching panel, I have a map and can know what to expect as I look ahead. I know – more or less – what will happen to this little girl now. She will meet me, then she will move into my home with me. Now, from my point of view, the prospect becomes more certain.

Curiously, that is reinforced by the fact that other people, the professionals, begin to refer to her as 'your daughter'. My daughter. A daughter I have never seen. How much of this was premeditated? How much was it designed to draw me in, to prepare me with glimpses and hints, much as a woman carrying a baby feels the quickening signs, or sees a prenatal scan?

But she, the child, 'my daughter', knows none of this as yet, cannot possibly grasp any of this, and most certainly has no say, no choice. She has not even been told that this has happened, that her whole future has been rubber-stamped and sealed. So what can that mean to her? How can she begin to imagine what will happen to her? Even when she is told, and this welcoming book showing glimpses of scenes of her new life is put into her hands, how can she envisage a future home, a future mother? I am a complete stranger to her.

I, on the other hand, have now spent three months thinking about her. I have seen one new picture to supplement the black-and-white photocopy that is still pinned to my bedroom door. I have read a lot of files. And so, even while I carry on imagining her little figure alongside me, even while I keep making my home into a home for her, all her losses, past and future, haunt me and challenge me, testing the home I am making.

In Sigmund Freud's famous 1919 essay on 'The Uncanny' he combs carefully over the meaning of the word in many languages and in many dictionaries. In English, the word derives from 'canny', 'knowing' or 'cunning', so it refers both to the 'known' and the 'unknown' or 'unfamiliar'. But in German the word is '*unheimlich*', so it is explicitly linked with '*heim*' ('home') as the 'familiar' place, and the *'unheimlich'* – the 'unhomely' or 'not homely' – is the strange place of discomfort, disorientation and distress.

The word, as Freud explains, 'develops in the direction of ambivalence': so *'heimlich'* can mean safe, familiar, 'of the home', but it can also mean secret, hidden, private, mysterious, or occult. It can refer precisely to the *unknown*. In this way the very idea of home includes the potential for alienation, loss, fear and pain. The apparent security of 'home' can only be invoked by imagining its disruption. And once you have imagined that disorder, the order itself is disordered.

But what then does this tell me about this child coming to live in my home? She has already lived in several places, whether or not she considered them home. She was torn abruptly and hastily from the first; taken by official decree from the second; left, without explanation, by the third; and then moved again and again by official decree. Each one of these moves is a small death, because her little body loses its place in the world, loses its old identity and familiar shape and takes on a new skin. But the ghosts of those old lost selves will still be there. Now, I – in effect – am making her suffer this again. I will be removing her from the only safe place she has ever known.

As I worry about this transition, transformation, transmutation, I consider my own long-ago experience as a child who was also moved many times. True, I changed places, but those places, at first, were similar and I did not change people as well. But the last move was as a child migrant, and even now I can see how that experience has cut across my sense of identity, my sense of belonging.

In my twenties, I revisited the paths of my childhood with my husband. My cousin Jenny gave us three tapes as we set off from her house in Sydney, along with plenty of water and an extra can of petrol. These tapes were: a recording of Australian birdsong set to meditative music; *A Feather on the Breath of God* by Hildegard of Bingen; and archive recordings of famous arias and duets by the likes of Gigli and de Luca, Melba and Ponselle. So we drove off through these familiar landscapes, encountering frilled-neck lizards basking in the middle of the road and tribes of kangaroos grazing at sunset, with the jarring contrast of the 'Ride of the Valkyries' or a medieval Te Deum sounding in our ears.

On the way into Booligal, on a dead-straight tarmac road, I wanted to get something out of the boot and so we pulled over. Even as we did it, I remembered. Too late. These dead-straight roads are bordered by red-dust piles that bog you in an instant. I knew that. I had forgotten that. I fumed and cursed that new and old knowledge.

In these days before mobile phones, there was nothing to do but to wait. The road was empty. Of course it was. After about an hour a car appeared. My husband waved and it pulled off the road, straight into the treacherous dust. A lot of apologies, a lot of commiserations.

Another forty minutes' wait, and another vehicle appeared in the distance. But this time it was an open-backed truck, obviously driven by a local, who pulled up calmly on the tarmac. The weather-beaten farmer got out, looked us over, sized it all up, asked no questions nor waited to hear our accents. Instead, he took some chains out of the rear of the truck and had both cars back on the road in no time.

I was mortified. I was born here, I had travelled these well-known roads all the years of my childhood, yet I could well tune in, ashamedly, to the laconic explanation that the farmer would later offer to his wife about the hapless Poms out on the Cobb Highway. I no longer belonged to this home.

The last time I was in Australia I drove down to Avalon Beach to meet a friend for an early swim, with the sunlit water flashing glimpses through the trees. The beach was empty, white, newly swept, but the ocean-cleansed pool in the rocks was busy. The handsome Anglican minister was there, thrashing up and down the favourite sea-wall side. I also noticed the local doctor and the man from the post office. I waved to my friend. 'What do you do for water in England?' he asked. For a moment I did not even understand the question, I could not recognize the language. He meant, 'Where do you swim?' I have become a foreigner in my own land.

Richard II – which includes one of Shakespeare's most famous paeans to England ('This royal throne of kings, this scepter'd isle') – both begins and ends with exile. In Act I, when the King condemns Mowbray to perpetual banishment, Mowbray complains that this act will rob him of speech:

> The language I have learn'd these forty years,
> My native English, now I must forgo;

Without speech, without a common language, there can be no identity, no community, no belonging, and therefore no respectful recognition of individuality. Mowbray's rival, Bolingbroke, is also banished, and his father, John of Gaunt, tries to persuade him that he can pretend it is only a holiday, or a business trip. But Bolingbroke knows that rhetoric and imagination will not change facts:

> O, who can hold a fire in his hand
> By thinking on the frosty Caucasus?

And yet Bolingbroke's speech enacts the condition of exile. The man who is banished is defined by home, or rather, by the absence of home. Only by speaking of home – which he has not – can the exile explain who he is. The very thing he has to use to name himself is what is absent, what he has not.

Towards the end of the play the deposed King Richard is on his way to prison in the Tower when he meets the Queen, who is to be sent away for ever, back to France. And then follows his final injunction:

> In winter's tedious nights sit by the fire
> With good old folks, and let them tell thee tales
> Of woeful ages long ago betid;
> And ere thou bid good night, to quit their griefs,
> Tell thou the lamentable tale of me
> And send the hearers weeping to their beds:

I remember this particular speech vividly. At Oxford, I was in an undergraduate production where virtually every single one of the other actors went on to a starry theatrical career. My own contribution was entirely inadequate. But Tim McInnerny played Richard, and I have never forgotten those words or the intense, intimate and moving power of his voice.

In Richard's vision, the Queen will make herself at home by remembering the place that she has lost. As the teller of that tale, she will acquire an identity and a home in the world, even while she is no longer at home.

Home is not a place. It is a story.

Chloe Hooper's book *The Tall Man: Death and Life on Palm Island* tells of the events that followed the death of Cameron Doomadgee in Australia in November 2004. He was, at the time, in police custody. Senior Sergeant Chris Hurley was accused of causing his injuries, but eventually cleared of manslaughter and assault on appeal, and Hooper's book explains the long, sad story of this bitter engagement in Australia's racial history.

In the course of the inquest into the death of 'the one who has gone away' – the one whom his sister wished to be named as *Moordinyi* – Lloyd Bengaroo (an Aboriginal police liaison officer present at the time) was questioned about the circumstances of the arrest. *Moordinyi* was arrested because his swearing was a 'public nuisance'. But Bengaroo agreed that there was plenty of swearing on Palm Island:

'Had he ever arrested anyone for swearing at anyone other than a police officer?' 'No.'

'Had he heard police swear on the island?' 'Yeah, everybody swears.'

'Had he ever heard of a police officer being arrested for swearing?' 'No.'

On Palm Island, everyone speaks English, but Hurley and his like do not speak the same language as *Moordinyi*'s people. Without a shared tongue there can be no resolving story. No one is at home.

On 13 February 2008, the then Australian prime minister, Kevin Rudd, delivered a formal apology to the country's indigenous peoples and to the so-called Stolen Generations, a general name for the practice of removing Aboriginal children from their birth families:

I move:

That today we honour the Indigenous peoples of this land, the oldest continuing cultures in human history.

We reflect on their past mistreatment [. . .]

The time has now come for the nation to turn a new page in Australia's history [. . .]

In February 2009, on the first anniversary of the National Apology, all Australian schools received a large reproduction of the Apology Motion calligraphy artwork 'as a permanent reminder of our shared Journey of Reconciliation'.

Years later, when she is about ten, for a short while my daughter will go to a school in Newport, NSW with my cousin's daughter. One day, waiting to pick her up from the reception area, I am startled to see this notice prominently displayed. I entirely understand and applaud the motives behind the Apology Motion but it is troubling. How does one restore a lost home; all those lost homes?

I realize now how invested in the idea of home I was that summer. But it was a curious two-way process. I thought about myself and my own experience of home in the past. As a child I never lived anywhere for more than two years, but even as an adult I had moved often, not staying in one place for very long. Now I was making a home that would be long term for me, because I wanted that sense of long engagement with a place, a setting, a frame. I wanted a place to dream and a place that would become the repository of dreams. This is what Antoine de Saint-Exupery spoke of in *Terre des Hommes*:

> Ah! the miracle of a house is not that it shelters or warms
> you, nor that its walls belong to you. But that it has slowly
> deposited in us all those stored resources of gentle joy. And
> that deep within the heart it forms the shadowy range of
> hills in which our dreams, like spring waters, are born . . .

I set about the task of removing as many modern accretions as I could, letting the house shine through as it once was, as itself. And gradually I noticed an odd thing. No matter the dingy bits, the grubby corners where I had not yet re-painted, the house photographed wonderfully. Magically, the camera showed a fairy mirror, an enchanted world on the other side of the lens. When I mentioned this to a friend who is a professional photographer, Robin knew at once what I meant. Then he laughed: 'I'll bet you wish you lived there.'

But now this strange other-world beyond the lens holds a different significance for me. That is the dreaming house, the contentment house that I need to hold on to so that I can offer it to the little girl who will come to live here. This home will also be long term for her. Put simply, because she will need that security and only time can build a sense of safety. Put more urgently, because she has never had a home, a whole family and community, because she has never (or only briefly) belonged.

While the social workers beavered away at their meetings and form-fillings, my most important task was preparing this home. Of course, a lot of that was practical, but a great deal was also an imaginative effort. In the weeks that followed the matching panel, I was accompanied everywhere by the shadow of the little self. I saw everything through her eyes, but I also felt everything through her skin, and the spectre of her pain distracted me. But then, this in turn directed me to practicalities.

I consider what will happen here in this place, which is so familiar to me, but which will be so strange to her. This child, who, one summer day, will suddenly arrive in my life, in this world of mine, is not a baby. She is a sentient being with thoughts and opinions and feelings. I know everyone in my village, but I know a lot of people in the local market town too, and they know me. But they know me as a single person without a six-year-old daughter.

So I decide to spend a day trawling around: the grocer, the

bookshop, the library, the chemist, the delicatessen – even the clothes shop I like. I tell each and every one that I am adopting a little girl. I ask each and every one this favour: that when she first comes into the shop with me, I will introduce her as my daughter and will they please say no more than 'Hello' and 'Nice to meet you.' If they have any questions, could they please ask me now.

Why do I do this? Because I want my little girl to feel right away that she belongs. And because I most definitely do not want anyone asking me awkward questions in her presence.

I am at once glad and relieved that I had thought of this. One shopkeeper gasps when I tell her. 'But what if it does not work?' she cries. 'That's OK. It will,' I say. 'She has no choice, and I am determined.'

One other way to appease this phantom, this still as yet only imagined child, was by working hard at cementing myself – and therefore her – into the community, building a theatre of home and connection, a frame of tradition and purpose. So, I kept busy and threw myself into the life around me. I agreed to help with the village fête, I took my niece strawberry-picking, my god-daughters to the farm park, and we all went to see Giffords Circus.

In the twenty and more years since Nell and Toti Gifford first set up the circus, every year's performances included many delightful scenes. As we settled into our seats, a couple of rabbits and three geese mooched around the circus ring, a group of young girls in tutus and fishnets chatted and laughed, and the clown fell over his feet and glared reproachfully at the geese.

Now, of course, we will always miss Nell, but in this particular year she performed in an extraordinary piece with one other rider, called 'Horse and Hawk'. The bird comes to his hand and he directs its flight. Nell and her horse ride round and round the ring. The horse rises up, lies down. The music is haunting. It swells and fades. Nell and the falconer hold each other's gaze without wavering, without a shadow of disguise or extraneous display. It is sinister, weird, moving.

But on this day, the weirdest thing of all happened at the beginning. To a big roll of drums the ringmaster announced that some birthday celebrations were in order. 'Sooo . . . Happy birthday! To Matthew, aged three; Susannah, aged nine; and to —, aged six! Hip hip hooray.'

My niece turns to me with an astonished look. 'Is that your girl? Did you arrange for that announcement?'

No, of course it isn't. Of course I didn't. But her little apparition is there beside me again. Because, yes, as it happens, that other child obviously has the same name and the same birthday, and today, this very day, is indeed the date of my little girl's sixth birthday.

It is the day before the village fête. I have invited Dan Cruickshank to come and open the proceedings, and I go to collect him from the train. Dan and Jim Howett, both part of the key Spitalfields crew, appear in pale jackets and smart brogues, looking like something out of the 1950s. As we are raising funds for repair work to the church, after lunch they set off to inspect the old building, then on for a walk. I plan a route that takes them past

a local great house, two interesting churchyards, the fanciest
farm shop in the world, and ends up at the pub.

In two hours, my niece Anastasia has made four big cakes and
a batch of fairy cakes for the fête, as well as a pudding for tonight.
I have got the stew into the bottom oven and finished typing up
my auction list for tomorrow. Two of my god-daughters and
their parents arrive. I suggest that Paul, the children's father,
goes to collect Dan and Jim from the pub. As he sets off, his wife
Vicky shakes her head. 'You do realize what you have just done?
Sending one man to fetch two other men from the pub? It's a
terrible mistake.'

She is right. An hour passes. After an hour and a half I get out
my list of numbers and set my teenage god-daughter to text the
same message simultaneously to all three men's mobiles: 'Come
home now. Dinner on the table.'

Fête day is brilliant with sun. All the stalls are set out. The guess-
the-weight-of-the-cake stall does a brisk business. Anastasia – much
to her chagrin – is half an ounce out. My god-daughter Georgia
is entranced by the old penny slot machines, some of them dating
back to the First World War. The band plays, and a crooner with
a dark velvet voice sings 'I've Got You Under My Skin'.

For months I have been trawling around my writer friends
and acquaintances, collecting signed copies. Dan auctions them
off with brio. Anastasia is the auctioneer's assistant and prances
about displaying the goods. Two of my friends see a flaw in my
arrangements and fill in forms for promised purchasers and collect cash. In the end, for some twenty books, we make over £500.

Much to our collective amazement, the whole fête, over all the events, raises some £10,000. Two days later, Anne, one of the churchwardens, hosts a drinks party to say thank you to everyone. By now they have all heard what is happening to me; that my unknown, never-seen little girl will shortly be arriving here into her new home.

Before I go in, I sit in the garden, listen to the birds, and have a little weep.

AND SO

AS THE SOCIAL workers go on with the official placement paperwork, they also consult about timing. The matching panel happened early in July. How soon can they get everything into order? The decision having been made, an end date has to be agreed, and they would like to make it as soon as possible. Eventually the date is set. This little girl will come to live with me for ever on 28 August. So, working backwards from that date, all the things that need to be tidied up between now and then have to be set in train as well.

Everything begins to happen at once. 'There is no point now in delaying,' Jessica explains to me. 'Catherine will be telling her tomorrow that you will be her new mother, so then we have to go as fast as we can.'

Catherine and Khadija and Jessica come to inspect my house. Fortunately, I had a certificate for my electric wiring issued comparatively recently. They note down the details. I have already painted the bedroom, made some curtains, and all this is approved. They check the fireguards around the (two) open fires. They worry a bit about the Rayburn. Jessica bounces on one stair tread and instructs me that it needs supporting. Then she looks again at the whole staircase. It is steep. 'You do know that she

191

can sleepwalk?' Well, no, I didn't. 'I think you will need guards at the top of the stairs.'

'Oh. And, of course, a fire extinguisher and a first aid kit in the kitchen.'

Of course. Sometimes I laugh about this. Only the homes of my friends who have recently adopted children have first aid kits and fire extinguishers prominently displayed. If you know the secret code it is an instant giveaway.

Another meeting. This time with another of my new daughter's therapists. The little girl has been having sessions three times a week in order to help prepare her for the move. She is barely six. I wonder what they talk about? Do they talk at all, or does she play, while the therapist observes? Does she have a grown-up person alongside her, in her imagination, as I have a small child in mine?

The clinic is in a big Edwardian house with a waiting room full of toys: a doll's house, a rocking horse, building blocks, children's books. The therapist is a gentle woman, very nicely dressed. She clearly has a soft spot for my girl. The child is bright, she assures me. But she is sensitive too, and works out many things for herself.

As I am about to leave, the receptionist accosts me. 'Are you going to be the little girl's new mother?' She is a cosy Irish lady. 'We all love her here. She is such a character. We will miss her so much.'

For some reason Coleridge's poem about his baby son comes into my mind. In 'Frost at Midnight' he is awake on a winter's night, the babe sleeping peacefully with all his future, so

unknown, before him; a future that will take the child far away
from his parents, from everything that they have ever known:

> My babe so beautiful! it thrills my heart
> With tender gladness, thus to look at thee,
> And think that thou shalt learn far other lore,
> And in far other scenes!

Who is this character so loved by the people around her? I wonder. I have no idea. And I am the one who is now to be her mother.

Another big occasion: the planning placement meeting. We have
to work out all the minute details of the introduction process.
Each person there represents one angle in the elaborate transition under discussion. As I sign in at the Social Services offices, I
am once again aware that this is merely a professional exercise
for everyone else who will be there. For me, the results of the
decisions made here will impact on my whole life. And hers.

We have coffee and nice biscuits. But the ceiling is low, there
are no windows, the lights are glaring. Susan, the team manager,
begins by asking me to sign two pieces of paper. It is, she says, a
mere formality. Reading them through I try not to focus too
hard on the immensity of the one and the horror of the other. In
the first document I agree to take her. For ever. I have seen a picture, read her papers, but that is all. I have never heard her voice.
I have never seen her face. In the second document I agree to
inform them if she is injured or dies in my care.

Two hours in and so far we have only dealt with the big-
picture issues, such as who will take responsibility for which part

of the process, how the ordering of day-by-day decision-making will work, and what the overall timetable needs to include.

Now we have to start planning out everyone's movements, contributions, phone calls and tasks for a whole three weeks. Again, I wonder briefly about how my life has been hazarded, hijacked, heisted. We start on the timetabled grid. Another hour and we have only done three days. In the end, the meeting takes more than four hours. There have been quite a few difficult sticking points, but someone has given way.

Then Moira, the little girl's foster carer, casually remarks that she and Bill won't be able to make one scheduled appointment because they will almost certainly be getting a new baby that day. The conversation continues, but Jessica is frowning. 'Wait a minute,' she says, 'what's this about a baby?' I had barely even noticed. Moira and Bill are professional foster carers. They specialize in babies. And this baby that Moira is expecting has already been taken into the care of the local authority *in utero*. 'That's right,' says Moira. 'The mother will be due that week and they will bring the newborn straight to us. We agreed it last week.'

For a moment I am shaken and distracted by the ghastly actualities behind this matter-of-fact statement. Some poor woman somewhere is big with child. She is about to go through the transformation (at the least) or the trauma (at the worst) that makes her baby a separate living being. And at the moment of that mothering labour, that effort of the work of mothering, she and her child will be separated not only in body, but in heart, in mind, in soul. All bonds broken. Probably for ever.

Jessica, ever the professional, does not pause. She shakes her head. 'I don't really think that can be right. Here you have an older child, who is about to be moved on to a new placement. She will feel that you have replaced her with this baby. That she has been displaced and rejected in favour of another child. Has anyone discussed it with the therapist?'

No one had. The meeting, for the most part, suddenly seems to see Jessica's point. Everyone shifts a bit uncomfortably. No one present at this meeting had (so apparently thoughtlessly) planned to place the newborn with Moira, but it had been someone in their department. One hand not knowing what the other is doing. Catherine, my little girl's social worker, speaks up. 'Jessica is right,' she says simply.

Moira gets irritated. 'But then what will happen? If we don't take this baby we've no idea how long it will be before we get another.' But Jessica is not having it. She is there to look after my interests. And it is in my interest to be taking home a child who is not buffeted by emotion – any more than is inevitable, anyway. And in this case, as she steams into her argument, no one in the team that should be looking after her is considering my little girl's interests. 'It may be your job,' Jessica says firmly, 'but this is her life and her psychological well-being at a crucial time when she is most vulnerable. It is out of the question.' The social workers look at each other.

But then Khadija steps in. 'Jessica *is* right,' she says. 'Catherine agrees with her too. I'm sorry. We should never have offered you that baby at this time. We'll have to think again. We will be able to find you a new baby once the placement has happened.'

Later on, I think about the significance of this moment. It was fortunate for me that Jessica was alert and noticed the problem instantly. And still more so for my little girl. These are the realities for hard-pressed adoption and fostering teams. They are supposed to look out for the children in their care, and plan sensitively for an adoption placement. Yet, at the same time, new children become 'looked after' hour by hour. They too have to be placed, so principles – all too easily – can be forgotten, and the consequences can be horrendous.

'OK,' says Khadija. 'Let's move on to talk about the annual outing to the zoo. Can you make that date?'

Now it is done. We are all exhausted. 'Oh,' says Susan. 'I forgot. The stuff. You can't take all that on the final handover day. Moira, will you pack up her things, except the most important, so that they can be collected beforehand? Then, on the day . . .' she turns to me '. . . you will just take essential things, like her Red Health Book, her passport and such. OK?'

Moira demurs. 'Have I got to pack everything? Even the broken stuff?'

'Absolutely', says Susan. 'All her clothes, all her toys and books – everything. And no bin bags, of course. We'll get you some proper suitcases.'

Again, as I discovered later on, this 'no bin bags' remark might sound like some terrible joke, but it was too often the reality for children moving from a foster home, whether to another such placement, or to an adoptive placement.

'Well, that's that. Thank goodness,' says Khadija. 'It's a terrible business. But if it's any comfort, when I was about to give birth to my daughter, I was petrified and told the midwife I had changed my mind. She said, "What goes up must come down," and told me to get on with it.' Then Khadija smiles at me a trifle ruefully and shrugs. 'Let's just hope the chemistry works.'

The appalling thing is that she is right. We plan and plan, consider and plan some more. But who knows? I just have to go on believing.

Introductions are a serious business. Ours will begin with one very short meeting at the foster carer's home. Moira will be present, and Catherine. It will last half an hour. For something so momentous it sounds like nothing. But believe me, having done it, half an hour is quite long enough for the amount of feeling involved.

Then, for six days a week, for three weeks solid, I will see my child every day. Half an hour, one hour, two hours each day, and so on. At her foster home to begin with, then elsewhere, but with the foster carers present, then on my own, all culminating in an overnight visit to my home. Our home. Hence all this meticulous planning. At what other time in my life have I ever known exactly what I will be doing every minute of every day for practically the whole month ahead of me?

She will attend the school where I have been volunteering already. I moved there after the nursery when I realized I would be adopting an older child and would need experience with primary-school-aged children. I know the staff and they know me. But it is the summer holidays, so I have to leave a message on the answerphone.

Three days later the headteacher calls me. He is irritated. As well he might be, with this new addition to his numbers so late in the day. 'I knew it was on the cards, but I would have liked to have spoken to you.' He is even more irritated when I tell him that my girl's Social Services agency have decreed that she cannot start school at the beginning of term. Given that she is being placed with me at the end of August, they reckon she needs time to settle in with just me alone. 'It is very foolish,' he says. 'She will already feel different and this will make it worse.'

He knows what he is talking about. That is why I know she will be safe.

And I do one naughty thing. I register my daughter at the school under my name. The official recommendation is that you register your child at school and with the doctor under their birth name, in case records are lost or information is not matched up – an all too frequent occurrence. But I decided that it would be possible to deal with that bureaucratic side of such things, and in this case I felt that belonging was more important.

After all, she was not going to be starting school until October so, as the headteacher had said to me, she would be different, not the same as all the other children. If she arrived with one name and was introduced as such, and then had to have a change of name six months or a year later, that too would arouse curiosity. I cannot do anything about the directive from Social Services on the date she starts school. But I can do this, so I do. I have so little control, but then, I think, she has none at all.

And then there is work. Now that we are through matching panel and the plan for the introductions is in place, I have to tell college and apply for adoption leave to begin pretty quickly. I make an appointment with my head of department. It will be a terrible headache for him, I know. My classes are already advertised, students are signed up, so he will have to rush about and find replacement teachers at once. All the same, he is lovely, warm, sympathetic, organized.

By the time of graduation, everyone knows. After the ceremony, and after the 'meet the parents and congratulate them on their wonderful offspring' reception – an event I honestly and particularly relish – there is a little party put on by Jenny and Bev and Faisal, and all our lovely administrative team for the brand-new graduates.

It is a sunny day and we are outside, laughing, happy. One of my colleagues has his little boy with him. The child proudly clutches a small Paddington Bear suitcase that he acquired on a flight when my colleague was travelling on a research trip. I make a mental note: must remember that. I notice how my friends and colleagues suddenly want to share stories about their children with me. Already I am part of the parental cabal. But that is where I wanted to be.

One warm, sweet-scented night, Anastasia and I are stripping redcurrants and watching the film *Far from Heaven*. ('But it's so terribly sad,' she says.) Afterwards, I go out to look at the mulberry tree in the garden. Tied to its trunk is a red ribbon, which I put there ages since.

Years ago, while I was still considering inter-country adoption, I read about the 'red thread', which was then an image used by many such adoption groups, promoting the idea of an inevitable destiny that links all those who come together in life.

It is a cheering image. And many people adopting from

abroad are heartened by this idea. It seems to provide some real link with their children; something positive, rather than this process being merely random, which is probably what it really is. So it is indeed a fairy tale. The parents of such children, longing for a baby, cannot really afford to allow themselves to think too much about the stark realities of their child's experience.

Now, I would agree with many of the sentiments expressed by Grace Newton, the author of the Red Thread Broken blog. She explains how the mystic idea of connection works: 'An ancient Chinese proverb says, "An invisible red thread connects those destined to meet, regardless of the time, place, or circumstance." [. . .] In the international (specifically Chinese) adoption community, these words have a very different meaning. The Invisible Red Thread proverb has been used to propagate and encourage adoptions.'

But then, Newton goes on to point out that there is a terrible inequality and sadness here: if children are 'destined' to be connected to their adoptive parents, then that means that they are also destined to lose their birth parents. Newton concludes that '. . . it is time to acknowledge that the invisible red thread is broken. [. . .]'

When I tied the ribbon to the mulberry tree it was bright and glad. Years have passed. Now it is faded, frayed and limp. I see that it has begun to cut into the bark where the tree has grown. It will damage the tree if I leave it there. I will leave it there for the moment. But in two weeks' time, after I have finally met my child, I will cut it off.

I wonder about misplaced desire and thwarted longing. Can

waiting cut off the sap, prevent growth and damage the soul? I wonder too about other kinds of damage. My child is six. She was once a new baby, bright and glad. Years have passed. Who is she now?

Domenico di Michelino's *Madonna della Misericordia* has been painted over many times, so it has not so much of the romance or mystery of Piero della Francesca's *Madonna del Parto*, but it still tells a powerful story. A young woman in a red dress, which clings suggestively, stands at the centre. Over her shoulders is draped a cloak of deep blue. This she holds out with both arms over two groups of much smaller figures of children in the hieratic scale, eight on each side: six older children in the uniform of the Ospedale degli Innocenti, some of whom look up to the Madonna with their hands held in prayer; six younger children in simple linen tunics, one of them clinging to her skirt; and four infants in swaddling bands, two of them breaking free from their bonds.

The image of the Madonna of Mercy was popular with artists across Europe from the thirteenth century to the sixteenth, and may have derived from a Byzantine icon of the Virgin where she is conceived as 'more spacious than the heavens' because she carried the Christ child in her body. Her association with the heavens is here reduced to the two stars that appear in the blue of her cloak, but Michelino's picture is specifically linked to the Ospedale degli Innocenti – the foundling hospital in the city of Florence – because the background is the distinctive arches of the loggia for Brunelleschi's building.

Mary's head is positioned at the apex of one of these, so that she embodies the very idea of shelter and succour, just as the portico offers shelter from sun and rain, then and now, to the people of Florence. The arcades and the cloak both represent the canopy of the heavens or the veil that divides life and death, much the same as the stagelike curtain that della Francesca used in his *Madonna del Parto*. In a similar way, the roundels of Brunelleschi's design – blank at this stage when the picture was painted in 1446 – flank and echo the gold line of the Virgin's halo.

Everything was ready. There were two weeks to go before I was to meet my child. All I had to do was wait, and in this interval I travelled to Florence to make a radio programme about the early twentieth-century composer Ethel Smyth.

Kate, my producer, was then living in a wildly romantic artist's studio in the garden of an ancient house. Once we had finished our interviews, she cooked dinner while I sat on her bed and wrote my script. Kate's seven-year-old son pulled up a small chair, placed his elbow on his knees, chin in his hand, and regarded me seriously, steadfastly.

So many things were coming together in this present moment, harnessing all the teeming pictures in my mind both from the faraway past and the future just round the corner. A short way up the street was Casa Guidi, where Elizabeth Barrett Browning had lived in the mid-nineteenth century, and where – much to her surprise, given her long-term ill health and her previous miscarriages – she had given birth to her one son, whom she saw as a kind of changeling and brought up in defiance of nineteenth-century gender stereotypes.

In my twenties, following my own private pilgrimage, I had visited her apartments there, along with her holiday home in Bagni di Lucca, and all the places she had travelled – from Vallombrosa to Siena. But that was the past. Now, the little figure in the green hooded coat that belonged only to my imagination sat alongside Kate's son and regarded me.

With time to spare before we recorded our programme, I made another pilgrimage to match that other, long-ago summer day when I saw Piero della Francesca's *Madonna del Parto*. This time, the scene was the square of the Piazza Santissima Annunciata and the buildings of the Ospedale degli Innocenti. Michelino's picture is housed in the museum there, and on this day I was the only visitor.

In history – and still today in countries and cultures all across the world – parents carried and carry their children, used their adult bodies to protect their small vulnerable bodies, kept them close, whether the child was wrapped in a cloth and borne on the back, or slung across a hip, or placed in a basket, or transported in a net hung from the forehead, or bound in a cradleboard decorated with symbols and signs for the safety and welfare of the child.

I have never, nor will I ever, bear a child of my body, but I can still do the work of mothering. I can still use my body – myself – to sustain and contain, nurture and provide, support and guide a child. So I stood before Michelino's picture and reviewed this new version of the mothering that I am about to undertake – the woman who stretches out her arms and her sheltering embrace to the nurslings and nestlings that look up towards her face and pull at her skirt.

*

As the day of our first meeting approaches, I wonder about what happens to other new parents – people expecting a baby, anticipating a birth, wondering about the child that is coming towards them. In some ways it might be the same – they too will have imagined this new being, created an image of that child for themselves, which may or may not be what they get. But there is, of course, one crucial difference. They will have to go through a birth – an extraordinary moment of physical transition that will certainly be unpredictable and may well be perilous. I do not have to do that. I am spared that. But, strangely enough, my unconscious puts me through it just the same.

Wake early after a restless sleep. Remembered in the middle of the night that I had left the window of the car open and it was raining, so got up in the dark to go and shut it. Then fell into a dream. A child – a little boy– is my responsibility and I struggle. He slips, literally, through my fingers, wriggling and resisting. The room is a mess. We are in some sort of ruined castle. I cannot dress him, bathe him, get him into bed. He evades me. And I am anxious too, for there is danger everywhere, both inside and out. I notice, as I make another attempt to grasp him, that his eyes are small and his skull oddly shaped – the physical characteristics of fetal alcohol syndrome. Also, his hair is thin, his skin pale – is he ill?

Wake again feeling overwhelmed by all I have to do. Try to calm myself by working out what really matters. Then I focus on the sounds I can hear, near and far: the cat purring, the wind in the trees, a dove cooing, a horse neighing.

I know that the dream is trying to face my fears. And I am

anxious. It is hard to focus. I cannot remember anything for two minutes together. There are butterflies in my stomach. I feel I can hardly breathe.

Tomorrow I am going to meet my daughter for the very first time.

FIRST WORDS

Go, said the bird, for the leaves were full of children,
Hidden excitedly, containing laughter.
Go, go, go, said the bird:

T. S. Eliot, 'Burnt Norton', *Four Quartets*

I MEET CATHERINE at her office. She shows me the bus route
and the way to the house. These are the paths I will walk every
day for three weeks and then never again in my life. Bill opens
the door. Moira is sitting on the sofa with the little girl standing
beside her. She is wearing a crown made of gold card. I know
that this has been made by her for me. Catherine told me so. But
now she wears it down over her eyes and peeks out at me, over it,
under it, beside it.

As I have said, half an hour is quite long enough. Too much
emotion, too much feeling, fear, imagination, hope and specula-
tion all crammed into thirty minutes. Now I have said goodbye
and 'See you tomorrow', and am walking away along this strange
new path that will become familiar. I think about other half-
hours 'close packed with sensation'. I remember Virginia Woolf

bidding for her house in a pub. I remember doing it myself. But with a house you can move out, move away, move on. I will never be able to move away from this. This commitment is for life, or until death, which is the same.

As I reach the train station some forty-five minutes later, my phone rings. 'That went well. She is fine about everything. But she is worried about your lipstick. She says it is too red.' Catherine has stayed, while I left after the agreed half an hour, and we are now having a de-briefing call. I wonder briefly about Angela Carter and the fear of being eaten. In 'The Tiger's Bride' she describes it thus: 'He will gobble you up. Nursery fears made flesh and sinew; earliest and most archaic of fears, fear of devourment.'

'What can we do?' says Catherine. 'Don't worry,' I reply, 'I'll go and buy a paler one before tomorrow.'

Day two and I went back again. Moira produced a complicated little mosaic puzzle for her. We sat outside in a garden shelter as it was drizzling a bit. She soon became absorbed and concentrated hard. Her little fingers were dextrous, her focus was complete. This was reassuring. Then an outing to an adventure centre. Bill and I had a cup of tea. He read the newspaper. She played, on her own. She played hard, her little face hard, as if she was deter-mined to enjoy it.

The next day we went to the park. We played hide-and-seek. And then she started to sing a song, apparently learned at school: 'Patching up a quarrel, making friends and then, saying, "I for-give you . . ."' For the very first time I thought: I can do this.

*

The first outing on our own was to Kew Gardens. We were both hungry by the time we alighted at the train station, and I turned into a restaurant for lunch. As I paid, the waitress remarked on my daughter's good manners. It was the first time anyone had taken it for granted that she is my daughter. I had not expected it. After all, I have been out in the world with other young children – my nephews and nieces, my god-daughters – but this has never happened before. One possibility is that it has, but I forgot because it was irrelevant to me. The other possibility is that this observing stranger saw something different, something in the way that I am behaving as I practise performing mother.

Then we had another outing to the Science Museum. When we passed by the Royal Albert Hall, I decided on the spur of the moment to take a tour. She listened attentively to everything. As we finished, the tour guide put her hand on my arm. 'Is your daughter home schooled? She reminds me of my daughter.'

Outside, I said, 'We will come here for a concert in one year's time.' And we did. (To a children's Prom, which included 'the loudest piece of classical music ever written' – Jón Leifs' 'Hekla' – and a talk by David Attenborough.) In Kensington Gardens, on the way to the children's playground, my phone rang. It was Anastasia, about to board a plane for New Zealand. 'Would you like to speak to your cousin?' I asked.

It was all strange. I find I remember very little. Most of the time I was numb. There was no space for emotion. It was all time-tables, keeping an eye on the time, being on time, keeping to time. And always being on show, having always to get it right, having to find the exact words, never saying too much. Or too little. It was all strange.

And none of it can be shared with anyone else. I am alone in these meetings. After the first few, it is just her and me. Of course, Jessica is there at the end of the phone and she checks in with me regularly to make sure I am coping. Of course I can call my friends. But that is not the same. And in any case, I am so exhausted, so filled up and overloaded with information that I do not have the energy to do that. And anyway, how could they understand? I have friends – one dear friend, in particular, who adopted a child as a baby. She understands a great deal. But there is no one beside me to whom I can say, 'Did I do that right?' or 'What do you think that meant?' But then, maybe even this is much the same for new birth parents. They too must feel alone in this new, uncharted world.

One day, towards the end of the introductions timetable, I join in with the adoption and fostering team's annual outing to the zoo. All the looked after children in this area, their carers, and various carers' family members come along. Yet another weird day in the many weird days. But one thing was cheering. As we queued for a helter-skelter ride I started a rhyming word game. 'Let's go with the flow.' 'But don't stub your toe.' 'This line is slow.' 'We should go for a row.' 'Or put on a show.' 'Or find a garden to mow.' The other kids look bored. But she gets it at once and joins in. And she is good at it.

In the Ladies, a foster carer puts her head round the door. She has lost one of her charges. 'Destiny,' she shouts. 'Where are you? Destiny, are you in here?'

Good question.

FIRST DAYS

That night we drove to hear about adoption
You jumped an unmarked junction, trying to find
The Social Work Centre . . .

I couldn't really tell
Just what we wanted. I wanted too much . . .

Robert Crawford, 'Winter'

IT IS 28 August. Today is the day she will come to live with me. I get up at 5 o'clock in the morning. By 8 a.m. I have to be in town. But there will be commuter traffic; the earlier I set off the better. Jessica has been strict with her instructions: 'You arrive on the dot. Remember the car seat. No chat. No coffee. Go to the loo before you get there. Once she is in the car, Catherine will give you the last box of documents and you go. No matter what.'

No matter what. As Bill opens the door to me, I hear her crying. She is clinging to her foster mother and weeping. Screaming with weeping. Her little face is streaked with tears.

'I don't want to go. I want to stay here.'

'That isn't going to happen,' says Moira. Over and over.

Moira coaxes her out of the house, down the path, towards the car. Catherine grimaces at me and indicates that we follow. We hover, but keep out of the way. Moira persuades her into the car seat, fastens the seatbelt. Catherine opens the boot, puts the box of documents in, and says, 'Drive.'

I drive. I make comforting noises. This route should be well known by now, but soon I am lost. We pass a big convent wall. More strange streets. The wailing doesn't end, nor the gulping for air. The fat tears running down her cheeks. I pass the convent wall for the second time and realize that in my distraction I have gone in a circle.

Eventually I make it on to the right main road. About an hour and a half later – at length, she falls silent – I glance in the rear-view mirror. Her head is turned away. Her cheeks are tear-marked. Eyes wide, she stares out of the window.

At home at last, she bops about. She plays the piano. She runs upstairs, she runs down. She runs out into the garden. She sits down. She gets up. She won't eat and refuses to drink. I decide to combat the psychic tumult with real noise and get out the lawn-mower. Then I have an idea. I find a portable CD player, pop in an audio recording of Michael Horden reading *The Lion, the Witch and the Wardrobe*, give her some earphones and go back to the garden. Six stripes further on I take a look. Half the sand-wich has been eaten, and she is lying on the sofa, talking to herself, 'Oh, Aslan. Poor Aslan!'

Three days in and, yet again, reviewing in hopeless fashion the events of that ghastly first day, I realize: I drove into the conges-tion charge zone. And now it is too late to pay. A penalty will be liable. Calling the office, I launch into a long-winded explanation.

The man on the other end of the phone listens patiently. 'That's OK,' he says. 'I'm cancelling it.'

The earliest days of an adoption placement are hard. A BBC producer I know, even a year in with her new daughter, just kept saying the same thing: 'What a shocker!' I did some things right. And a lot of things wrong. But I learned to make better mistakes: 'Try again. Fail again. Fail better,' as Beckett says in 'Worstward Ho'.

My family and my friends were wonderful. I vividly recall Edith Hall's encouraging words: 'The worst times are as bad as you can possibly imagine them. But the best times are so far, far beyond your expectations that you cannot imagine them.'

But in many ways the most useful supporters were those in the same situation, and by this time I had quite a few friends with adoptive children. Just as new birth parents might share horror stories about long labours or unsympathetic midwives, so we shared appalling stories of the arrival day: the screaming child, the child who hid under the table, the child silent and withdrawn.

We were all obsessed. Birth parents will sometimes tell you that the memory of a difficult birthing fades. But for an adoptive parent, this live birthing, which is the child suddenly arriving in your life, can never disappear. Because birth parents know where their child was before they appeared. They can (more or less) guess at their mute past because, the mother at least, was always there. But adoptive parents know that the advent of their child in their lives marks a radical break from the past of the child's life, and – no matter how much official paperwork we read – none of us can know, or guess at what went on there.

Even many months on, it occurred to me that the key subject of conversation with such parents always revolved around our children. This was very much the case with one couple whom I had met first at the nursery because one of their children attended it, then another of their children went to the school where I volunteered later on. I would run into Beth on the train to London. We would talk and talk. By the time we got to Slough (an hour and ten minutes), she might say, 'Are you coming to ballet on Tuesday?' Or I would go over to see them for supper. Two hours in and Tom might ask, 'How's work?'

Before my little girl first came to me, the mother of one of my god-daughters gave me a pile of clothes. She also talked my god-daughter and her sister into writing a letter of welcome. And then she had the two girls pick out all the toys and books and other paraphernalia that they were prepared to offer – at the ages of twelve and nine – to give to my new little girl, aged six.

So when my daughter came to live with me there was a loving letter addressed to her by name and a big laundry basket full of toys. She read the letter very seriously. She looked over the basket very seriously.

A couple of days later I ran into a neighbour in the village. It was her dear mother who was really my neighbour, but the mother had died – at a great age, and at home, and in the way she would have wished – the previous Christmas. I stood chatting to her daughter about this and that, and my new girl played with the daughter's dog.

Jaffa is the most obliging dog in the world. My little girl threw a stick. Dog ran after it and brought it back again. She threw another. He did the deed. For a clear twenty minutes, dog and child were entirely happy.

When we got home – after a very emotional parting with the dog – my daughter marched straight to the laundry basket. She picked out a toy dog. A puppy border collie, black, with a white stripe down his nose. 'This is Jaffa,' she announced. Well, it was. This one of the toy dogs did indeed look like Jaffa. And so it was that he came to her new school with us on her very first day. And so it was that she slept every night with her arms tight around him.

Birth parents will know about the importance of 'comforters' for very young children. 'Snuggie', 'Cuggie', 'Cuddly', 'Blankie' and 'Wah-wah' are examples that I can think of immediately among my family and friends. But interestingly, I have seen very little on this for adoptive children, whether younger or older, and I was particularly pleased that my daughter had found her own, specifically associated with me and my home.

It was just a lucky accident for me, but afterwards I wondered about the circumstances. In their book *Real Parents, Real Children: Parenting the Adopted Child*, Holly van Gulden and Lisa M. Bartels-Rabb talk about 'pebbling' as a strategy for talking to children – dropping little conversational openings that might allow your child to discuss difficult issues with you if they are minded to do so. Was this an example of such physical 'pebbling'? Perhaps the fact that the toys were just left lying around for her to find was a useful ploy.

D. W. Winnicott is the important theorist on the function of comforters, or 'transitional objects' or the 'not-me' possession, which is associated with the (usually birth) mother and which helps the child to make the transition to thinking about herself as separate from the mother and as an individual being. Of course this makes sense when mother and child literally were one, in one body, but perhaps it has some relevance too for the adopted child, who also needs to find a place to balance the sense of a separate individual self with the need to belong.

I might also mention here that the German translation for 'cuddle blanket' is '*Schmusedecke*' – 'soothing layer', or cover – which seems to me a lovely interpretation.

In that first week we expanded the territory very slowly. At first it was just a walk to the pond and back. Then to one end of the village, where there is a shadowy path beside an old apple orchard. Then to the other end of the village, where one of my neighbours, away in the United States, had invited us to help ourselves to their vegetables. Then beyond the village, to the river where we played pooh sticks under the bridge.

One day, in the neighbour's vegetable garden, we ran into the lady who was looking after their house. She watched my little girl on the swing for a while, in silence. And then she said slowly, 'I wish I'd done that.'

Soon after that terrible first day, I was looking for a way to exhaust her energy. We walked up to the field behind the church and she played at being Billy the pony, coming to her call as she offered food. After several canterings away and more canterings back, we went into the church.

This was late summer. Hot, staring and unshaded outside. Cool and damp within. She inspected the kneelers, danced up the aisle, piled up the hymn books.

I was tired. So tired. Suddenly, in this cool, dark place it was all too much. I felt the tears pricking. As she started to read out the inscription on each accessible monument, I approached the big copy of the Gospel, open on the lectern.

And there I read:

And Jesus called a little child unto him . . . whoso shall offend one of these little ones . . . it were better for him that a millstone were hanged about his neck, and *that* he were drowned in the depth of the sea.

I was still tired. But I was no longer impatient.

Long before I knew that I would be in this position, I had agreed to chair a discussion at the Cheltenham Literature Festival. A one-time student and colleague of mine was running it at the time, so I knew we could manage. Now I have only one image of my new daughter there. In the green room, surrounded by people coming and going, talking and laughing, she sat in a corner with her banana and honey sandwiches, watching, silent, looking lost.

A week later it was a friend's daughter's birthday party at the local pool. Again, I recall my own daughter, wary and reserved. The noise went on around her. She had joined in the swimming with glee, but afterwards sat silent and still, watching. As the roaring kids danced around with their pizza, as wrapping paper flew all over the room and the birthday girl's father tried to marshal some order for a photograph, my daughter propped her elbows on the table and put her head in her hands.

It is a sad thing to see a child of six with their head bowed in their hands. But then I realized something. In those months immediately past, from May till August, my world had been possessed by the otherworldly spirit of the little girl I was imagining into being. Now, for her, a curiously inverted process was taking place. In her mind she was still herself, but this new world around her was apparitional, remote, eerie.

At this point there were so many gulfs and gaps to negotiate. I had no right to ask questions or to invite intimacy. I was a stranger. And for her, this world was strange. I remember deciding early on to expect nothing, to ask for nothing. In those first days I treated it as a job of work and cast her notionally as one of my students. That meant: responding quickly, speaking clearly, behaving respectfully, waiting patiently, meeting all physical needs, keeping a consistent routine. This may sound forced and unnatural, but none of this was natural – I needed the structure and shape quite as much as she did.

Writing this now, I might make it appear straightforward, but some of it was hard to stick to, especially adhering to a routine. For instance, when I first read in an article from *Adoption Today* – 'Ten Ways to Promote Secure Attachment' or some such – that you should stay with your child until they fall asleep every night, I was appalled. But I prepared to grit my teeth and go through with it. In fact, it was brilliant advice, and not hard at all. Our bedtime routine was down to ten minutes in no time – clean teeth, hot water bottle, comforter (Jaffa), quick back massage over her pyjamas, one chapter of *The Famous Five*, and lullaby. Or not – quite often she was sound asleep by then. And after a while I found that it worked just the same even away from home and no matter what was going on downstairs.

In her book *Our Own: Adopting and Parenting the Older Child*, Trish Maskew lists some recommendations for promoting healthy attachment, including reading a bedtime story, 'perhaps as part of a larger, elaborate bedtime ritual', rocking to sleep, creating set routines, and finding opportunities to touch, such as back rubs or feeding each other ice cream.

From the very first, I never offered to kiss my little girl, nor did I ask her to kiss me. As I began to introduce them, I also asked my family not to ask, not even in the most casual way ('Give us a kiss!'). I know this was the right thing to do, but it has to be a clear and professional choice because, in some ways, it may be contrary to 'ordinary' expectation.

For birth parents welcoming a new baby, touch is all important and reassuring, keeping up the physical connection and duality that is cut across with parturition. Touch might also be important for an adopted baby, a swift way to establish connection. But this was an older child who has had a separate life away from me. And people too easily assume that physical expression – hugging, wrestling, tickling – with children is acceptable, normal, straightforward. But no one can know what might have gone on in the past. Much better to let the boundaries stand. To keep a physical distance and wait.

Gradually she would kiss me when she felt I was not noticing. After about a year and a half she suddenly became more demonstrative, would jump up to kiss me in the middle of dinner, or reach across as we were driving to school. She also began to ask for kisses and hugs. But the key thing is that I left her to set the pace.

About a month in, I took my new daughter to meet my mother, my brother Jeremy, his wife Stephanie, and Holden, their eight-month-old baby son. Stephanie sat on the sofa and stroked my daughter's long hair as she sat on the floor with the baby in her lap. My daughter is good with babies, having seen so many of them in her foster home. Then she asked for a pen. Coloured pencils and paper were produced. She drew a little card with stick-figure pictures of us all: 'Dear Gran and Jeremy and Steph. Thank you for inviting me to your beautiful home.'

My mother, who had neither encouraged nor criticized my decisions, but just taken them as they were, blu-tacked it to the kitchen cupboard where it stayed until the day she died many years later.

Preparing for the day when she will eventually start school, my daughter and I drive into a local town to buy her uniform. We park in the multi-storey and set out to find the shop. Though it is a weekday, the streets are full of people, and the pavements, the noise and the bustle seem strange, even to me, after so many quiet days at home. She begins to lag, pulling at my hand, and eventually comes to a full stop, her little face screwed with weariness.

She puts out both her arms. I recognize this from when my god-daughter was little. 'Carry her,' she used to say. So I do. I pick her up and march on, muttering reassuring words into her hair, and taking no notice of the passers-by who look askance at me and my big baby. My big baby who still has to be sustained by the fact of my life, protected by my body, sheltered under my cloak.

Halfway through October, at last, my daughter started school, beginning with just a morning session. We took ceremonial pictures of her in her new school uniform, with Jaffa in her arms. And then arrived at school so very early that no one was there and we had to take a walk up the street and back again.

Once my daughter had started school, the first review took place there. This inspection is a statutory requirement for looked after children in a new placement, and it was conducted by Matthew, the independent reviewing officer, a man I had never met before. Catherine and Jessica both attended, as her social worker and mine, along with the headteacher and Mrs Hathaway, my daughter's new teacher. Pretty much inured now to all this public scrutiny, I am fairly confident, as my daughter does seem to have settled into school. Apart from anything else, I know that the school secretary gets a phone call every single day from Social Services: first, to check that my daughter is in school; second, to ask how she is doing.

One thing I cannot now recall is whether or not my daughter was brought into the room at any point. Which is odd, because a quick glance at the guidelines for such reviews says under the heading 'Invitations and the Child's participation' that the first person to be invited should be the child.

What I do remember is this. At one point there was some discussion about her emotional well-being. Glancing up, I saw that the headteacher had tears in his eyes. Mrs Hathaway discreetly touched his arm. Much later on, he explained to me. He was adopted from Vietnam, having been left at an orphanage when he was three days old. 'When my own son was born,' he told me, 'I took him in my arms when he was three days old, and I made him a promise.'

The reactions of others who have no experience of adoption can be a real difficulty. Some take a prurient interest, and are occasionally keen to hear gory details of the child's past. But the adoptive parents I know would never tell, and carefully avoid all questioning. First of all, it is not their story to tell – that belongs only to the child. And secondly, children too have a right to privacy, these children perhaps more than most.

Other people see adoption as an over-simplified 'happy ending': 'Well, everything is all right now, isn't it?' Smiley face. Partly yes, partly no, and that partly no can never go away. Some other people have no idea of the correct terminology. Too easily they may refer to a child's 'natural mother' or, even worse to my mind, their 'real mother'. This one drives me mad. Two or three times I have found myself saying sternly, 'Birth mother. I am her real mother.'

But I did have the help of my friends who were also adoptive parents. Beth and Tom lived in the next village, with their three sons and one daughter. If I thought it was bad that my daughter arrived at her new home in the summer, and I had to delay her starting at school, they experienced much worse. All their children were placed with them in late December. They had experienced an arrival day quite as horrendous as mine, but in their case it was, of course, much multiplied.

And then came Christmas. Now, for obvious reasons – too great an expectation, little time and much pressure – Christmas can be an overwrought time in the most well-ordered of households. But for looked after children, Christmas may be especially difficult – for not so obvious reasons connected to the child's past, unknown to us, but all too well known, perhaps, to them. As the holiday set in, Beth and Tom did exactly as it says in the textbooks and went into siege mode. They got in supplies. They walked no further than the river in the village. They invited no one. They went nowhere. Their oldest boy just retired to bed and slept and slept. When he was not in bed, he slept on the sofa.

Fortunately, because Beth and Tom had carefully prepared their neighbours, they were understanding. All the same, on Christmas morning they came out of their door to find chocolate coins and sweets and little presents tied all over the tree in their front garden.

As my daughter became more used to her new surroundings, I knew I could take her over to Beth and Tom's place to play. From my point of view, it was safe because they had the same attitudes, ideals and boundaries. I knew they would never make assumptions or take anything for granted. From her point of view, she was not different there. She was exactly the same as these other kids, they could talk about their past if they wanted to, and none of it was odd or curious, bizarre or weird.

*

At one point my daughter went through a period of getting up in the night and coming into my room. This was pretty wearing. In the end, I caught a terrible cold – not surprisingly. So, on the fifth night, I lie awake with a bad cough, but this time she does not disturb me.

The following night, once again, she sleeps through. I still do not get much sleep because of the cough. Then it comes to me. 'Behaviour is a child's first language,' as my social worker would so often recite. Question: why had she been coming into my room? Answer: to check that I was there. Once I started coughing, she knew for certain that I was there. She could hear me, and so she felt safe.

When I told this story to Beth, she said, 'Maybe you need to get a reverse baby monitor?' I never did. But as my cough lasted a good two weeks, she returned to a proper sleeping pattern pretty rapidly.

I suspect in retrospect that I was low at this time and 'post-adoption depression syndrome' played its part. Like any parent – however you have got there – there might be that teasing 'what have I done?' moment. But it is also purely physical and emotional. You are tired, new routines are in place, new responsibilities loom, new priorities emerge, and the period of adjustment is tricky. Once again, one foot in front of the other.

In December, the week before school broke up for the holidays, I agreed to help with the children's Christmas lunch and undertook to make some brownies to Mrs Rivers' recipe. They turned out, as it happened, really well. 'These are *so* good, Mum,' she remarked. The headteacher approached me. 'It must be nice to hear her call you Mum?' It is, but it has taken a while and she has done it in her own time.

But this means something else as well. I am now 'Mum', and when she speaks of me to others I am 'my mum'. As I was once possessed by her imaginatively, so she has now decided to possess me; to own me for herself. Except that I realize there is an odd lack of reciprocity here. Consciously, I think about her all the time: she is my first waking thought and my last before-sleeping thought. Yet I do not dream about her at all. Ever. Or if I do, it is not her real, living, day-by-day self, but that wraith that lived alongside me all those preparation years. It took, if I can remember correctly, some eight or nine months before she, her real living self, entered my dreams. When this did happen, I pondered for a while on that 'eight or nine months', on that very interesting number.

In fact, there is one part of that account that is not true, because I clearly did not think about her all the time. On one occasion during those early months – I am glad to say only the one – I was absorbed in writing an article and finished a paragraph vaguely thinking I needed to remember something. Then it came to me. She was at school. It was already 3.30 p.m. and I should have picked her up a quarter of an hour ago. I had forgotten her. I had forgotten me, the me that was now a mother. School did not mind. She did not seem to mind. (Though I discover to my chagrin that she does recall this event.) And I was embarrassed.

So much so that I confessed it all to my own mother on the telephone that night. Mummy said, 'Oh well, I used to forget you. Or rather I used to forget that I had you; that I had someone else to think about.' And so I felt forgiven.

That is another thing. In those very early days I used to call my mother a lot. Not necessarily to talk about anything very important. Just to check that she was there.

It is Christmas Day. Our own very first Christmas Day, so we won't be doing much. At the crack of dawn she comes into my room with her Christmas sack. It was once my Christmas sack, a sixties pillowslip depicting a garish, red-cheeked Santa dishing out presents. She pulls out all the little bits and pieces down to the orange at the bottom, and makes very careful piles in the dark. I get up in my pyjamas and make Nigella's Christmas Morning Muffins, which is something I had never done before.

Like many people, I can read some cookbooks as if they were novels – Jane Grigson, Marcella Hazan, Nigella Lawson – and I had been seduced by Nigella's account of the need for Christmas traditions in families. So the waft of nutmeg scented the air as my daughter sprinkled the final topping of sugar and cinnamon. (Fast forward: this does indeed now happen every year.)

After the morning service, my immediate neighbours have invited us for a drink. Under their tastefully decorated Christmas tree are several little parcels labelled with my little girl's name. Everything is lovely, and my new daughter has beautiful manners and is fulsomely appreciative. But the loveliest thing of all is a tiny parcel, which contains a miniature version of Jaffa. He has become such a celebrity, at church and in the village, that my neighbour has noticed, and then – when she saw this smaller, even more puppy version in a local store – pounced on him. My girl is in raptures. Now we carry them both around. The puppy is called Lassie.

IN THE END

MY (NOT) OWN child has her own name. Not Angel. By this time I have begun to tell her all the stories of what went before. She is not keen on the names I would have chosen for her had I had her as a baby. She considers it a lucky escape

Through all this new experience there were the social workers. Every week someone came to visit us, either Jessica or Catherine – sometimes both. Occasionally we might meet in a café while my daughter was at school. More often, I would pick them up from the train so that they could see her when she came home from school. After a while, I began to realize that these visits made her agitated, but I could not change them. So I used to choose not to tell her in advance, but only on the way home, when the meeting was imminent. In retrospect, I do wonder if that was a mistake? If it made her more anxious, gave her even less power?

Susan Hill once said to me, 'Not every child has an unhappy childhood. But every child has an anxious childhood.' Why? Because they have no autonomy, no choice, no control. And what happens if they also have no family, no explanations, no consistency, no one always there to take their side?

*

We are at my nephew's first birthday party. Another mother –
one of my brother's friends – is contending with her toddler.
'Mum! Mum! Can I have a biscuit?'

'Yes, Maya, darling, but eat two more tomatoes first, please.
And what was the word?' 'Please!' The child stomps out before
running off.

The place is crawling with babies. I am sitting on the sofa
with my mother and trying to pay attention as she tells me
about two DVDs that interest her about China and Tibet. I am
vaguely thinking that I must get on the internet and see if I can
find them for her. At the same time I am lending half an ear to
Stephanie, my American sister-in-law, explaining about Oba-
ma's inauguration: 'I just decided I had to go. My friends told
me where to park and I had to walk for three hours [Is that
really what she said?] to get anywhere close to Capitol Hill, but
I had a great view, even though we were packed in like sar-
dines.' She does an imitation, raising her shoulders up to her
ears. 'And we had to squeeze sideways if anyone wanted to go
in or out.'

Then I hear: 'Mummm! *Mum!*' I mutter an apology to my
own mother and head towards the stairs to the basement. She
meets me halfway up, tears on her cheeks, hand outstretched.

'What is it, darling?'

'I shut my hand in the door . . .'

'OK, honey, come on.'

I scoop her up and take her back to the sofa. My mother says,
'Let Gran have a look. Oh, it's not so bad. I'll rub it for you.
How's that? Better now?'

The point about this story is that I heard her. A lot of the time in those early days, I found myself worrying about not quite being able to spot her in a crowd of other little fair-haired children. But her voice, in whatever crowded circumstance, called to me instantly, particularly, distinguishably, umbilically.

Then the snow falls. Snow on snow on snow. I get her to school, but the secretary calls two hours later to say that they are closing. A neighbour comes by with a plastic sledge, so we take it up to the hill behind the church. Quite soon I realize just how brilliant this is for a parent. That is, you stand at the top of the slope and admire the view, while the child whizzes down with squeals of delight, then trudges back up again, glowing and energetic. She'll be worn out in no time. I just wish I'd thought to bring a hip flask.

That night, as she falls asleep, weary beyond measure, she says, 'Mum, I've just had the best day in my whole wide life.'

Her whole wide life. She is six and a half.

At the second review I let her fill in the form by herself. There are questions about her home, what she does with her days and who she sees, and scores about how happy she is. (I steal a glance and discover she marks ten out of ten. Phew.)

When she gets to a section headed (unhelpfully), 'What else do you need to move on?' she writes, 'Learn to canter.' At another question labelled (similarly unhelpfully), 'Is there anything else you would like to see?' she writes, 'Dolphins, sharks, giant elves.'

That's my girl!

*

My friend is going to Paris, so I decide that we too will go for a few days in the Easter holidays. It might be a risk. Most of the adoption gurus advise against any travel abroad for at least the first year. But this was part of my original plan. Just as my parents had visited many places with us in tow as children, so I wanted to take my child to see different things, to know different views. This was the kind of excursion that I had once talked over with my friends Angela and Harriet. So I called up Catherine and explained, and asked if she could write me the necessary permission letter from Social Services to enable me to take her abroad.

When we get there it's fine. We hang out at Shakespeare and Company. My little girl plays with Colette the dog, and cuddles a white kitten with bright blue eyes called Henry (for Henry Miller). She chats happily with the owner, George, who is ninety-five. She flings her arms around Sylvia, his daughter, who is in her twenties and beautiful, funny, warm. The shop puts on an Easter egg hunt for her, complete with clues from Poe and Dickens. We all take a boat trip up to the Eiffel (or as the guide pronounces it, 'Awful') Tower. We admire its coat – what the guide calls 'Awful Tower Brown'. My daughter paddles in the pools by the pyramid at the Louvre. My friend purchases six consecutive rides for her on the merry-go-round by the Hôtel de Ville.

But on the way home, the mood is different. In quick succession she plays out a series of scenarios. It begins with her as the little girl who asks me – in this game, a stranger she has just met on the train – to look after her because her mother has gone off to Paris and left her alone at home. Then she is a little white kitten at the vets, and I have to come and choose her and take her home. Finally, she is a beggar girl on the streets, and I am the lady passing by, who asks her if she would like to come home and live with her.

I am pretty done in by the time we get back, but she is delighted to be at home. She rushes all over the house seeking the cats, greeting her toys and settling her favourite cuddly dog back on her bed. We have a very quiet day. Nothing but a long walk over to the next village.

Then. 'I've had a lovely day, Mum,' she says at bedtime. 'And I had a lovely time in Paris.'

'Did you, darling? What was your favourite thing?'

'The kitten. And George. But yes, definitely the kitten.'

'OK . . . So, in the game, you come to the door and find me and I am a little girl living on the street.'

'Ooookay . . . I get it. Hello, little girl! Who are you? Where do you live? Where is your Mummy?'

'Hmmm . . . Ooh . . .' She runs away, whimpering.

'Don't be scared, little girl. I won't hurt you. Let me help you. Where do you live?'

'I live here.'

'Where?'

'Here in the snow.'

'In the snow! But that's terrible! Why are you here?'

'Well, I had a mummy and a daddy, but I got stolen away. And I have lived here ever since and made a bed in the snow and now I'm four years old.'

'But what have you been eating?'

'I stole food from that house,' she points at the Wendy house in the garden, 'and I would come and listen at the door of your house and that's how I learned to speak. And I learnt how to read because I found some letters about how I was kidnapped when I was a baby. But I'm very cold and sad and people run away from me.'

'Well, that *is* all very sad. Would you like to come into the house, and sit on the sofa and have some hot chocolate?'

'Yes please. I know about hot ch . . . ch . . . How do you say it? Hot chocolate, because I read about that in a book I stole from that house too. Do you think they will mind?'

'No. I think they will be fine about it. Come on. Let's go in.'

To my mind, the astonishing thing about this exchange is how closely it resembles Mary Shelley's description of the Creature's introduction to human society in *Frankenstein* as he lives in the hovel adjacent to the De Laceys' cottage. The stealing of the food, the listening in on the language are the same. But – most intriguing of all – is the idea of the 'letters of origin' about her putative kidnapping, for the Creature similarly happens to have fled Frankenstein's laboratory with the scientist's creation journal in his pocket, and thus learns the facts of his own beginnings – just as Mary Shelley herself learned of hers, through reading her mother's works, and her mother and father's letters to each other. My daughter was only seven at the time of this incident, and I am pretty sure I had never told her the story of *Frankenstein*, but perhaps I am mistaken?

I have constructed so many stories about this child in the years when she was first of all just an abstract idea, and then a still unknown – though real – name and identity. Now, in her young years, she is constructing her own stories all the time about how she got here, how her history works. I have to remember that this is right. I tell my story. But then she will tell hers. And hers will be the one that is most important because she is her own person and her version will be the truth of her life.

At the end of the summer we went to visit our friends Helen and David in Perthshire. My daughter spent the journey becoming acquainted with a dog on the train, so the hours passed swiftly.

Once arrived, we gathered with other friends and Helen's parents round the fire. It might have been late August but it was Scotland. My daughter casually remarked that this was 'our anniversary'. It was a whole year, to the day, since that frightful time when she had first come to live with me.

David stood up and left the room. A moment later he reappeared with a bottle of champagne and a tray of glasses, including one the size of a thimble for my daughter: 'This calls for a celebration.'

A short while later she was in her pyjamas and ready for bed, a velvet-covered hot water bottle supplied by Helen under one arm, Jaffa under the other. I watched her rearranging the selection of bedtime reading offered by David and considered timings: I had written the words that first began this story – 'It is hard now to recall when she – if she is a she – came into my life' – in this house. And that visit, when I wrote those words, took place seven years ago. Which meant that when I first wrote those words my daughter had only just been born.

*

I put her in a red velvet dress handed down by a neighbour, and we catch the train to London. This is the day of the final formal adoption ceremony. At the family division in High Holborn we meet Jessica. My mother has already arrived and gone in. The courtroom is huge, but there are only six of us present: Judge Robinson, the clerk to the court, me, my mother, my daughter and Jessica. It does not take long. My daughter gets a special certificate saying she belongs. And a bear. We go and have lunch. There are no photographs.

On the way home, my little girl pointed out the train window. 'That's a buddleia, isn't it?' 'Yes, darling,' I replied. 'And the purple one on our wall is a wisteria, and the pink one outside school is a tamarisk?' she goes on. We may have been sealed and stamped today, but this is more of an endorsement. My mother's classes continue.

One day I returned home late, having been at an examiners' meeting for hours. Out playing in the garden, she was all dressed up in a pirate costume made for her by Jayne, complete with a curved wooden sword carved by Jayne's husband, Julian. She rushed to greet me. 'Mummy, Mummy, Mummy!'

After her childminder had gone, she declared, 'Mum, I feel sad.'

'Do you, sweetie? What brought that on? What made you feel sad?'

'I don't know, really.'

Later on, she said, 'Mum, I've been thinking about it. I feel sad when you're not the one looking after me.'

As a single parent, I reflected that there was not much I could do about this one. But in one way I was happy about this observation. She was seeing me as her first-choice person, her safe place, her source of comfort. I was reminded of John Bowlby's words from his 1988 book *A Secure Base: Parent–Child Attachment and Healthy Human Development*: 'All of us, from the cradle to the grave, are happiest when life is organized as a series of excursions, long or short, from the secure base provided by our attachment figures.'

As the years go by, we travelled just as I had planned. My family story became her family story because she is my family. The first time we went to Australia, my cousin Jenny met us at the airport. My eight-year-old daughter was suddenly shy, and hid behind me. I had forgotten that it can be cold, even in Sydney, in the winter. So Jenny installed us in my aunt Gillian's flat, and then took us down to the op-shops to buy my daughter some jeans, a coat, a scarf. I am reminded of Litzi marching my family to Oxford Street after the boat had docked at Southampton all that long time ago.

My daughter makes friends with her new cousins. My uncle Eric, who is in his eighties, greets her with, 'G'day.' They hold hands in the street. I visit my father's sister – my aunt Annette – and my daughter plays in the garden, inspects the hive of native bees. Annette gives her a beautiful shell.

When I get home I apply for an adoption visa. Australia is still my home and so it should become her home too. She needs to be the same as the rest of her family, and all her cousins have Australian passports by right of their parents having been born there. I had imagined this would be straightforward for my daughter too. But no. Because she is adopted I have to apply for an adoption visa. When I discovered this, I ranted to my brothers and sister: 'So when is adoption not adoption?' But bureaucracy, strangely enough, paid no attention.

I filled in the (long and complicated) form. I paid the (expensive) fee. I took her to the (also expensive) required medical. This adoption visa will give her a right of residence. I have five years to get her an Australian passport. Just in case she ever wants to make Australia not only her home, but also the place where she lives.

Much later, on another visit, my daughter, my niece Anastasia and I drove to West Wyalong. At a café on the road, the Italian-Australian owner quizzed me over Brexit. 'What on earth do you Brits think you are doing?'

We stayed at the golf club because there was nowhere else to stay. We ate at the pub at Top Town because there was nowhere else to eat. I found my grandmother's house instantly. Newly built when they moved into it in the 1920s, now it looked neglected, run down. There was another house on the lot beside, once a lush garden and a vegetable plot. I decided not to knock on the door. That way the inside remains a place of glamour, of mystery and delight. The girls preferred it that way too.

But then we could not remember the exact location of the gate dedicated to the memory of my grandfather Ernest Fisher, who for many years was the local doctor. We asked at the library. 'Oh, look, here's Ray. He'll be able to tell you.' 'Well,' says Ray, 'the person you should ask is Eric Fisher. He lives in Sydney.' We all laugh. 'Yes!' says my daughter, 'he's my great uncle – my mum's uncle.'

But then we remember. It's in the grounds of the new hospital. A nurse offers to take a photograph of the three of us standing in front of it.

Never mind the official channels and their form-filling. Eric is my daughter's great uncle. She said so. Ernest is her great grand-father. Anastasia is her cousin. She is my daughter and I am her mother.

Like many people (well, women and girls), around the time when she first came to live with me, I watched the film of *Mamma Mia!* Edith, who had seen the musical, had warned me about one scene towards the end when Meryl Streep sings 'Slipping Through My Fingers', which is about everything you plan to do but just don't get around to in the end, as the brief time of childhood goes by. When I first saw the film, I still had only an imagined child. Once my daughter really was my daughter the song became unbearable. It still is.

I think I have actually done pretty well with some of those things. We never did get to the Schubertiade, though we have done a lot of travelling and seen a lot of opera. But, for me, in my situation, time is shorter than most ('slipping through my fingers'). I will never have the eighteen years of growing up that birth parents might hope for; I only get twelve. And, strangely, now I find that my heart aches for the parts of her life that came before, that I miss and long for the little child that she was, the baby that she was, the toddler, the three-year-old in pigtails that I never knew, and never can know.

*

We are reading L. M. Montgomery's *Anne of Green Gables*, a favourite of mine, woman and girl. At first, when I started reading it at bedtime, I skipped the poetic descriptions of the scenery and converted the long words into simpler vocabulary. But then it became clear that she was easily absorbing the words and liked the descriptions, so I read it straight and she loves it. We have to stop every so often as she exclaims, 'But that's not fair!' when Marilla accuses Anne of losing her brooch, or 'How could he!' when Gilbert pulls Anne's hair and whispers, 'Carrots, carrots.'

It suits me too. The straightforward moral landscape of this world helps me to focus, and surely it can do her nothing but good? And then I love the writing, love revisiting the old stories, though this must be my thousandth time.

All the same, sometimes it catches me unawares. I find I had quite forgotten the episode when Anne, dared by the self-satisfied Josie Pye to walk the ridge-pole of the Barry's kitchen roof, falls and breaks her ankle. I had quite forgotten too what happens next:

Marilla was out in the orchard picking a panful of summer apples when she saw Mr Barry coming over the log bridge and up the slope, with Mrs Barry beside him and a whole procession of little girls trailing after him. In his arms he carried Anne, whose head lay limply against his shoulder.

At that moment Marilla had a revelation. In the sudden stab of fear that pierced her very heart she realized what Anne had come to mean to her. She would have admitted that she liked Anne – nay, that she was very fond of Anne.

But now she knew as she hurried wildly down the slope that Anne was dearer to her than anything else on earth.

'Mum! ... Mummy! Why have you stopped? Keep reading! Mum!'

I hold her tight and smell her hair. For a little while I cannot speak and have no words.

QUESTING

. . . Superman was a foundling.
Sylvia Green was adopted.
Tiggist was orphaned . . .

Lemn Sissay, 'Superman
Was a Foundling'

FOR THE LONGEST time I thought that that was the end of the story. You have shown me otherwise. I wanted a child. Now I have a daughter. This is not about instinct, or hormones, or chance, or social expectation, or sharing with another. It was a choice – a deliberate, conscious choice, growing, yes, out of feeling, but brought into existence by sustained and long-maintained intellectual effort. So now I have a daughter.

But I know that I do not have, nor ever will have, a child 'of my own'.

In concluding her book on the desire for a child as portrayed in literature, *A Child of One's Own: Parental Stories*, Rachel Bowlby writes that, in the end, children belong only to themselves. She is not, first of all, thinking of adopted children, but her words are relevant especially to them because for them there is always a 'was', a lost family that went before:

> There always is, or was, or will be another person or
> institution or social world in the life of the child, with whom
> or with which it has been or will be divided. With relief,
> with grief, or with pleasure; sometimes with all of these.
> There is never, once and for all, a child of one's own [. . .
> only a] letting go.

For adoptive parents especially, letting go has to be there, even before the gathering in.

But Bowlby's title raises a wider question. Why does anyone want a child? Specifically, why does anyone want 'a child of one's own'? There are many answers, and some of those I recognized and encountered and reviewed in my long journey. But now that I do have a child, that 'have' bit seems to me to be ever more suspect, ever more impossible.

Because all of the reasons for wishing for a child only take account of the adult, the grown-up – would be (or would not be) – parental perspective. I can only tell this story from that adult point of view. But I now know clearly that no child is 'one's own'. All of the common phrases 'to want a child', 'to long for a child', to want 'your own child' seem grossly improper. Because they take no account of that child. But now, for me, I have to take account of the child who is you, or the child that you were, because you are a child no longer.

*

On the other hand, I do know that Toni Morrison was right about how being a mother makes you into a different person. Or helps to make you try to be a different person. A different whole person. And I have found the place to put that 'kind of love' that Jacqueline Rose spoke about. Jacqueline has also written, in *Mothers: An Essay on Love and Cruelty* about the ways that 'maternal joy' can shatter 'the carapace of selfhood'. This is another thing that I have discovered. Other perspectives, other views, other scenes open out before me all the time through you. And Edith Hall's predictions have come true: those shining moments of surprise and delight that are your doing, your showing, your being.

At the end of *Mother: An Unconventional History*, where she writes about the work of mothering, Sarah Knott watches her own little son in a halo of morning sun:

> For a split second, he is everychild: small, unmarked, outside culture and history.
>
> But, of course not. There are no everychildren any more than there are everymothers.

At other times, in other places, other people knew this. In the 1440s, when Brunelleschi built the graceful arches of the loggia for the Ospedale degli Innocenti in Florence, he incorporated round spandrels between each. For years they remained empty, but at the end of the century they were filled with distinctive roundels, or *tondi*, of white-glazed terracotta on blue backgrounds by Andrea della Robbia. They depicted swaddled infants, and were the particular emblem of the city's foundling hospital. From the fifteenth to the late-nineteenth century, the hospital tried to help all the children left at the 'turning wheel' in the same way: feeding them, educating them, finding a place for them. To this end the children were dressed in uniform and made to look the same. But della Robbia's images tell another story. For each one of his ten roundels is the same but different: the *bambini* turn their faces to left or right; they hold out both arms or only one; some are tightly swaddled from shoulder to toe; others break out of their bands. Their faces and bodies are all different. Every child is not everychild. Every child is one, singular, particular, specific.

I was also really lucky because of who you are, because you are you. You have something – something, as it seems to me now, unknown to anybody that knew you before this time. Unknown, because nobody knew you. And this unknown thing is a secret treasure. It is that you have the most blessedly positive nature, an attitude of optimism, a gift for happiness that is all your own, an alertness always to glad scenes and delight And who knows where that comes from? Certainly not from your early experience. But that too is for you to tell.

Of your effect on me there is much to say. I know now that I need to pay attention, to be fully present, to really see another perspective, to really hear another voice. Not that I always manage it. You know that. Sorry. I try. Quite a lot of the time I don't do very well. But it is something to know what I am aiming for – the things that might make me a better mother, a better person, a better self in the world.

Two small stories of yours are important. I hope you will not mind if I tell them? When you were little, there were times when I got frustrated or upset or angry – with colleagues, with the social workers, with the traffic, with the cats, with the politician on the radio. Whatever. And you would ask, 'Is it my fault?' It never was, of course. But children who have experienced loss, or losses, see that the common denominator in each of those scenes is them – their very selves. Therefore it must be their fault, and so that was your default position too.

And one other thing. In your young years there were the ordinary anxieties of childhood. At about nine you were worried about me dying because (remember?), 'I don't have any money and I don't know your PIN number.' But there were also the not so ordinary anxieties – terrors, even – created by the impact of your particular start in life. When you were about seven you were also worried about me dying. 'It's OK, darling,' I said, trying to be reassuring, 'it won't be for a long time, and by then you will have children of your own.' And you replied, 'But they will be taken away from me.'

I also, now, think about death. Because of the proximity of your young life. I watch the changes in the seasons, the growth and the decay and the growth. Autumn has to be managed with fires, candlelight, and soup in the bottom oven of the old Rayburn. Spring is intense and painful. There is a wood full of bluebells on the way to school, and every time I pass it I think of the many, many days and springs and years to come when I will not be driving past; when I will not be, but the bluebells will bloom just the same. Except that they won't be the same, because they too will be new bulbs, new growth.

'And nothing 'gainst Time's scythe can make defence / Save breed, to brave him when he takes thee hence,' says Shakespeare's Sonnet XII and all the others of that odd procreation sequence, including Sonnet II:

> When forty winters shall besiege thy brow,
> And dig deep trenches in thy beauty's field,
> . . .
> Then being asked, where all thy beauty lies,
> Where all the treasure of thy lusty days;
> . . .
> How much more praise deserv'd thy beauty's use,
> If thou couldst answer 'This fair child of mine
> Shall sum my count, and make my old excuse,'
> Proving his beauty by succession thine!
> This were to be new made when thou art old,
> And see thy blood warm when thou feel'st it cold.

But Shakespeare was wrong about the 'breeding' bit. Because this fair child that is you will indeed 'sum my count, and make my old excuse', though I did not breed you.

He was wrong too about the beauty thing. Because the beauty you will own will be your own, and not derived from me, or any heritage but yours. As it should be. So I think again about Jackie Kay and her poem to her adoptive mother. Her lovely poem in the voice of the lovely mother who wants her daughter to be who she chooses to be:

> . . . Now when people say 'ah but
> it's not like having your own child though is it',
> I say of course it is, what else is it?
> she's my child, l have told her stories
> wept at her losses, laughed at her pleasures,
> she is mine . . .

In another version of this poem, Kay writes, '. . . I suppose there would have been things / I couldn't have understood with any child.'

I try to understand. And know I will not understand that much. And quite often don't. And you tolerate the paradox. On the one hand, you put up with knowing (maybe you don't?) that you will always be my little girl. As Toni Morrison says in *Beloved*, 'Grown don't mean nothing to a mother. A child is a child. They get bigger, older, but grown? What's that suppose to mean? In my heart it don't mean a thing.' Yet you also, rightly, insist on difference and independence. And I know that your view is the truth, the right view.

Sometimes I wonder how anyone has the determination, the endurance, the *chutzpah*, the obstinacy – the arrogance, even – to adopt. There are so many gaps, so many times when one has to try to catch the whisper of what is lost or hidden or unknown. Very often we have sat before a doctor who is asking if anyone in the family suffered from this or that. We look at each other. Sometimes we explain. Sometimes we just stare out the puzzled and impatient looks and say, 'We don't know.' And that's just the physical stuff.

Adoption is not easy. It is hard at the beginning. It is hard in the middle. It is hard at the end. And there is no end. But as I contemplate the adoption triangle, I believe now that it is adoptive parents who get the easiest corner.

Religion and culture tell us to care for children without families. Orphans have the right to zakat, or to the gleanings from the vineyard. Literature and myth tell us stories about children without families. Very often unhappy stories. I sometimes suggest to students that they might gauge the moral compass of a fictional character by considering that character's attitude to children not their own.

Adoption means that a child starts off at birth in one place. A place where – for whatever reason – that child cannot stay. But for that child – when the child finds, or has found for him or her a place where he can stay – then that adoptive family still belongs to the child, even if the child is not 'their own', or anyone else's. In her book *Mothers*, Jacqueline Rose tells this story.

'How could you do it?' one friend asked me as he clutched his new-born to his chest. 'I wanted,' he admitted with just a touch of embarrassment, 'to see my DNA grow and spread, my biological heritage and all that.'

Jacqueline replies, 'But to nurture another's baby is to be part of the DNA of the whole world.'

*

In 2014 the poet Lemn Sissay composed a written installation for the walls of a room at the Foundling Museum in London. It is titled 'Superman Was a Foundling' and goes on to detail a list of fictional characters whose stories make them displaced, or re-placed, or parentless or other-mothered: 'Pippi Longstocking was orphaned. [. . .] Jane Eyre was fostered. [. . .] Anne Shirley was adopted.'

At the opening of the installation, Lemn made a speech in which he said three key things: that he had always been told that his childhood spent in residential homes was only about his childhood, when in fact, it affected the whole of his adulthood; that because he did not have a family, he came to realize what family is for ('separating and coming together for the rest of your lives'); and finally, that children and young people who have experienced living in care have astonishing insight because they have to relive and address and overcome the trauma of their loss every single day of their lives.

These are stories of power. These are stories bright with prospect.

THE BRIGHT FIELD

You are neither here nor there,
A hurry through which known and strange things pass
As big soft buffetings come at the car sideways
And catch the heart off guard and blow it open.

Seamus Heaney, 'Postscript'

SHE IS ELEVEN, nearly twelve. We are in France – in Fontaine-de-Vaucluse – and, much against my better judgement, we are going kayaking. 'The hardest bit,' says the cheery young guide, 'is near the beginning. You have to push your kayak over the weir and into the centre of the river. Then there are a couple of little rapids near the end. You just bump over those.' What he did not tell us was that the whole route would take just over two hours.

We got over the weir OK, and I was just beginning to get my paddle arm in and be able to appreciate my surroundings – the peace, the birdsong, the light speckling the water – when she screamed, 'Mum! There's a bear!' We peered into the greeny gloom. There was indeed something round and brown and furry. It was the rear end of a donkey.

Rapids bumped over, we collapse on to the return bus. Back at base, the car park is nearly empty, and dusk is falling as we hand over our life jackets and paddles. As we turn back to our car, a kingfisher flashes blue across the sunset. We high-five.

Then she hugs me. 'Do you know, Mum, while I was on the water I prayed not to die. I wanted to have lived with you for half my life.'

She is ten, nearly eleven. It was early, the campsite at Les Ormes silent and still. But it was raining – a fine, steady, penetrating rain. Penetrating into our too-hastily pitched tent. We bundled everything into the car. We ran to the shower. Only the donkeys were awake. We had to knock up the *patron* to pay – he rather grumpy after too much late-night enjoyment of his own hospitality. A sudden beginning to the day, but a good thing really; we had to be in Orange by lunchtime. We pulled out of the campsite, through the village, and on towards the main road.

The night before, as I had been putting up the tent as fast as I could in the fading light, she had stood, half on tiptoe, wistfully watching an impromptu game of football. One of the dads waved. 'Come on. Join in. Cover that corner.' A glance at me for permission and she was off. An hour later she came back to ask for some euros to buy a hot chocolate. The football group had all lit a campfire and were toasting marshmallows.

Now, as we drive on to meet our friends, my ten-year-old daughter is telling me a story about another girl she had met there. I remember the emptiness, the green forest on the left, the shining yellow harvested fields on the right, the rain, the swish of the windscreen wipers. Suddenly I was filled with joy – an irrepressible, exquisite delight. And why? Because she is my daughter and I am her mother and the world is full of promise.

And so now I see that this is my bright field, just as in R. S. Thomas's poem. My present with my daughter is one that relies neither on a 'receding future' nor an 'imagined past', but is present in a now in which I turn aside and pause before 'the miracle / of the lit bush'.

Very often R. S. Thomas writes about space, emptiness, absence. The idea of a 'gap' is one of his key words and images, and his poetry encases and encloses the silence, the space between, the absence which is really a presence. In 'The Bright Field', Thomas begins by speaking about something that he *did not* see, that he *did not* recognize in its full meaning: 'I have seen the sun break through /[. . .] and gone my way / and forgotten it [. . .]'. Then he remembers, and in retrospect he gives it meaning, acknowledges its power: 'But that was the / pearl of great price, the one field that had / treasure in it. I realise now [. . .]'. And at the end, there is no 'hurrying on', but only the pause of recognition. I wanted this child to belong in my home. Now this young person is in my life. Or, more to the point, she is in hers.

This is what has happened to me. This is how I listened to the wild track. This is how I followed that wild track. How I arrived at a place where I knew I had arrived and knew that it was the place – the bright field. This is not the end of the story, because there will never be an end. And because this is not the only story.

AD LUCEM —
TOWARDS THE LIGHT

Between the dark and the daylight,
When the night is beginning to lower,
Comes a pause in the day's occupations,
That is known as the Children's Hour.

Henry Wadsworth Longfellow,
'The Children's Hour'

ADOPTIVE PARENTS MIGHT wonder how they are going to cope with the problems of a child who has particular needs, sometimes forgetting that all children – all humans – have problems and needs, which are all different, depending on the person. My needs were not too dissimilar to those of a normal child – love, stability, a sense of belonging, and so on. But, because I had not had them before (at least not consistently), they had become voids in my life which needed filling more than in the average child. This is the same for all adopted, looked after and displaced children.

I think most of all that we need something in our lives that will make us realize that we are deserving of those fundamental human rights. As children, we are often counted as second-rate humans, with few rights, and fewer still that are regularly upheld. As someone who had been through more difficult things than most at such a young age, who had been constantly told they were useless, unworthy and that their opinions didn't matter, I felt like what some people might call a third-rate human, though I don't believe in the concept of different grades of human value.

Between the ages of about three and nine, I suffered from eczema. It was the kind of eczema that left raw skin oozing.

One time, when I was in the bath, my mum caught me itching it. I couldn't help it. 'You naughty girl,' she exploded. I don't think she'd had a particularly good day. It was quite soon after I'd come to live with her, and I'm not sure she'd figured out how to respond to children yet. She moved my arm away and glared at me so hard that the lines on her forehead bunched into each other.

I took one look at her and burst into floods of tears. I felt so guilty. I didn't think I deserved to be shouted at – I couldn't help the itching – but at the same time, I had disappointed her. 'I'm not,' I blubbered. 'I'm not a naughty girl. It's just sometimes, I do naughty things.' Her anger passed as quickly as it came and her face softened. 'Of course. I'm sorry, darling. Mummy didn't mean to shout. Let's put some cream on your arms so that it doesn't hurt as much.'

I realize now that the most likely cause of eczema for me was stress and anxiety. Many studies have shown that those who have been through trauma in their lives are much more likely to suffer with skin conditions such as eczema than those who have not.

I had trauma written all over me, though it has taken a long time to admit. I had been traumatized, neglected and moved more times than my age at the time of adoption. It took around two years after this for my eczema to clear up. It reappeared when I contacted my biological 'family' for the first time, and when I sat my GCSE exams.

Within my first week of coming to live with Peggy, I had received a beautiful box of goodies from a then stranger, who later became known as my 'Butterfly Grandmother' Mona (so called because her whole house was decorated with butterfly stickers and orna-ments) but also a basket from my mother's godchildren: a collection of hand-me-downs, which included a toy border collie whom I named Jaffa and carried around everywhere for several years. At the age of eleven, after years of subtle hints and serious campaigning, this toy became a reality. I named this one Faith, which seemed appropriate at that particular point in time and she has indeed lived up to her name. She is a faithful companion.

While I was excited by these gifts, I also felt honoured. For me it felt like, for the first time, someone really cared about me. They were the most thoughtful presents that I had ever been given and, I was assured, they were not going to be taken away from me. They were mine and they were honest displays of affection and acceptance by strangers who would go on to be great influences in my life. I'd never had anything like that before. I felt, in that fleeting moment, as if I were special, as if I finally had somewhere to belong, somewhere that wanted me to belong. The fact that the items were not new added to the feelings of honour and acceptance. It was as if I was worthy enough to be in possession of items that were once precious to the already well-loved people in my 'new' life.

Of course, all this was still so novel because I received them almost immediately after I came to live in the quirky, queer little seventeenth-century cottages with no central heating or TV that were now home. The realization that I had been 'snatched', that this was to be for the foreseeable, had not hit me yet. Then, it was just a dizzying carousel ride in a fairy tale and it had not yet stopped. You see, I was never told by the social workers, therapists, or even Moira and Bill, that this would be my life for the future. I wasn't told, in a way that I understood, what adoption was and that I was going to live with Peggy. I hadn't yet fully realized that she would become my mum, permanently.

Being a child who had suffered so much disappointment and trauma in my short life, I never expected anything to be permanent, whether that be a stable supply of food or a stable home. I had learned, in my little life of experiences, to take what you were offered quickly and be happy about it then and there, for it was likely that, at some point in the near future, it would be taken away again. It's a mentality that I likely still have to this day, though it doesn't manifest in the same way.

I do find it upsetting that I was never properly told that I wasn't going to go back to Moira and Bill. I can only hope this isn't a common occurrence with children who are being adopted. If it is not fully explained to them in a way that they understand, it can lead to even more turmoil.

In fact, I only saw them three times after leaving, and I would never see my biological parents during my adolescent life. From what I recall, the social workers promised me contact with my birth father. They were perhaps thinking that it would help me in the transition period. Perhaps they thought, 'She's just a child, she will forget in a few weeks in her lovely new home.' Needless to say, I didn't forget that promise; I've forgotten very little about what happened prior to adoption.

I think that is what those adopting or working with adopted children in their day-to-day lives, such as teachers, sometimes forget about once the child has been adopted: that there was a life before adoption, that there are bound to be many memories that will impact the child in question daily, and that they will likely be bad ones. No matter the child's ability and no matter the warmth of their new home, they are unlikely to forget about what has happened to them quickly, if ever. It's something they'll have to carry with them throughout their lives.

However, that doesn't mean that child is any less easy to love, or less rewarding. Some people say that they couldn't cope with a child who has been abused, because it would be too hard for them emotionally to hear what the child has been through. To some extent I can understand that. Yet, that child is living with the effects of that abuse every day. If an adult can't cope with the stories, how can the child be expected to do so?

Of course it will be hard for an adoptive parent to hear how much pain their child has been through. It must be terrible to think about your child's suffering and to wish that you could have protected them from the start of their lives. But how much harder it is for the child.

Once a child or any person starts telling people what they've been through, the healing process can begin. It is a positive, redemptive thing.

The official adoption came in the late autumn, just a few months after a year of me living with Peggy had been celebrated. While I do remember it, I remember it for the people I was with and not the legal significance of the day. When you're seven years old, a year feels like a long time, particularly for me as this was the longest I'd stayed in one place. I'd become entirely used to my new routines and, in general, relished them. I couldn't quite comprehend the importance of the day as, for me, nothing was changing. I remember the excitement in the air, combined with the lingering nervousness and impatience of my mother – I assume she just wanted the day to be over. For her, the day was of far greater significance.

The Family Division of the High Court felt, at the time of them looming over me, like very important buildings indeed, though I knew not why they were important. We had to go through security, similar to at the airport and, in typical fashion of my ever-imagining self, I pretended that I was a secret agent with a goal of getting to the other side without being discovered. The courtroom was almost empty, aside from what I then thought was just a rather sinister-looking old man at the 'table' at the far side, though at that age, anyone who looked remotely old seemed sinister. I softened my prejudgment of him a bit when I saw that his eyes sparkled near the end of the proceedings. They were kind eyes.

There were questions. I gave answers. I didn't really know what was going on – why questions were being asked, what some of the things that were being said meant — so the secret-agent game continued inside of my head for the duration. The end of the formal affair drew to a close and the kind old man with sparkling eyes, the judge, gave me a small but rather handsome bear in a knitted jumper. His name is Freddie.

For me, my sense of identity has always been significant, I think even more so because I'm adopted. During my early years I was always moving between different people, being told different things about myself: some truthful; some not. It's about having somewhere to belong, somewhere that will never abandon you, because it's a part of you and you are a part of it.

Now, I often wonder whether belonging is good. I wonder why we, as humans, should have to choose only one thing, person or place to belong to, for we are not one-dimensional — something we often forget. However, it was important to me then. Because I didn't know my biological family very well, I felt as if I didn't really know who I was or who I was supposed to be. I was missing out on a culture that, by birth, I felt that I deserved to have.

I had a hole that needed to be filled, questions that needed to be answered. I needed to know where I came from so that I could do the genealogy 'discover your ancestors' homework I seemed to be given at the beginning of each school year, and so that I could answer the questions I was constantly being peppered with. Particularly the questions I sometimes ended up being given with regards to my race. Questions that left me standing awkwardly because I simply didn't know the answers to them. I felt upset. Angry. Everyone else seemed to know who they were, where they came from.

Why shouldn't I?

It was a difficult few years. In any teen's life, this is the stage at which you are just starting to find out about yourself – your interests, your passions, what makes you tick. It's why, when I was fourteen, I decided to do some serious research into my biological roots because, at the time, I needed closure to help me move on and process the difficult things in my past.

It's scary not knowing who you are. Or thinking that you don't know who you are. Most people have a fair sense of identity that helps to guide them through certain parts of their lives. I didn't have that foundation. This can be either a good thing (you can shape who you are yourself), or a bad thing (your brain is pulling you in multiple directions and you don't know which way to go because you don't know yourself). Are you the rebel who sets off the fire alarm, or are you the kind person who cares about everyone and everything? Or are you both? I realize now that it's much more complicated than black or white.

When I was younger, I was confused. Was I from the countryside or London or the North? Should I actively try to live up to the expectations people had of me (which were sometimes prejudiced) because it's easier? Or should I fight to be accepted as who I truly am? Was I English because I was born here? Was I African because of my biological father? Australian because of my mum?

Once, when in Australia, one of my cousins proclaimed very loudly to her friends, 'She isn't Australian or my cousin. Not really, cos she's just adopted.' This was a very big blow to my ten-year-old self. I felt hurt, confused, insecure and unworthy, all at once. I was Australian, wasn't I?

I feel Australian. I feel just as Australian as my mum feels, as my cousins feel – perhaps even more so than some of them because it's something I've clung on to, having never felt like I'd belonged anywhere before. Yet I don't just want to feel Australian, I want to be accepted as Australian, insofar as someone who is not Aboriginal can be.

I have a permanent resident visa – something my mum fought hard for – but I don't have full citizenship: I don't have an Australian passport. After my passport application was first rejected (though we have now reapplied), I was devastated. Though I am legally the daughter of an Australian, because I am 'only' Australian by adoption and not 'by blood', I have to fill in a different form. I cannot just apply as a daughter of an Australian, though that is who I am.

I was told by my family that I belonged, but in that moment I didn't feel as if I did belong. In my mind, at the time, this 'official' rejection showed that I was still different and that in some ways I was still an outlier. I've visited Australia more times than some of my cousins have. Nonetheless, they are automatically entitled to dual nationality because one of their biological parents was born in Australia.

Perhaps I shouldn't have been surprised at the rejection or the lengthy process we had to go through even just to meet the criteria for applying. After all, you need only to look at how the Australian government treats refugees in the current day, or even Australian-born ethnic minorities, to know how they deal with 'outsiders'. Perhaps, despite what they say, they really have forgotten how the Australia as we know it came to be.

*

Even without citizenship, Australia feels like home. One of my many homes. I feel free there, new life is sparked inside me when I go, when I think about it. I miss Australia when I'm not there. Sometimes, I feel as though I could stay for ever.

I love my Australian cousins. We play dares, run barefoot everywhere, tell one another stories around a makeshift fire, climb the roof, swim when it's shark hour. Adults do not control us and tell us what to do or where to be. As long as we know we are on the same beach, we are left alone. We don't get into trouble for letting our imaginations run wild here. Mum is happier here. I feel like me here. Everyone is more laidback than in England – we can combine intellectual debates and politics with sand and barbies. No one I meet feels uptight or hostile, and we say what we feel, even if we sometimes disagree. I am me here.

Over the years, Tom and Beth have become particular allies of mine, especially recently. We talk about politics, the growing concerns and disasters in the world, the books we are reading and recommend, the injustices of the system, and, of course, adoption.

We don't talk about it a lot, but when we do, we usually talk about the concerns they have with their children, our possibly similar concerns, and the misunderstandings both adopted children and adoptive parents face. There is much to be misunderstood when it comes to adoptees, particularly when it comes to adults with no experience of adoption or its processes. Often these misconceptions will be most prominent in those who are responsible for a child's welfare at school, as that is where most children spend the majority of their time.

A particular teacher was in charge of pastoral care for one of Beth and Tom's children's needs with regards to perceived 'difficulties' (in our standardized world), many of which had sprung from emotional traumas in the past. This teacher expressed, in a meeting, that it was her belief that their child should not, in certain situations, still be struggling with the impact of past traumas on his behaviour. These traumas had occurred 'too long ago', and coming to live with parents such as Beth and Tom should have been an end to his issues. Another occasion led to me also meeting with this teacher. I tried to explain why I was struggling with a particular thing, which related to events of my childhood, and her response was, 'Well, we all have our own little problems.'

One day, Beth had picked me up early from school and we managed to get into a conversation where we were talking about the relation of birth parents to adopted children. One thing she said stuck in my mind. It was something along the lines of 'I never think about the children as my own, for I understand that they do not belong to me, just as no child should be the belonging of anyone. I think of them as beings I have been lucky enough to have crossed paths with and helped grow, gifts that I have a responsibility to look after but not mould their personalities how I want them to be – to let them have ownership of themselves and to decide for themselves what they want to do.'

She is a truly remarkable person. Both she and Tom are people for whom I have great admiration.

There is never a 'too long ago'. Even subconscious feelings and memories impact us, memories that are branded on our bodies. No matter how well an adoptive parent or a teacher knows a child, there are always going to be things that they don't know – things that happened in the child's past but that nonetheless will always affect the now. It's a common misconception – as demonstrated with the incident with the teacher – that once a child is adopted or taken from an unhappy situation into a happy one, their past problems are forgotten as they move on in their life.

I was flicking through a small book called *Eeyore's Little Book of Gloom*, and one quote that particularly resonated with me was 'You can give the donkey a happy ending, but the miserable beginning remains for ever.'

It was just before the summer holidays of 2016 when I signed myself up to participate in a study analysing the different emotions in teenagers. It included a written and verbal test, as well as an MRI scan to see which part of my brain was responding to different prompts. It was something that genuinely intrigued me – at school we had been learning about how MRI scanners worked – but a £20 Amazon voucher was also at stake.

I went to the MRI scanner, but before that were the rigorous interrogations: 'Have you had sex recently?' 'Do you have any hidden piercings or tattoos?' 'Do you have any metal plates implanted?' 'Is there any chance of you being pregnant? Don't worry if you are, we don't have to inform your guardian. It's all confidential here.'

So we talked. It was decided that I had the all clear.

I was given a variety of stimuli on a screen – pictures of animals, carefully selected words, people without homes – different situations occurring in the same place. Then it came to the part where I was asked to look at the screen and to try to move the bar into the green area using my brain. I was told it would move in response to my emotions, and the strength of those emotions, so it was suggested that I think of different things. Good memories; bad memories. Situations I'd been in and situations I'd imagined.

I started off with what was then the most obvious thing to me: bad memories and situations I'd been in. I thought that had to work. I was pushing with all the concentration I could muster. The bar flickered occasionally, but it would not move to the green area. My brain felt like it was about to explode. Why wasn't it moving?

I was growing increasingly agitated and it was becoming obvious. I was almost crying with the frustration of not being able to perform the required task, but the bar, though now much closer to the green line, was still not close enough. I then moved on to trying to imagine myself in some of the situations previously shown to me. That didn't prevail either.

Finally, I unclenched my fists, reined in my emotions and breathed, which was something that I may or may not have been doing throughout the process of conjuring up the thoughts and memories. I didn't realize how tense I'd become. I let my mind wander, hoping, with high levels of doubt, that my brain would lead me to somewhere, something, anything that would make that bar move.

I was suddenly filled with overwhelming happiness. I felt snow. My first snow came flooding back to my memory. The moment when we had finished sledging and she was pulling me on the hefty wooden sledge, something she had found in a local antique shop. I was giggling with ecstasy, blurring everything out but the speed and the snow; she was telling me a story.

'Perfect' – a loud clear voice, back to now. I opened my tear-stained eyes and looked up. The bar had shot to the very top of the green line, off the scale. My happiest day.

Every child deserves to feel the strength of those happy memories. The thing that is amazing about humans – children, in particular – is how one powerfully joyous memory can outweigh hundreds of negative memories, even if those negative memories will never truly be erased and will continue to impact our lives. How that one memory had more power than everything else I had thought of. Perhaps that is why we have survived this long.

AFTERWORD —
THE BEGINNING

Come away, O human child!
To the waters and the wild
With a faery, hand in hand,
For the world's more full of weeping than you can
   understand.

W. B. Yeats, 'The Stolen Child'

I CAN'T SLEEP. Nothing unusual for me, but today is different. I glance at the white clock hanging to the right of me:
5.27 a.m. Over two hours of life left. I try to make myself
numb, as if throughout the night I'd been attached to a drip
sucking my blood from my veins and arteries. I mustn't let
myself feel, for I fear feeling will break me. If I cry, I'll never
stop.

What have I done so wrong to deserve being sent away again?
Am I evil? I know I took some food into my bedroom the other
week, when I wasn't supposed to, for a midnight feast; that I'd
thrown up two nights ago, but surely I'm not so bad that I have

265

to leave? I don't love my life here, I feel suffocated, but I love the people in my life here – mostly.

These were the people who had always been a constant, the people who I'd always gone back to when I'd come back into foster care. These were the people I sometimes even call 'mum' and 'dad', something my foster brother had always reprimanded me for. This had been my first period of rough stability.

I do not want to leave. I miss Santa – the black moggy – already, and I haven't even left yet. I imagine stories and different lives with him, and tell him everything. A part of myself is in him, stories I no longer remember.

I can't find my Tamagotchi either. I'm beyond stressed about that. The creature to whom I'd told my deepest fears, the creature whom I'd invested so much time into feeding and making sure it went to sleep on time, the ritual routines that kept me sane in my world otherwise absent of routine. I'd given the creature the care I wished for myself. All for nothing if I cannot find it to keep it alive. Perhaps next time I am here I'll get him back.

I run my left hand along the wall. The textured bumps provide some comfort, some feeling. I run my right hand between my mattress and the metal it sits on. All I find is dust that wedges itself into my fingernails. I hang upside down from my bed as I look under it for things I might have left. I feel the blood rush to my brain and become lightheaded – and not in a good way. I feel inside as I look to others outside, truly upside down. I retch but restrain myself, before my emotions engulf me completely. Looking for a picture of an imagined family that I'd drawn the other day, I let myself slide on to the wooden floor.

It was 5.58 a.m. when I started crying, uncontrollable sobs. I couldn't breathe. Out of all my other experiences prior to adoption, this was the one that caused a complete breakdown of both my mind and body. I hadn't been told I was leaving for ever, yet in my heart I knew that I would never be here again.

I lay on the floor a while, letting the tears cascade. When I thought I couldn't cry any more, I directed my eyeballs to look up. I could just make out on the end of my bed – even with my clogged-up eyes – *The Lion, the Witch and the Wardrobe*. The copy she gave me. Too much, too soon. I started again.

I close my eyes, wet lashes clinging to my tear-streaked face. If I hurt the people I love so much that I have to keep leaving, I don't want to be on this planet any more.

I feel like Edmund and Lucy all in one; Edmund the betrayer and Lucy the betrayed. A storm of feelings I do not understand. A body racked with emotions it should not yet be old enough to feel.

It was just before 7 a.m. when I stopped crying and stared at the wall, spaced out as in a state of catatonia, unblinking, my body on the hard wooden floor. The time seemed to slip from me, as though I had no sense of it. I didn't have any sense of it. Emotions don't run by seconds and milliseconds, hours and minutes. Time is, after all, a made-up human concept and something particularly hard to comprehend for a child, especially a child going through the tumult of being taken from everything they know.

I heard the doorbell ring in my head. I wasn't ready. Let me stay. I cried all the way back to the two little cottages. I never got my Tamagotchi back.

EPILOGUE

The wild track. In our lives and in the world, there is no perfect. We know that. But we don't need perfect to make this work. Success is not perfect. It is having the determination to carry on. The resilience to carry on. The wish to carry on, in spite of the inevitable imperfect. We grit our teeth, roll our eyes and argue. We keep silent. We make the best of what we have, and we do what we need to do. In the end, we know that we both want the same thing, even if we disagree about the best way to achieve that thing.

Our happiest times leave us beyond contented, and it is in these moments that our connection is most profound. But these moments are rarely planned. Often, these are times that come when we have made no arrangements, times that come out of nowhere and are the result of chance or when we're circumstantially brought together – on long journeys or in moments of crisis. They're the times when we both rant about the same thing and recognize ourselves in one another; when we are driving along, blasting out seventies music and laughing at the lyrics with a merriment that we share; when we are – the two of us – holding back our laughter in a situation that does not seem quite appropriate, or when we need only to glance at each other to know what is being thought or felt. They are the moments when the understanding after a misunderstanding clicks into place over dinner and we take it in turns to tell the story from our individual perspectives. Our often silent but intimate contracts, made and re-made between ourselves. A look, a touch, a word.

March 2020 and the world stands still. The world as we know it has been shaken into disarray. Three months of lockdown. Sometimes difficult, but often valuable for our relationship.

July 2020 and we decide to take our chance. Like everyone else, all our summer plans had been cancelled. But now the ferries are running again, so we pack the camping gear and round up the dog – or, rather, she rounds up us. The boat is quiet, there are fewer passengers than usual, and it is late, so we snuggle down in our bunks, rise to the harp-music morning call, and set off into the fresh French day as the pearly clouds fade into the blue.

Working through the alphabet we find a song for each letter to while away the journey: 'Angie', 'Get It On', 'Home Again', 'In questa reggia', 'The Sound Of Silence'. The motorway miles fall away as we head south. We have a favourite campsite, discovered by accident some years since but an easy four hours' drive from the ferry – well, six really, including food and dog-walking breaks. Years ago, we visited the evening *son et lumière* at the nearby chateau. The magic garden was full of giant pumpkins, avenues of moonlight, parades of topiary, and we entertained ourselves by imagining a fairy welcome in one of the more modest farm cottages in the grounds: the lit fire, the pure linen, the savoury stew, all set out by invisible hands.

This year, of course, as with everywhere else, the chateau sees fewer passers-by; fewer people drawn in by the soft lights and inviting music. And now, as we pull in to the campsite, we can see that here too all is quiet. We are the only non-French camping here and, in many ways, this is nicer. We pitch our own tent, foray out to the shops in our masks to buy dinner, and go swimming in the river.

As we head back to the bank, we realize that Faith is not with us. We can hear her scrabbling in the reeds downstream. Absurdly, foolishly, we both turn around and swim towards her, but, of course, she is a dog. Before we are even in the shallows, she is on the shore, shaking herself vigorously and wondering what all the fuss was about. But then, as we paddle back in her direction, a pair of kingfishers dives into their nest in the riverbank right by our tent. In this moment, we know that we are where we are meant to be.

Further on south, and installed in our village abode – uninhabitable when first found but now known universally as 'Chateau Marianna' – we wake to the bread van sounding its horn in the early morning, and stagger out to buy croissants and fresh baguettes by the medieval bridge. We go to a jazz concert, and sit in the castle courtyard under a swing of stars. We eat freshly made pizza at the *marché nocturne* in the next village, after a long day helping our neighbour – and friend – to weed his field. And we swim, all three including Faith, in the river.

At Nîmes we dawdle around the Roman arena, baking under the sun, skipping from shade to shade. Waiting in the queue to enter the temple of the Maison Carrée, a child asks us what kind of dog Faith is. '*Elle est une border collie.*' The child nods. '*Elle s'appelle Foi.*'

And we talk. About our past together. About our future, which will be both together and apart. And we talk about children, all the other many children, now more than ever, who have troubled pasts, precarious presents and uncertain futures.

And then: 'Mum, what can we do? How can we change things? Who will really listen?'

NOTES AND REFERENCES

R. S. Thomas, 'The Bright Field', *Laboratories of the Spirit* (London: Macmillan, 1975), and ed. Anthony Thwaite, *R. S. Thomas*, Everyman's Poetry (London: J. M. Dent, 1996), p. 87.

First Light

Louis MacNeice, 'Snow', *Louis MacNeice: Collected Poems*, ed. Peter McDonald (1935: London: Faber & Faber, 2016), p. 24.

Christina Rossetti, *Goblin Market, The Prince's Progress and Other Poems* (London: Macmillan and Co., 1875). Also in ed. R. W. Crump, *The Complete Poems of Christina Rossetti: A Variorum Edition*, Vol. 1 (Baton Rouge, LA and London: Louisiana State University Press, 1979), pp. 216–17.

'In the Bleak Midwinter', *Soul Music*, BBC Radio 4, producer Sara Conkey (December 2004).

Neville Symington, *A Healing Conversation: How Healing Happens* (London: Karnac Books, 2006), p. 19.

Simone de Beauvoir, *Le Deuxième Sexe : Les faits et les mythes* and *L'expérience vécue* (Paris: Gallimard, 1949), *The Second Sex*, trans.

Constance Borde and Sheila Malovany-Chevallier (London: Vintage, 2015).

Melanie Klein, *The Collected Writings of Melanie Klein* (Vol. 1), *Love, Guilt and Reparation: And Other Works 1921–1945* (Vol. 2), *The Psychoanalysis of Children* (Vol. 3), *Envy and Gratitude and Other Works 1946–1963* (London: Hogarth Press, 1975).

D. W. Winnicott, 'Hate in the counter-transference', *International Journal of Psychoanalysis*, 30:2 (1949), and in *Through Paediatrics to Psychoanalysis: Collected Papers of D. W. Winnicott* (New York: Basic Books, 1958).

Adrienne Rich, *Of Woman Born: Motherhood as Experience and Institution* (1976: New York: W. W. Norton & Co., 1995), p. 21.

A few more recent books on mothering include Ayelet Waldman, *Bad Mother: A Chronicle of Maternal Crimes, Minor Calamities, and Occasional Moments of Grace* (New York: Doubleday, 2009); Elisa Albert's novel *After Birth* (Boston, MA: Houghton Mifflin Harcourt, 2015); Rebecca Solnit, 'The Mother of All Questions' (2015) in *The Mother of All Questions: Further Feminisms* (London: Granta, 2017); Orna Donath's analysis of the experience of a range of women, *Regretting Motherhood: A Study*, (Berkeley, CA: North Atlantic Books, 2017); Meaghan O'Connell, *And Now We Have Everything: On Motherhood Before I Was Ready* (New York: Little, Brown & Co., 2018); and Sheila Heti's novel of ambivalence *Motherhood* (London: Harvill Secker, 2018).

Eavan Boland, 'The Other Sylvia Plath', in ed. Patricia Dienstfrey and Brenda Hillman, *The Grand Permission: New Writings on Poetics and Motherhood* (Middletown, CT: Wesleyan University Press, 2003), p. 70.

Eavan Boland, 'The Journey', *The Journey and Other Poems* (Manchester: Carcanet Press, 1987), p. 39.

Eavan Boland, *Night Feed* (Manchester: Carcanet Press, 1982).

'Four Women Poets', BBC Radio 4, producer Beaty Rubens (1992).

Buchi Emecheta, *The Joys of Motherhood* (Oxford: Heinemann, 1979).

Julia Kristeva, '*Hérethique de l'amour*', *Tel Quel* (1977), translated as 'Stabat Mater' by Arthur Goldhammer, published in *Poetics Today* (1985), and translated again by Leon S. Roudiez in ed. Toril Moi, *The Kristeva Reader* (Oxford: Blackwell Publishers, 1986), pp. 160–86.

Julia Kristeva, 'Motherhood Today' (2005). Available at: http://www.kristeva.fr/motherhood.html

Rachel Cusk, *A Life's Work: On Becoming a Mother* (London: Fourth Estate, 2001).

Rachel Cusk, '*Shattered: Modern Motherhood and the Illusion of Equality* by Rebecca Asher – review', *Guardian*, 3 April 2011. Available at: https://www.theguardian.com/books/2011/apr/03/shattered-rebecca-asher-motherhood-equality.

Jacqueline Rose, *Mothers: An Essay on Love and Cruelty* (London: Faber & Faber, 2018), p. 210.

Sarah Knott, *Mother: An Unconventional History* (2019: London: Penguin Books, 2020), p. 264.

Clover Stroud, *My Wild and Sleepless Nights* (London: Doubleday, 2020).

Claire Howorth, 'Motherhood is hard to get wrong. So why do so many moms feel so bad about themselves?', *Time*, 19 October 2017. Available at: https://time.com/magazine/us/4989032/october-30th-2017-vol-190-no-18-u-s.

Jill Bialosky and Helen Schulman, *Wanting a Child: Twenty-two Writers on Their Difficult But Mostly Successful Quests for Parenthood in a High-tech Age* (New York: Farrar Straus and Giroux, 1998), p. 6.

Sylvia Plath, 'Morning Song', *Ariel* (London: Faber & Faber, 1965) and in ed. Ted Hughes, *Sylvia Plath, Collected Poems* (1981: Faber & Faber, 1989), p. 156. Also in Sylvia Plath, *Ariel: The Restored Edition: A Facsimile of Plath's Manuscript, Reinstating Her Original Selection and Arrangement* (London: Faber and Faber, 2004), p. 5.

Carol Ann Duffy, 'Lessons in the Orchard' (2014). Available at: https://www.charleston.org.uk/lessons-in-the-orchard-by-carol-ann-duffy.

Virginia Woolf, 'A Sketch of the Past' (1939) in *Moments of Being*, ed. Jeanne Schulkind (London: Pimlico, 2002), pp. 78–9.

Carol Ann Duffy, 'Snow', *The Bees* (London: Picador, 2011), p. 62.

Toni Morrison interview with Bill Moyers, 11 March 1990. Available at: https://billmoyers.com/content/toni-morrison-part-1. Also quoted in Danille K. Taylor-Guthrie, *Conversations with Toni Morrison* (Jackson, MS: University Press of Mississippi, 1994), pp. 270–1, and Andrea O'Reilly, *Toni Morrison and Motherhood: A Politics of the Heart* (Albany, NY: State University of New York Press, 2004), p. 19–20.

Sappho, fr. 98 ('purple headband'), fr. 104 a) and b) ('Hesperus'), fr. 122 ('a tender girl picking flowers'), fr. 132 ('golden child'), edited and translated by David A. Campbell, *Greek Lyric I: Sappho and Alcaeus*, Loeb Edition (Cambridge, MA: Harvard University Press, 1982), pp. 123–5, 131, 143, 149.

H. V. Morton, *A Traveller in Italy* (1964: London: Methuen, 1982), pp. 528–9.

Lisa Jardine interview with Jenni Murray, *Woman's Hour*, BBC Radio 4, 8 November 2013. Available at: https://www.bbc.co.uk/programmes/b03ggllw.

If

George Eliot, *Adam Bede* (1859), ed. Margaret Reynolds (London: Penguin, 2008), p. xviii.

Sarah Knott, *Mother: An Unconventional History* (2019: London: Penguin Books, 2020), p. 89.

Home

Elizabeth Bishop, 'One Art', ed. Robert Giroux and Lloyd Schwartz, *Elizabeth Bishop: Poems, Prose & Letters*, No. 180,

Library of America Series (New York: Farrar, Straus and Giroux, 2014), pp. 166–7.

Virginia Woolf, *The Diaries of Virginia Woolf*, Vol. I, 1915–1919, ed. Anne Olivier Bell, introduced by Quentin Bell (London: Hogarth Press, 1977), pp. 286–8.

A. B. Patterson, 'Hay and Hell and Booligal', *The Bulletin*, 25 April 1896, and *Rio Grande's Last Race and Other Verses* (Sydney: Angus and Robertson, 1902). See also *The Collected Verse of A. B. Patterson*, with an introduction by Frederick T. Macartney, (Sydney: Angus and Robertson, 1951), pp. 122–3.

In 1962, Australia sent a small group of military advisers to assist the government of South Vietnam in their struggle with Communist-run North Vietnam. Under the National Service Act (1964) compulsory military service for males aged twenty was introduced. Over the following decade, as the conflict escalated to war, approximately 60,000 Australians served in Vietnam. Five hundred and twenty-one were killed, and more than 3,000 were wounded. Australian troops were finally withdrawn in 1973.

'At the time I was evacuated I used to tell myself that one day the war would be over and I could go back home . . .' This quotation by Jim Bartley from a display card at the exhibition at the Imperial War Museum is not included in the companion book, but for the effects of the war on the child population of Europe, see Juliet Gardiner, *The Children's War: The Second World War through the Eyes of the Children of Britain* (London: Portrait, an imprint of Ratkus Books in association with the Imperial War Museum, 2005), pp. 200–3.

Shaun Tan and John Marsden, *The Rabbits* (Sydney: Lothian Books, 1998), p. 1.

Chloe Hooper, 'The Tall Man', *Monthly* (March 2006), and in *The Best Australian Essays 2006*, ed. Drusilla Modjeska (Melbourne, Black Inc., 2006), pp. 111–37. Chloe Hooper, *The Tall Man: Death and Life on Palm Island* (2008: London: Vintage, 2010), p. 9.

Maybe

On the practice and implementation of the home study, see: Nick Allen, *Making Sense of the New Adoption Law: A Guide for Social and Welfare Services* (Lyme Regis, Dorset: Russell House Publishing, 2003); Maria James, *An Adoption Diary: A Couple's Journey from Infertility to Parenthood* (London: BAAF, 2006); Julia Wise, *Flying Solo: A Single Parent's Adoption Story* (London: BAAF, 2007). BAAF – the British Association for Adoption and Fostering can supply materials on this element of the adoption process. The children's charity Coram, based in London, now provides adoption services for many local authorities: https://www.coram.org.uk.

OASIS – Overseas Adoption Support and Information Service – was a voluntary organization for people who wished to adopt or had adopted from overseas. The Department for Children, Schools and Families had responsibility for adoption in the UK from 2007 to 2010. Today it is the Department for Education. The Inter-country Adoption Centre can be contacted at www.icacentre.org.uk.

'At the time, the China Center of Adoption Affairs . . . accepted single women as prospective adopters.' As of March 2007, these criteria for inter-country adoption from China no longer apply. The China Center of Adoption Affairs (CCAA) then notified the Department for Children, Schools and Families of new criteria with effect from 1 May 2007. The main changes were that applications are prioritized where the prospective adopters are: a married couple; both husband and wife are at least thirty years old and under fifty years old (this age limit is extended to fifty-five years old if the couple is applying to adopt a child with special needs); the couple has been married for at least two years. If either partner has been married before (and they cannot have had more than two previous marriages), the couple has to have been married for at least five years. See the websites for the China Center of Adoption Affairs and China Center for Welfare and Adoption: http://www.cccwa.cn/index_en.shtml; http://cccwaen.mca.gov.cn.

Kay Ann Johnson, *China's Hidden Children: Abandonment, Adoption, and the Human Costs of the One-Child Policy* (Chicago, IL and London: University of Chicago Press, 2016).

Mei Fong, *One Child: The Story of China's Most Radical Experiment* (New York: Houghton Mifflin Harcourt, 2016).

Daddy

William Blake, 'The Little Boy Lost', *Songs of Innocence* (1789). Copy B (1789), Library of Congress, object 22. Available at: http://www.blakearchive.org/blake/indexworks.htm.

C. Harlow, 'Accountancy, new public management and the problems of the Child Support Agency', *Journal of Law and Society*, 26:2 (1999), pp. 150–74. See also G. Bates, D. Hutchinson, T. Robertson, A. Wadsworth and R. Watson, 'Identifying the cause of the Child Support Agency's problems: A case of new public management failure or an issue of inapt accountability?', Stage 3 students: BA Business Management, University of Newcastle upon Tyne, December 2002. Available at: http://www.childsupportanalysis.co.uk/guest_contributions/newcastle_paper/index.htm.

Wilfrid Bion, *Learning from Experience* (London: Heinemann, 1962), *Elements of Psycho-Analysis* (London: Heinemann, 1963), and *Transformations: Change from Learning to Growth* (London: Heinemann, 1965).

D. W. Winnicott, 'Transitional objects and transitional phenomena', *International Journal of Psychoanalysis*, 34 (1953), pp. 89–97; 'Clinical varieties of transference', *International Journal of Psychoanalysis*, 37 (1955–6), p. 386; and 'Mirror-role of the mother and family in child development' in ed. P. Lomas, *The Predicament of the Family: A Psycho-Analytical Symposium* (London: Hogarth Press, 1967), pp. 26–33.

John Bowlby, *Attachment and Loss: Attachment* (Vol. 1), *Separation: Anxiety and Anger* (Vol. 2), *Loss: Sadness and Depression* (Vol. 3) (London: Hogarth Press, 1969, 1972 and 1980). See also Jeremy Holmes, *John Bowlby and Attachment Theory* (Hove and New York: Brunner-Routledge, 1993), pp. 23–4.

Jacqueline Rose, *Mothers: An Essay on Love and Cruelty* (London: Faber & Faber, 2018), p. 1.

Sir David Henshaw, 'Recovering Child Support: Routes to Responsibility', a report to the Secretary of State for Work and Pensions, July 2006. Available at: https://www.gov.uk/government/publications/recovering-child-support-routes-to-responsibility.

Alan Dolan, '"I've learnt what a dad should do": The interaction of masculine and fathering identities among men who attended a "dads only" parenting programme', *Sociology*, 48:4 (2014), pp. 812–28.

Ethel Turner, *Seven Little Australians* (1894: Camberwell: Puffin Books, 2003), p. 176.

E. Nesbit, *The Railway Children* (1906: London: Puffin Books, 1994), pp. 265, 266–7.

Roger McGough, 'The Way Things Are', *Selected Poems* (London: Penguin, 2006), pp. 181–2.

Venturing

Vahni Capildeo, 'Windrush Lineage' from 'Windrush Reflections' in *Odyssey Calling* (Bristol: Sad Press, 2020), p. 16.

MSS letters, Kenneth Reynolds to Charles Reynolds (1952–4).

'Booligal', *Sydney Morning Herald*, 8 February 2004. Available at: https://www.smh.com.au/lifestyle/booligal-20040208-gdkpyi.html.

Almost

Audre Lorde, 'From the House of Yemanjá', *The Collected Poems of Audre Lorde* (New York: W. W. Norton & Co., 1997), p. 235.

Jackie Kay, *The Adoption Papers* (Hexham: Bloodaxe Books, 1991), p. 23.

David Batty, 'Council slated for substandard adoption procedures', *Guardian*, 24 October 2001. Available at: https://www.theguardian.com/society/2001/oct/24/adoptionandfostering.adoption.

Children Who Wait, published for members of AdoptionUK. *Be My Parent* is published by BAAF (British Association for Adoption and Fostering).

Daniel Hughes, *Building the Bonds of Attachment: Awakening Love in Deeply Traumatized Children* (1998: Lanham, Boulder, New York: Rowman & Littlefield, 2017) and *Attachment-focused Family Therapy Workbook* (New York: W. W. Norton & Co., 2011).

Classrooms

Imtiaz Dharker, 'Tissue' from *The Terrorist at My Table* (Hexham: Bloodaxe Books, 2006), p.14.

Charles Dickens, 'Scenes and Characters No. 1', *Bell's Life in London*, September 1835. Available at: http://thecircumlocutionoffice.com/sketchesbyboz/scenes/chapter-5.

Charles Dickens, ['Autobiographical Fragment'] in John Forster, 'Hard Experiences in Boyhood 1822–1824', *The Life of Charles Dickens*, Vol. 1 (London: Cecil Palmer, 1872–1874), chapter 2. And in Claire Tomalin, *Charles Dickens: A Life* (London: Viking, 2011), p. 29.

Gladys Storey, *Dickens and Daughter* (London: Frederick Muller, 1939), p. 94. And in Fred Kaplan, *Dickens: A Biography* (London: Hodder and Stoughton, 1988), p. 399.

Marjorie Newman, *Mole and the Baby Bird*, illustrated by Patrick Benson (London: Bloomsbury, 2002), p. 24.

But

According to the 'National Minimum Standards', the role of an adoption approval panel is to 'make timely, quality and appropriate recommendations/decisions in line with the overriding objective to promote the welfare of children throughout their lives . . . ', July 2014. Available at: https://assets.publishing.service.gov.uk/government/uploads/system/uploads/attachment_data/file/336069/Adoption_NMS_July_2014_for_publication.pdf.

The Independent Review Mechanism (IRM) started operating in April 2004. Its brief is to provide adoption applicants in England with the option of applying to an independent body to review the adoption agency's determination not to approve them as adopters or to withdraw their approval. It is now operated by Coram Children's Legal Centre on behalf of the Department for Education. From 1 April 2009 this service was expanded to include consideration of fostering cases. Available at: https://www.gov.uk/government/organisations/independent-review-mechanism.

Classrooms

Alice Walker, 'Expect Nothing', *Revolutionary Petunias & Other Poems* (New York: Harcourt Brace Jovanovich, 1973) and in

Collected Poems: Her Blue Body Everything We Know: Earthling Poems 1965–1990 (1991: New York and London: Weidenfeld & Nicolson, 2005), p. 191.

This is an extract from the website for the Inter-country Adoption Centre (IAC), September 2017: 'Some families come to IAC very clear about which country they wish to adopt from. They may have family connections locally, or are originally from that country, or they might be adopting a child who is related to them. Others are less certain and seek guidance to help explore their options. When adopting a child from overseas, prospective parents need to be respectful of a child's culture, particularly if it is not the same as their own. They must be willing to engage with their adoptive child's background and to ensure that they grow up with a full sense of their cultural heritage.

'When adopting from abroad, it is important to note that you must be eligible to adopt both within the UK as well as from the relevant country overseas. Sometimes that country's eligibility criteria might be different or more stringent than the UK's, so the first step for potential adopters is to check their eligibility by contacting the Advice Line. IAC works with many individuals seeking to adopt from many countries around the world and our world map illustrates the range of countries our families have adopted from. Not all countries are "open" for adoption – some because the country itself does not wish to place children overseas and others because the UK currently restricts adoption from a country, due to concerns about the processes in country. Cambodia, Guatemala, Haiti and

Nepal are currently restricted.' Available at: http://www.icacentre.org.uk.

Christina Rossetti, 'Later Life: A Double Sonnet of Sonnets', *A Pageant and Other Poems* (London: Macmillan & Co., 1881). Also in ed. R. W. Crump, *The Complete Poems of Christina Rossetti: A Variorum Edition*, Vol. 2 (Baton Rouge, LA and London: Louisiana State University Press, 1979), pp. 140–41.

Anton Chekhov, *The Cherry Orchard* (1904), Act I.

William Shakespeare, *The Winter's Tale* (1623), Act III, Scene 2, lines 192–3.

Emma Smith, *This Is Shakespeare* (London: Pelican Books, 2019) and Charlotte Scott, *The Child in Shakespeare* (Oxford: Oxford University Press, 2018).

'Benjamin Waugh and the Founding of the Society' in Anne Allen and Arthur Morton, *This Is Your Child: The Story of the National Society for the Prevention of Cruelty to Children* (London: Routledge & Kegan Paul, 1961), pp. 15–33. Benjamin Waugh, *The Gaol Cradle: Who Rocks It?* (London: Strahan and Co., 1873) and Jane Abbott, 'The Press and the Public Visibility of Nineteenth-Century Criminal Children' in eds. Judith Rowbotham and Kim Stevenson, *Criminal Conversations: Victorian Crimes, Social Panic and Moral Outrage* (Columbus, OH: Ohio State University Press, 2005), pp. 23–39.

For South Sudan's ratification of the Convention of the Rights of the Child, see 'UN lauds South Sudan as country ratifies landmark child rights treaty', *UN News*, 4 May 2015. Available at: https://news.un.org/en/story/2015/05/497732.

Research supported by the Joseph Rowntree Foundation found that only one in three of the 120 authorities in England and Wales were using independent visitors. The study estimated that just 4 per cent of children and young people who would have been eligible for a visitor actually had one. Among disabled children being looked after, who were the particular focus of the study, it appeared that just 1 per cent of those eligible were seeing an independent visitor. Yet interviews with disabled young people who did have a visitor indicated that such schemes were popular. See Abigail Knight, 'Most authorities neglect duty to recruit Independent Visitors', February 1998. Available at: www.jrf.org.uk.

Alexandra Gordon and Kris Graham, 'The National Independent Visitor Data Report', January 2016, p. 2. Available at: https://www.barnardos.org.uk/sites/default/files/2020-02/National%20Independent%20Visitor%20Data%20Report.

John Bingham, 'Public less "outraged" by neglect of children than elderly, says Children's Commissioner', *Telegraph*, 9 January 2014. Available at: https://www.telegraph.co.uk/news/politics/10559537/Public-less-outraged-by-neglect-of-children-than-elderly-says-Childrens-Commissioner.html.

Lucy Johnston, 'Doubled in a decade, tally of the children placed in care', *Daily Express*, 10 June 2018. Available at: https://www.express.co.uk/news/uk/972075/Number-children-social-services-care-doubled-decade.

In December 2019, new figures released by the Department of Education showed that in the year ending March 2019, the number of looked-after children in the UK stood at 78,150, while the number adopted and ceasing to be looked after fell to 3,570. Available at: https://www.coram.org.uk/news/coram-responds-new-figures-looked-after-children-england.

Unless

Nancy Newton Verrier, *The Primal Wound: Understanding the Adopted Child* (Baltimore: Gateway Press Inc., 1993), p. xvi.

Hannah Pool, *My Fathers' Daughter: A Story of Family and Belonging* (2005: London: Penguin Books, 2006).

Maja Lee Langvad, *Hun er vred, She Is Angry (A Personal Account of Transnational Adoption)*, trans. Paul Russell Garrett, *Versopolis: European Review of Poetry, Books and Culture* (2014). Available at: www.versopolis.com/poet/173/maja-lee-langvad.

'*In April 2016, one British agency, Parents and Children Together (PACT), decided to withdraw its inter-country adoption services.*' Available at: pactcharity.org/news-events/latest-news/pact-cease-intercountry-adoption-services.

The International Adoption Guide gives some information on the situation with regard to Russia. Available at: https://international adoptionguide.co.uk/from-which-countries-is-it-possible-to-adopt-from/criteria-for-adoption-from-russia.

Carol Lefevre, 'Kissing It Better', in ed. Sara Holloway, *Family Wanted: Adoption Stories* (London: Granta, 2005), p. 225.

Venturing

Adrienne Rich, 'Diving into the Wreck', *Diving into the Wreck: Poems 1971–1972* (1973: New York: W. W. Norton & Co., 2013), p. 23.

Daddy

Maxine Kumin, 'Spree', *The Long Approach: Poems by Maxine Kumin* (1985: New York: Viking, 1986), p. 10.

Dorothea Mackellar, 'My Country', first published as 'Core of My Heart' in the *Spectator*, 5 September 1908. Later published in Dorothea Mackellar, *The Closed Door and Other Verses* (Melbourne: Australasian Authors Agency, 1911), pp. 9–11.

Han Suyin, *The Mountain Is Young* (1958: London: Sheridan, 1995), p. 431.

William Shakespeare, *The Tempest*, Act I, Scene 2, lines 55–6.

Jenifer Neils, 'Children and Greek Religion', in eds. Jenifer Neils and John H. Oakley with the assistance of Katherine Hart, *Coming of Age in Ancient Greece: Images of Childhood from the Classical Past* (New Haven, CT and London: Yale University Press, 2003), p. 144. In the naming of a child, too – which took place on about the tenth day after birth – the paternal line has priority, the firstborn son being named for the paternal grandfather and the second son for the maternal grandfather.

Aeschylus, *Eumenides*, trans. Herbert Weir Smyth, Loeb Edition (Cambridge, MA and London: Harvard University Press, 1999), pp. 334–5.

Paola Bressan, 'Why babies look like their daddies: Paternity uncertainty and the evolution of self-deception in evaluating family resemblance', *Acta Ethologica*, 4:2 (Heidelberg: Springer Berlin, 2002), pp. 113–18.

Eds. Stephen Beckerman and Paul Valentine, *Cultures of Multiple Fathers: The Theory and Practice of Partible Paternity in Lowland South America* (Gainsville, FL: University of Florida Press, 2002).

Sylvia Plath, 'Daddy', from *Ariel* (1965: London: Faber & Faber, 2001), pp. 48–50. See also Sylvia Plath, *Ariel: The Restored Edition: A Facsimile of Plath's Manuscript, Reinstating Her Original Selection and Arrangement* (London: Faber and Faber, 2004), pp. 73–5.

William Shakespeare, *King Lear*, Act I, Scene 1, lines 58, 160, 89–92, 200–3, 248 (Oxford: Oxford University Press, 1965), pp. 908, 909, 910, and Act IV, Scene 6, lines 154–5 (Oxford: Oxford University Press, 1965), p. 935. And William Shakespeare, *King Lear*, Act IV, Scene 7, lines 59–76 (Oxford: Oxford University Press, 1965), p. 937.

Or

More information on preparation courses can be found at Adopters for Adoption or First 4 Adoption: www.adoptersfor adoption.com; www.first4adoption.org.uk. For an overview of the process see 'Child Adoption' at https://www.gov.uk/child-adoption/overview.

BAAF, the British Association for Adoption and Fostering, Coram and Barnardo's also offer advice and guidance on their websites.

Children Who Wait includes helpful articles on case studies and strategies for managing the arrival and continuing care of adopted children as well as notice of seminars and other courses for social workers and adoptive parents. See www.adoptionuk. org/finding-child/children-who-wait. The BAAF also offers a similar service, and a magazine and website called *Be My Parent*: www.bemyparent.org.uk.

Louis MacNeice, 'Entirely', *Louis MacNeice: Collected Poems*, ed. Peter McDonald (1940: London: Faber & Faber, 2016), p. 171.

Angela Leighton, 'The Sand Children' in *Sea Level* (Nottingham: Shoestring Press, 2012), p. 65. By kind permission of the author.

The NHS Choices website gives this account of the adoption health assessment: 'As part of the adoption assessment process, potential adopters are required to have a comprehensive health assessment. Adoption agencies need to check whether there are any physical or mental health issues that might affect your ability to provide a safe, stable and loving home until a child reaches adulthood and, ideally, beyond [. . .] Your medical will take up to one hour and will include the following areas: 1) your health history; 2) a review of your lifestyle; 3) your family medical history; 4) a complete physical examination including your height, weight and blood pressure.' Available at: https://www.nhs.uk/live-well/ healthy-body/adopting-a-child-your-health-and-wellbeing.

Lois Raynor, *The Adopted Child Comes of Age*, National Institute Social Services Library No. 36 (London: George Allen & Unwin, 1980). See also Rita J. Simon and Howard Altstein, *Adoption, Race and Identity: From Infancy to Young Adulthood* (1992: New

Brunswick, NJ, Transaction Publishers, 2002) for an account of interracial adoption.

Kathy Tyler and Joy Drake, *The Angel Cards: Inspirational Messages and Meditations* (1981: New York: Narada Productions Inc., 1999).

Charlotte Moundlic, *La Croute* (2009) with illustrations by Olivier Tallec, *The Scar* (London: Walker Books, 2011).

Shaun Tan, *The Red Tree* (London: Hachette, 2001).

The First4Adoption website gives a quick overview of the processes for matching panel: www.first4adoption.org.uk. Mumsnet also carries a substantial discussion on the topic, see: www.mumsnet.com.

Home

Christina Rossetti, 'At Home', *Goblin Market and Other Poems* (London: Macmillan, 1862). Also in ed. R. W. Crump, *The Complete Poems of Christina Rossetti: A Variorum Edition*, Vol. 1 (Baton Rouge, LA and London: Louisiana State University Press, 1979), p. 28.

Sigmund Freud, 'The Uncanny' (1919), in *The Standard Edition of the Complete Psychological Works of Sigmund Freud*, James Strachey, Anna Freud, Alix Strachey and Alan Tyson, *An Infantile Neurosis and Other Works*, Volume XVII (1917–1919) (London: Hogarth Press, 1955), p. 226.

William Shakespeare, *The Tragedy of King Richard II*, Act I, Scene 3, lines 159–73; Act I, Scene 3, lines 294–303; Act V, Scene 1, lines 37–50 (Oxford: Oxford University Press, 1965), pp. 385, 386, 403.

Chloe Hooper, 'The Tall Man', *Monthly* (March 2006), and in *The Best Australian Essays 2006*, ed. Drusilla Modjeska (Melbourne: Black Inc., 2006), pp. 111–37. Chloe Hooper, *The Tall Man: Death and Life on Palm Island* (2008: London: Vintage, 2010), p. 72.

On 13 February 2008, the then Australian prime minister, Kevin Rudd, delivered a formal apology to the country's indigenous peoples. Available at: https://www.aph.gov.au/About_Parliament/House_of_Representatives/Powers_practice_and_procedure/Practice7/HTML/Chapter9/Motion_of_apology.

Antoine de Saint-Exupery, *Terre des Hommes* (Paris: Gallimard, 1939). Published in English as *Wind, Sand and Stars*, trans. William Rees (London: Penguin, 1995), p. 40.

Gifford's Circus performance of 'Horse and Hawk' from *Caravan* (2008). Also see Nell Gifford, *Gifford's Circus: The First Ten Years* (Stroud: History Press, 2014).

And So

Samuel Taylor Coleridge, 'Frost at Midnight' (1798), collected in *Sybilline Leaves: A Collection of Poems* (London: Rest Fenner, 1817), and in ed. William Keach, *Samuel Taylor Coleridge: The Complete Poems* (London: Penguin Books, 1997), p. 232.

In 2015, The Children's Society was still urging councils and social workers to provide luggage and packing boxes for

children moving from foster homes: www.childrenssociety.org.
uk. In 2014, Dave Linton founded a community interest company called Madlug – 'make a difference luggage' – where profits
go to provide proper bags for children in care. Best practice today
advises social workers to keep a suitcase in their car, in case a
child needs to be re-homed in an emergency: www.madlug.com.

Grace Newton, Red Thread Broken blog: https://redthreadbro-
ken.wordpress.com.

Mei Fong also quotes the same passage from Newton's blog in
One Child: The Story of China's Most Radical Experiment (Boston
and New York: Houghton Mifflin Harcourt, 2016), p. 189. Children's stories that use this image include Karen Acres' *Little Miss
Ladybug & Her Magical Red Thread* (Quebec: Ladybug Productions, 2003) and Grace Lin, *The Red Thread: An Adoption
Fairytale* (Park Ridge, IL: Albert Whitman and Company, 2007).

Domenico di Michelino's *Madonna della Misericordia*. Curated
by Lucia Sandri, *Gli Innocenti e Firenze nei Secoli: Un ospedale,
un archivio, una città* (Firenze: Studio per Edizioni Scelte, 2005),
p. 71.

'A Portrait of Ethel Smyth', BBC Radio 3, producer Kate Bolton-
Porciatti (27 September 2008).

First Words

T. S. Eliot, 'Burnt Norton', *Four Quartets* (London: Faber &
Faber, 1936), and in T. S. Eliot, *Collected Poems: 1909–1962* (London: Faber & Faber, 1974), p. 190.

Angela Carter, 'The Tiger's Bride', *The Bloody Chamber and Other Stories* (1979: London: Vintage Books, 2006), p. 74.

First Days

Robert Crawford, 'Winter', *Masculinity* (London: Jonathan Cape, 1996), p. 56. By kind permission of the author.

'I learned to make better mistakes.' This is what the hopeful adoptive parents say in the comedy-drama *The Odd Life of Timothy Green* (2012), starring Jennifer Garner, Joel Edgerton and CJ Adams, written and directed by Peter Hedges and produced by Walt Disney Pictures.

Samuel Beckett, 'Worstward Ho' (1983), published together with 'Company' and 'Ill Seen Ill Said', in *Nohow On* (New York: Grove Press, 1989).

Holly van Gulden and Lisa M. Bartels-Rabb, *Real Parents, Real Children: Parenting the Adopted Child* (Chicago, IL: Independent Publishers Group, 1995).

D. W. Winnicott, *Playing and Reality* (New York: Tavistock Publications, 1971), pp. 1–14, 52. This research was originally published in the *International Journal of Psychoanalysis*, 34:2 (1953), and in D. W. Winnicott, 'Transitional objects and transitional phenomena' (1951) in *Collected Papers: Through Paediatrics to Psycho-Analysis* (New York: Tavistock Publications, 1958), pp. 204–42.

'And Jesus called a little child unto him'. Matthew 18: 1–6.

Trish Maskew, *Our Own: Adopting and Parenting the Older Child* (New York: Snowcap Press, 1999).

For more information on looked after children reviews see: https://lawstuff.org.uk/childrens-services/looked-after-child-reviews-lac-review.

In the End

Mary Shelley, *Frankenstein: or, the New Prometheus* (London, 1818), chapters 12–14.

John Bowlby, *A Secure Base: Parent–Child Attachment and Healthy Human Development* (London: Routledge, 1988), p. 27.

L. M. Montgomery, *Anne of Green Gables* (1908), chapter XXIII, 'Anne Comes to Grief in an Affair of Honor'.

Questing

Lemn Sissay, 'Superman Was a Foundling', written installation at the Foundling Museum, Brunswick Square, London. By kind permission of the author. See: https://foundlingmuseum.org.uk/events/superman-was-a-foundling.

Rachel Bowlby, *A Child of One's Own: Parental Stories* (Oxford: University Press, 2013), p. 233.

Jacqueline Rose, *Mothers: An Essay on Love and Cruelty* (London: Faber & Faber, London, 2018), p. 200.

Sarah Knott, *Mother: An Unconventional History* (2019: London: Penguin Books, 2020), p. 259.

William Shakespeare, 'When I do count the clock that tells the time . . . ', Sonnet XII (Oxford: Oxford University Press, 1965), p. 1107.

William Shakespeare, 'When forty winters shall besiege thy brow', Sonnet II (Oxford: Oxford University Press, 1965), p. 1106.

Jackie Kay, 'The Telling Part', *The Adoption Papers* (Hexham: Bloodaxe Books, 1991), p. 23. By kind permission of the author.

Toni Morrison, *Beloved* (1987: London: Vintage, 2016), p. 54.

'Orphans have the right to zakat, or to the gleanings from the vineyard': 'They ask you, [O Muhammad], what they should spend [in charity]. Say, "Whatever you spend of good is [to be] for parents and relatives and orphans and the needy and the traveller. And whatever you do of good – indeed, Allah is Knowing of it."' Al-Baqarah 2: 215.

'When thou gatherest the grapes of thy vineyard, thou shalt not glean *it* afterward: it shall be for the stranger, for the fatherless, and for the widow.' Deuteronomy 24: 21.

'Literature and myth tell us a story about children without families. Very often an unhappy story.' See Lemn Sissay on his written installation 'Superman Was a Foundling': "Superman was a Foundling" upraises the fictional stars of popular and classic culture who are fostered, adopted or orphaned. They range from Romulus and Remus of Rome's foundation myth, to Lisbeth Salander of *The Girl with the Dragon Tattoo*. Their adventures have enriched our lives, but we do

not recognise the connection between the fictional characters and the fostered, adopted and orphaned children in our midst. Did Superman have ADHD? Did Harry Potter have an uncontrollable temper? Was Lisbeth Salander unable to form lasting relationships? For all their complexity and pain, these characters are shining examples of how to be your best. Young people in care enrich our lives in a similar way.' Available at: https://foundlingmuseum.org. uk/events/superman-was-a-foundling.

At the opening of 'Superman Was a Foundling', Lemn Sissay made a speech in which he said three key things. Available at: https://www.youtube.com/watch?v=pJgomzEcGiU.

Jacqueline Rose, *Mothers: An Essay on Love and Cruelty* (London: Faber & Faber, 2018), p. 202.

The Bright Field

Seamus Heaney, 'Postscript', *The Spirit Level* (London: Faber & Faber, 1996), p. 70.

R. S. Thomas, 'The Bright Field', *Laboratories of the Spirit* (London: Macmillan, 1975) and ed. Anthony Thwaite, *R. S. Thomas*, Everyman's Poetry (London: J. M. Dent, 1996), p. 87.

Ad Lucem – Towards the Light

Henry Wadsworth Longfellow, 'The Children's Hour', *The Complete Poetical Works of Henry Wadsworth Longfellow*, Cambridge Edition (London: George Routledge and Sons, 1895), p. 201.

Eeyore's Little Book of Gloom, inspired by A. A. Milne and illustrated by E. H. Shepard, (London: Egmont Children's Books, 1999), p. 19.

Afterword – The Beginning

W. B. Yeats, 'The Stolen Child', ed. Timothy Webb, *W. B. Yeats: Selected Poems* (London: Penguin Books, 2000), p. 18.

ACKNOWLEDGEMENTS

Thanks to the many people who helped to bring this book into being: particularly Robert Caskie, the most engaged and encouraging of agents, and my editor, Helena Gonda, for her thoughtfulness and dedication to the project. But I would also like to thank Rebecca Wright for her meticulous copy-editing and patience, and Josh Benn, Tabitha Pelly and all of the team at Transworld.

Grateful acknowledgement is due to those who read all or parts of this book and offered their expertise and advice: Edith Hall, Angela Leighton, Antonia Reynolds, Hilary Reynolds, Jacqueline Rose. All errors are my own.

Most especially we would like to thank and pay tribute to all of those who offered support through the time of this story, including friends, neighbours, colleagues and students in the School of English and Drama at Queen Mary, University of London.

Thank you to Faisal Abul, Louise Angus, Patricia Atkinson, Benjamin Ball, Georgia Ball, Gerry Bastable, Gillian Brierley, Dinah Casson, Charlotte Dormandy, Nigel Farrow, Andrew and Louise Fifield, Helen Fraser, Charles Gledhill, Edith Hall, Patricia Hamilton, James Howett, Marianna Kennedy, Angela Leighton, Suzi Lewis, Harriet Marland, Bel Mooney, Alan Moses,

Philip Ogden, Christylle and Nicholas Phillips, Elspeth Pickin, Richard Poynder, Georgia and Sarah Poynder, David Profumo, Caroline and Richard Pye, Daphne Ransom, Jacqueline Rose, Mia Rose, James and Sara Ross, Anne and Alan Smith, Beverley Stewart, Liz Warner and family, Jayne and Julian Wilkinson, Veronica Woodford, Linda Young. And finally to our family, Antonia Reynolds and Nic White, Philip and Hilary Reynolds, Jeremy Reynolds and Stephanie Lieber, and all our aunts and uncles, cousins, nephews and nieces in the UK, New Zealand and Australia.

Margaret Reynolds is a writer, academic, critic and broadcaster. Her critical edition of Elizabeth Barrett Browning's *Aurora Leigh* won the British Academy's Rose Mary Crawshay Prize. Other books include *The Penguin Book of Lesbian Short Stories*, *The Sappho Companion*, *Victorian Women Poets: An Anthology* (with Angela Leighton) and a series of study guides on contemporary writers, *Vintage Living Texts*. She is Professor of English at Queen Mary, University of London and a Life Member of Clare Hall, Cambridge. She is the presenter of BBC Radio 4's long-running *Adventures in Poetry*.